Customer Communications
2006–2007

The Chartered
Institute of Marketing

Customer
Communications
2006–2007

Maggie Jones

ELSEVIER

AMSTERDAM • BOSTON • HEIDELBERG • LONDON • NEW YORK • OXFORD
PARIS • SAN DIEGO • SAN FRANCISCO • SINGAPORE • SYDNEY • TOKYO

Butterworth-Heinemann is an imprint of Elsevier

Butterworth-Heinemann is an imprint of Elsevier
Linacre House, Jordan Hill, Oxford OX2 8DP, UK
30 Corporate Drive, Suite 400, Burlington, MA 01803, USA

First edition 2006

Notice
No responsibility is assumed by the publisher for any injury and/or damage to persons
or property as a matter of products liability, negligence or otherwise, or from any use
or operation of any methods, products, instructions or ideas contained in the material
herein. Because of rapid advances in the medical sciences, in particular, independent
verification of diagnoses and drug dosages should be made

British Library Cataloguing in Publication Data
A catalogue record for this book is available from the British Library

Library of Congress Cataloging-in-Publication Data
A catalog record for this book is available from the Library of Congress

ISBN-13: 978-0-7506-8003-5
ISBN-10: 0-7506-8003-2

For information on all Butterworth-Heinemann publications
visit our website at books.elsevier.com

Typeset by Integra Software Services Pvt. Ltd, Pondicherry, India
www.integra-india.com
Printed and bound in Italy
06 07 08 09 10   10 9 8 7 6 5 4 3 2 1

Contents

Contents

Preface
welcome to the CIM coursebooks

An introduction from the Certificate level verifier

Customer communications is one of the four modules for students at the Professional Certificate level. The Professional Certificate is part of a suite of qualifications which can eventually result in students of marketing embarking upon a study path to take them through the first 5 years of their marketing career, from marketing assistant through to marketing manager and hopefully one day to marketing director.

Elsevier Butterworth-Heinemann have worked with the authoring team to produce a book for each of the four modules that accurately reflects the learning outcomes being tested by the Certificate level syllabus.

The revisions to the Customer Communications coursebook this year are mostly structural, with the level of content of each unit changing to more accurately reflect the weighting of the five elements of the syllabus.

Technology continues to change the way we operate within the working environment. We have a unit dedicated to the effect of ICT on the communication process but as time progresses we will see certain communication methods move out of this unit into the more generic units covering written and verbal communications.

As Level Verifier I am responsible, along with the Senior Examiners, for the four Certificate modules, for establishing parity across the four modules and the two assessment methods available for Professional Certificate in Marketing. As you progress through your Certificate studies you will be signposted to areas of other modules that relate to the module you are currently studying, and how the four modules interlink.

Maggie Jones
Level Verifier Certificate

An introduction from the academic development advisor

The authoring team, Elsevier Butterworth-Heinemann and I have all aimed to rigorously revise and update the coursebook series to make sure that every title is the best possible study aid and accurately reflects the latest CIM syllabus. This has been further enhanced through independent reviews carried out by CIM.

We have aimed to develop the assessment support to include some additional support for the assignment route as well as the examination, so we hope you will find this helpful.

The authors and indeed Senior Examiners in the series have been commissioned for their CIM course teaching and examining experience, as well as their research into specific curriculum-related areas and their wide general knowledge of the latest thinking in marketing.

We are certain that you will find these coursebooks highly beneficial in terms of the content and assessment opportunities and as a study tool that will prepare you for both the CIM examinations and the continuous/integrative assessment opportunities. They will guide you in a logical and structured way through the detail of the syllabus, providing you with the required under-pinning knowledge, understanding and applications of theory.

The editorial team and authors wish you every success as you embark upon your studies.

Karen Beamish
Academic Development Advisor

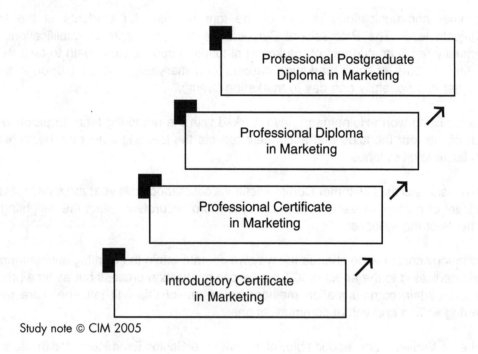

Study note © CIM 2005

How to use these coursebooks

Everyone who has contributed to this series has been careful to structure the books with the exams in mind. Each unit, therefore, covers an essential part of the syllabus. You need to work through the complete coursebook systematically to ensure that you have covered everything you need to know.

This coursebook is divided into units each containing a selection of the following standard elements:

- ○ *Learning objectives* – tell you what you will be expected to know, having read the unit.
- ○ *Syllabus references* – outline what part of the syllabus is covered in the module.
- ○ *Study guides* – tell you how long the unit is and how long its activities take to do.
- ○ *Questions* – are designed to give you practice; they will be similar to those you get in the exam.

o   *Answers* (at the end of the book) – give you a suggested format for answering exam questions. *Remember* there is no such thing as a model answer – you should use these examples only as guidelines.
o   *Activities* – give you a chance to put what you have learned into practice.
o   *Debriefings* (at the end of the book) – shed light on the methodologies involved in the activities.
o   *Hints and tips* – are tips from the senior examiner, examiner or author and are designed to help you avoid common mistakes made by previous candidates and give you guidance on improving your knowledge base.
o   *Insights* – encourage you to contextualize your academic knowledge by reference to real-life experience.
o   *Key definitions* – highlight and explain the key points relevant to that module.
o   *Definitions* – may be used for words you must know to pass the exam.
o   *Summaries* – cover what you should have picked up from reading the unit.
o   *Further study* – provides details of recommended reading in addition to the coursebook.

While you will find that each section of the syllabus has been covered within this text, you might also find that the order of some of the topics has been changed. This is because it sometimes makes more sense to put certain topics together when you are studying, even though they might appear in different sections of the syllabus itself. If you are following the reading and other activities, your coverage of the syllabus will be just fine, but don't forget to follow up with trade press reading!

About MarketingOnline

Elsevier Butterworth-Heinemann offers purchasers of the coursebooks free access to MarketingOnline (www.marketingonline.co.uk), our premier online support engine for the CIM marketing courses. On this site you can benefit from:

Fully customizable electronic versions of the coursebooks enabling you to annotate, cut and paste sections of text to create your own tailored learning notes.

The capacity to search the coursebook online for instant access to definitions and key concepts.

Useful links to e-marketing articles provided by Dave Chaffey, Director of Marketing Insights Ltd. and a leading UK e-marketing consultant, trainer and author.

A glossary providing a comprehensive dictionary of marketing terms.

A frequently asked questions (FAQs) section providing guidance and advice on common problems or queries.

Using MarketingOnline

Logging on

Before you can access MarketingOnline, you will first need to get a password. Please go to www.marketingonline.co.uk and click on the registration button where you will then find registration instructions for coursebook purchasers. Once you have got your password, you will need to log on using the onscreen instructions. This will give you access to the various functions of the site.

unit 1
introduction to customer communications

In this unit you will:

- o Understand the focus of the Customer Communications module and its place within the certificate level syllabus.

- o Focus on the learning outcomes for the modules and how to plan your studies.

- o Understand the methods of assessment available for the module.

- o Begin to focus on the importance of the customer within the marketing process.

- o Look at the different types of customers that you and your organization deal with. See syllabus section 1.1.

- o Examine the various ways you and your organization communicate with customers. See syllabus section 1.5.

By the end of the unit you should be able to:

- o Explain what is meant by the terms 'customer', 'stakeholder' and 'user' (1.1).

- o Demonstrate the fundamental importance of customers to all forms of organizations, including the services and the need to clearly define them (1.2).

- o Appreciate the need for internal and external customer communications and their link to and role in maintaining customer focus, developing and sustaining good customer relations and relationships in creating loyalty and customer retention (1.1.4).

- o Describe the decision-making unit (DMU) and the roles of its constituents (2.3).

This unit relates to the statements of practice

- o Manage or support customer relationships

- o Exchange information with others inside and outside the marketing function.

Key definitions

Customer communication – In business, it is the process by which information is transferred between one individual or group and another, both within and outside the organization. The communication can take place verbally or non-verbally and may be transmitted through a variety of communication methods, such as reports, presentations, letters, and advertising or in meetings.

Stakeholders – Stakeholders are people who affect an organization or are affected by its activities.

DMU – All the individuals who participate and influence the buying decision-making process. This is applicable to both business purchases and family purchases.

Introduction

The customer communications module is one of the four modules required for study at the certificate level. It is expected that the student studying this module will be conversant with the Marketing Fundamentals module, as much of the content of the coursebook assumes the student has an appreciation of the Marketing Process and the importance of the customer within that process.

The module aims to provide the student with a working knowledge of customer buying behaviour and the use of the promotional mix to influence that buying behaviour. The overall development and use of appropriate communications techniques required for a range of audiences and situations will also be addressed.

The key point to be made here is that, although 'customers' are dealt with on each syllabus, in this module you are dealing with customers purely from the perspective of how you communicate with them and the resultant impact on service delivery, and not from a broad marketing perspective as with the Marketing Fundamentals syllabus.

Study Guide

This unit provides an overview of the relationships the organization needs to maintain in order to operate effectively. It covers indicative content 1.1, 1.2, 1.4 and 2.3 of the syllabus.

You should take 2 hours to read this unit and a further 2 hours to complete the activities. References to examination questions relating to the content of this unit are signposted at the end of the unit.

Communications in a marketing context

The process of marketing, as defined by Michael Baker, University of Strathclyde, is being 'Concerned with the establishment and maintenance of mutually satisfying exchange relationships.' In order that this process can actually embed itself within the organizational culture, we must, by definition, ensure that our customers become aware of the products and services that have been developed in order to meet their needs. Communication is, therefore, key to the continuance of the marketing process and continuous evolution of the products and services offered.

Baker's definition also encompasses the communication between the organization and its immediate environment. It is essential that relationships with other stakeholders such as suppliers, distributors and the internal audience are fully developed to ensure mutually beneficial communication will result in sustainable competitive advantage for all involved in the process.

This process of communication must exist against the backdrop of a new type of consumer that is emerging. Lewis and Bridger (2000) identify the 'new consumer' as being free thinking and individualistic. Newfound affluence has resulted in consumers considering what they want to buy rather than just what they need to buy. This behaviour will be explored further in Unit 2. The new consumer is short of time rather than short of cash, seeking to purchase a lifestyle. Communication can demonstrate to them how this can be achieved but Lewis and Bridger (2000) observe that they are 'sceptical of figures of authority, including Government politicians, big business and brands'.

As consumers we receive over thirty times the amount of messages we are physically able to process in any one day. Many of these are concerned with our everyday life and therefore will be accepted into our memory without problem. As marketing-focused organizations, we must ensure the messages sent to our customers are worthy of being remembered and are delivered to the recipient in the most effective and efficient manner, in order that the one chance we get maximizes our opportunity.

Communication is, therefore, a core skill that marketing professionals need to use daily. Consequently, the module Customer Communications, that this textbook relates to, forms the bedrock of the CIM qualification and the foundation to other subjects you will study. Table 1.1 demonstrates how this textbook provides the underpinning knowledge required to enable you to gain a successful outcome to your studies.

Table 1.1 Learning outcomes – unit guide

Learning outcomes	Study units
Recognize organizations as open systems and explain the importance of relationships between the organization and its suppliers, intermediaries, customers and other key stakeholders in a changing environment	Unit 1
Explain why it is important for marketers to understand consumer and industrial buying behaviour for marketing decisions	Unit 2
Develop internal and external communications using appropriate tools to suit a variety of target audiences and using an understanding of customer behaviour and customer information	Units 2 and 3
Select appropriate verbal and non-verbal communications with people inside and outside the organization	Units 4 and 5
Explain the elements of the promotional mix and its fit with the marketing planning process	Units 7 and 8
Explain the advantages and disadvantages of the range of communications tools available to an organization	Units 7 and 8
Demonstrate the importance of customers and customer service and apply customer care principles to create positive relationships with customers in a variety of contexts	Unit 10

Assessment options

There are two available methods of assessing the level of knowledge achieved for the Customer Communications module. The first is an examination where you are required to answer one compulsory question and three optional questions. The second is assignment-based which has a core compulsory element and two optional elements. Each has its own advantages and disadvantages and these will be different for each student depending upon their preferred style of learning. The assessment methods available to you may be determined by the study centre that you attend. Both methods are dealt with in detail within Appendices 1 and 2 of this study text and samples of examination questions and assignments used can be viewed on the CIM Learning Zone accessible with your CIM student number at www.cim.co.uk.

Why do people communicate in business?

If you consider whom you communicate with, why, how and how often, you may be surprised at just how many people you actually communicate with, and the balance between those inside your organization and outside of it. You should also consider the people and organizations from which you receive information. How much of that information do you actually use and take in? How effective is your communication in relaying the intended message accurately?

The main reasons for people to communicate in business organizations, internally and externally, are as follows:

- To *build relationships*, internally and externally, with individuals and groups.
- To give *specific instructions* to others on a range of business matters, both procedural and strategic.
- To *disseminate information* on a range of corporate matters such as the mission statement, policy issues or, in the case of the external market, on price changes or new promotional initiatives.
- To *share ideas and values* on general organizational issues, possibly to maintain or subtly change the corporate culture.
- To *negotiate* matters of policy such as a joint venture or merger.

- To *discuss* or negotiate personal or professional matters such as remuneration and other factors affecting their performance within the workplace.
- To *motivate*, *interest* and *stimulate* employees for commitment and loyalty to the firm.
- To *create an awareness* of the organization, its products or services and *persuade* the external market, for example, to make a purchase decision or to request further information.
- To establish a *two-way communication process* to ensure messages sent are received and understood, and outstanding issues resolved through receiving *feedback*.

If, for instance, you are working in the marketing department of a firm that makes and sells garden furniture, and you have responsibility for the organization's marketing communications, then in an average working day you may communicate with a large number of people in a variety of ways . . .

Communication method	Communicating with	Possible purpose of communication
Post	Customers	Complaining about an element of product or service
	Suppliers	Informing you of their services
Telephone	Suppliers	Chasing or placing or negotiating terms on an order
	Colleagues	Arranging meetings Clarifying information
	Media	Talking to the press about a forthcoming launch
E-mail	Suppliers	Confirming details of an order
	Colleagues	Confirming details of a meeting Providing information
	Distributors	Confirming details of their order
Fax or ISDN	Advertising agency	Confirming copy changes to a new press ad
Letters or direct mail	Customers	Informing the customer of a forthcoming price promotion
Meetings/ presentations	Colleagues	Presenting the last quarter's sales figures to the rest of the team
Report	Colleagues/ suppliers	Presenting items for discussion to enable decisions to be made

The purpose for any communication can be broken down into four main areas. Most communication will have at least one of these four factors as their main objective and it can be useful to analyse which of these are required when putting a message together. These factors can be remembered by the mnemonic *DRIP*.

Differentiate – Identifies for the message receiver the key difference between the products/services you provide and those provided by competitor, for example Daz washes whiter.

Remind – Includes within the message product/service attributes they may have forgotten, for example now it's winter, it's nice to drink hot chocolate.

Inform – Includes within the message details of what the product/service can provide and any action required by them, for example now that the DVLA have an improved database of car owners, you will be fined if you do not renew your Car Tax on time.

Persuade – Usually applied to products/services we want rather than need, giving us a reason to buy, for example Crunchie – get that Friday feeling.

Below is an example of how Dyson used the DRIP factors.

DRIP Dyson

Dyson manufactures a revolutionary type of vacuum cleaner and has 52 per cent of the UK market. Its communications have needed to:

Differentiate it from conventional products – use of innovative technology.

Remind/reassure customers that the cyclone system works better than any other and to resist the competition's attempts to gain top of mind awareness.

Inform and educate the market about what is wrong with conventional appliances.

Persuade potential customers to consider Dyson as the only option when next purchasing floor-cleaning appliances.

 ## Activity 1.1

As a good start to your communications diary, look closely at a daily newspaper or weekly magazine and cut out at least ten different advertisements for a wide cross section of products/ services. Analyse how many of the DRIP factors you can apply to each advertisement and construct a table showing which advertisement incorporates which DRIP factors. Has your analysis allowed you to come to any conclusions about the types of messages that different categories of products/services tend to use when communicating with the consumer?

Who are an organization's customers?

In the traditional sense of the word, *customers* are the people who buy an organization's products and services. To communicate with them effectively, an organization needs to know who they are, what needs the products or services are required to meet, where they are located and the most cost-effective methods of communicating with them. By doing this, it will be easier to develop effective communications, such as advertising, sales literature, packaging and product instructions, that appeal to, and are understood by, the customer. However, there are some discreet differences between customers that will have an effect on how we can communicate with them effectively.

Customers fall into two main categories, external and internal – each having very different needs and expectations of the organization. We will deal first with the two distinct categories and then discuss how some of the boundaries are becoming less distinct in today's competitive environment.

External customers

These are individuals who have no connection with an organization, other than that they may have purchased goods or services in the past, or are purchasing at present. They can be either the traditional customer/consumer who buys a multitude of goods and services for their own use or that of their family, this category is referred to as Business-to-Consumer market (or B2C) or the business consumer who is buying on behalf of their organization, known as Business-to-Business (B2B). Further distinctions are as follows.

The consumer/user

The most obvious customer is the consumer or person who purchases the product or service; the end-user is the person who actually uses the product or service and is sometimes different from the purchaser. Therefore, although the person who pays for the product may also be the user or the consumer of the product this is not always the case.

For example, a manufacturer of toys needs to communicate with both the children who will use the product, so they will exert pressure on parents, and the parents themselves, as they will be the purchaser/decision-maker. The required message therefore has a dual purpose – first to *persuade* the children how exciting the toy is and secondly to *inform* the parents of its educational value.

When the purchase becomes more important and/or more expensive, such as a car, holiday or furniture, then again more people become involved in the purchase and certain members of the family become members of the DMU (decision-making unit). Each member of the DMU will have a different perspective and often take on similar, but less formal, roles to those identified below for B2B purchases.

The decision-making unit

In B2B marketing, it may be relevant for an organization to communicate not only with the purchaser but also with others who could be involved in the decision to purchase. The people involved in the purchase decision tend to have quite formal and closely defined roles; these individuals who make and influence buying decisions in a B2B environment are known as the *decision-making unit* (DMU).

For example, a firm that supplies photocopiers to small businesses needs to communicate with a variety of people, including the admin assistant who will use the machine, the office manager who has encountered other machines working in other organizations, and the finance director who will be interested in how much it will cost. These are not direct customers, but may influence the decision to buy and therefore need to be communicated with. These members of the DMU will be discussed further in Unit 2 which discusses buying behaviour of both consumers and organizations.

Targeting via children

A widely known beneficial use of children as conduits is the 'Five a Day' campaign, currently being run by the Department of Health, to promote healthy eating by ensuring we all eat five portions of fresh fruit and vegetables each day. The D of H distributed leaflets and promotional material in primary schools to reinforce the message being transmitted to parents.

In light of this increased emphasis on health, Kraft Foods, who are responsible for brands such as Dairylea, Angel Delight and Toblerone, are to alter their policy on advertising to children.

The company, which already has a policy of not advertising to children under 6 years of age, will extend the policy to children under 12 on products that could be considered to be unhealthy.

The move comes after sustained pressure on the food industry giants who are knowingly promoting unhealthy food to children despite child obesity levels soaring. The Jamie Oliver School meals campaign has also led to an increased interest in this area.

Mark Berlind, Kraft executive vice-president of global corporate affairs said:

'We recognize parents are concerned about the mix of food products being advertised to young children.'

Where Kraft believe that products do meet the new healthier nutrition criteria they will continue to be promoted but in a media environment seen by parent and all-family audiences rather than those viewed solely by children.

Kraft are hoping other food manufacturers will follow their lead on this issue.

Source: Media Guardian.

 Activity 1.2

Consider the use of communicating to parents via the children. What other companies are you aware of that have used this technique? Has it worked well for them? Look at your communications diary, have you picked up any examples already?

Recently, two large companies have been in the news for allegedly misusing this technique. Cadbury Ltd was accused of encouraging child obesity by linking promotional vouchers to chocolate purchases. Cadbury defended their actions by saying that, as the vouchers were for schools to buy sports equipment, this in fact demonstrated a responsible link by trying to get the 'couch potato' children to become more active.

Walker's crisps were similarly berated for their Books for Schools promotion.

The stakeholders/publics

Most organizations also have a mix of stakeholders or publics, that is internal and external individuals or groups, who come into contact with an organization or who affect or are affected by its activities. From a communication point of view, they can be considered as important customers or target audiences with whom the organization must communicate.

It is important to appreciate the importance of knowing about an organization's stakeholders and why they might want to communicate with them. An organization may choose to communicate with these publics, such as the media or the local community, because it is good for its public relations image and ultimately good for its business. Or it could be a legal requirement for an organization to produce an annual report for shareholders. It is often essential for an organization to form a close relationship with suppliers or distributors, in order to become more competitive. Thus an organization may establish an intranet to provide suppliers with up-to-date stock requirements or provide distributors with automatic access to orders to help them plan their distribution schedules.

In addition, most organizations wish to communicate effectively with current and potential employees to attract and retain the best staff in the marketplace. An organization's stakeholders might comprise the following (see Figure 1.1).

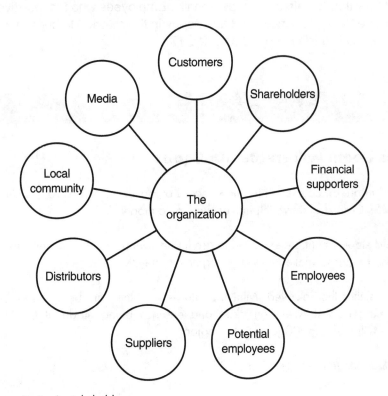

Figure 1.1 An organization's stakeholders

Let's consider the example of a car manufacturer such as Land Rover, who, although they are part of the American company of Ford, have a UK manufacturing plant in Solihull. Its *customers* will receive many forms of communication ranging from national advertising to attract new customers to direct mail shots targeting existing users to upgrade. The financial supporters, such as the *banks and city analysts*, will be concerned not only about the financial health and viability of the owner company, this can be communicated via the annual report, but also by the level and type of media coverage the organization receives. These stakeholders are usually communicated via PR techniques.

The *suppliers and distributors* are heavily dependent upon Land Rover's survival for their own financial stability, they will need to ensure that their own systems are as efficient and effective as possible in order to lower costs and be closely attuned to current and future customer needs. Regular communication is required often using an intranet facility to replace many paper-driven processes such as ordering from suppliers and analysing stock availability.

The *local community* will be interested in the stability due to the need for jobs and the financial well-being of the community, both now and in the future, for their children. Land Rover, who employ 3000 people in Solihull, can build links with the community by sponsoring local events or teams to engender a more pastoral edge to their corporate image.

Customers are obviously an important group. Traditionally, communications within marketing was concerned only about communicating with this group. However, the potential customers' interaction with the other stakeholders may influence their purchasing decision. An employee of a supplier will be more likely to consider buying a Land Rover if the relationship between the two organizations is a good one.

Employees, the internal resource covered later in this unit, will need to be reassured of the company's ability to provide work. They need to be told what the company's plans for the future are and how that will affect them personally. Employees who feel positive about who they work for are more likely to be motivated and happy in their work. Methods of communicating with this group are detailed in Figure 1.3 an page 17.

Insight

Mini sales boom will create 6000 jobs

Sales of the Mini are on course to hit a new record of more than 200 000 this year, providing a further boost to BMW's Oxford plant which makes the iconic model.

Production and employment are expected to rise further when BMW launches a new generation of car in 2007 and also begins to make the Mini's engines in the UK.

BMW estimates that the so-called 'Mini triangle' – with the cars being assembled in Oxford, body pressings coming from its Swindon plant and engines being made at the Hams Hall plant near Birmingham – will create 6000 jobs in the region.

Source: The Independent – September 2005.

 ### Activity 1.3

Identify more stakeholders that Land Rover may need to communicate with. Use the list of stakeholders mentioned in Figure 1.1 and add to them if you can. Briefly explain what methods of communication might be used, what messages might be communicated and why it is important for the organization to communicate with these stakeholders.

Wal-Mart Stores

Wal-Mart is a classic example of a company that has embraced a marketing orientation. Listed below are some quotes from a report on Wal-Mart.

'Every morning at 5.30 a.m. the previous day's results for each region, store, department and merchandise are provided to the managers, who in turn pass on pertinent information to their associates (employees).'

'Stories about Sam Walton and those associates who have made exceptional efforts to please customers are told regularly. These have become the informal way to communicate expectations and behaviours to other associates.'

'Wal-Mart make the customer the focus of everything they do. The company empowers all associates closest to the customer to do whatever it takes to satisfy them. This can go beyond the normal, helpful, friendly service and can include a cashier giving a customer a price reduction based on the customer's word that the product was cheaper elsewhere, or replacing at no charge an item left in the parking lot.'

'Wal-Mart consider themselves to be "students" of customers' buying habits, demographics, wants, likes and preferences through data gathering and personal contact. They see their role as the "customer's agent" – seeking out the best products, negotiating the best price and passing on savings to customers. The policy of EDLP (Every Day Low Prices) drives the company, but price is not the sole determinant of their success.'

The company is willing to try out many new ideas and to adjust them depending upon their success.

Wal-Mart is a proactive company that makes exceptional effort to please its customers. They want to make shopping a pleasurable experience and they are willing to change or adapt anything in order to remain relevant to the needs of customers.

Source: Adcock *et al.* (2001) *Marketing Principles and Practice*, 4th edition.

Internal customers

Consider your internal customers and how important it is that there is good internal communication in an organization. Think about how sometimes you are the customer and someone else is the service provider.

For example, when you receive your payslip from the finance department, you are the customer and expect it to be correct, to be delivered on time and the salary payment actually credited into your bank account. If there is a problem, you expect to be dealt with courteously and promptly. You do not expect to have to engage in lengthy correspondence to rectify a mistake. If you do receive information from the finance department – say, for example, about a new profit-related pay scheme – you expect it to be clearly written and well presented.

At other times, you could be the service provider to your colleagues or line manager; for instance, when you are asked to find out the costing of producing a sales promotion item as part of a future promotional campaign. Your internal customers will expect you to have completed the task on time, accurately, and to present it clearly at the next planning meeting.

So internal marketing is about working together with colleagues and providing them with a good service so that, as a team, your organization achieves its goals.

Internal marketing

Just as individuals have internal customers, such as colleagues and line managers, that they have to deal with, organizations have internal customers in the form of their staff.

From an organization's perspective, internal communication is vital to internal marketing, and the maintenance of employee motivation and company competitiveness. Simple methods of communication can be used to keep staff informed about new products/services, internal restructuring or how well (or not) the organization is doing. In dynamic environments, where firms need to manage change effectively, communication needs to be harnessed to help staff adapt and become familiar to changes in their working environment.

According to Berry and Parasuraman (1992) who are widely credited with recognizing the importance of internal marketing;

'A service company can be only as good as its people: if they aren't sold, customers won't be either.'

The point here being that most organizations provide at least some level of customer service as part of their product offering and increasingly it is seen as a way of differentiating products in an overcrowded market. Without a culture of internal marketing and effective internal customer communications, the employees within an organization face the following problems:

o   Communication problems
o   Frustration and non-cooperation
o   Time-wasting and inefficiency
o   Stress and lack of job satisfaction
o   Poor quality of work.

All of these problems eventually lead to poor service to the external customer, which eventually leads to reduced profit in the long term.

To foster strong relationships and an atmosphere of shared values, communication and information should flow in two ways. Information will obviously flow downwards from senior management to employees, but mechanisms should be put in place to ensure that it also flows upwards from employees to senior managers.

It is important for many marketers to market their department or services internally to colleagues and other departments. Problems can be raised by other people unaware of the marketing department's full range of services and the contribution it can make to the business.

Future challenges for internal communications

The changing environment in which organizations operate means that it may be difficult for some organizations to communicate with staff in the traditional way, and pressures upon staff may mean that they are less inclined to be committed to the organization's values and culture.

Factors influencing change
o The combination of downsized organizations and flatter management structures has removed layers of management and this means that employees are nearer to the decision-makers and that the communication process is speeded up. However, staff that are less secure in their jobs and more pressured to work faster and harder are less likely to communicate openly with their colleagues and managers.
o The trend of teleworking and home-based workers results in more people working away from the office, this means it is more difficult to create a corporate culture and a sense of belonging where people feel happy to communicate on an informal basis.
o The trend for some organizations to provide a 24/7 service often means that all employees do not meet each other and probably end up sharing personal space, such as a desk, with two others whom they have never met. This can be quite isolating.
o The merging of companies across the UK and elsewhere in the world is creating global organizations that do not have local identities and which cross over into different cultures, languages and operating systems. This can make it difficult for senior managers to communicate effectively with employees.

Communicating with the extended organization

Earlier in this unit, it was stated that the distinction between the internal and the external customer is becoming more blurred in many organizations. This has largely occurred due to the increased use of ICT replacing less efficient written and verbal communication processes. Good customer communication goes beyond your own immediate organization. The relationship your staff have with your organization's suppliers, distributors and the like can have a critical impact on the service your customers enjoy. More efficient communication via ICT using Intranets and Extranets results in quicker, cheaper and more effective use of resources for all members of the distribution channel, especially when linked into quality systems such as Just in Time (JIT).

For example, the Body Shop, the retail chain that sells health and beauty products, ensures that its staff work closely with the firm it retains to distribute its merchandise to its retail network, and the distributor actually has office space within the Body Shop factory. This arrangement ensures that close relationships and good communication are achieved.

This improved communication can result in staff enjoying as close a relationship with someone working for a supplier or distributor as the person at the next desk. This is where the difficulty of deciding where the boundaries between internal and external customers arises, with some groups previously considered external now becoming part of the extended organization.

Even end-users, although still very much categorized as external customers, are now able to order goods and services through digital, web-based or voice-activated systems requiring little, if any, human intervention.

A good working relationship with suppliers and other 'partners' can produce dramatic effects, such as:

- o   Innovation
- o   Improved performance
- o   Lower costs
- o   More holistic solutions to problems
- o   Better understanding of the needs of all parties
- o   New ways of working together
- o   More co-operation.

Argos – Changing the culture

Argos is one of the UK's largest non-food retail chains with annual sales exceeding £3 billion. In 1998, a successful, but hostile, takeover by GUS plc led to a change in management. It was the role of the new Managing Director, Terry Duddy, to reverse a previously disappointing performance.

One of his key areas of focus was concerned with the level of customer service. However he realized that to enable change he had to create an environment within Argos that motivated staff to work with him.

His new approach to make Argos more customer-focused was concerned with creating a new set of attitudes and beliefs for the employees to buy into. Those values are encapsulated in the newly created 'employer brand' which seeks to confirm:

Change makes us better and more successful –
- o   We are impatient to win
- o   As much opportunity as you can handle
- o   Teams work.

This approach was successful in gaining the commitment of Argos employees. Individual training programmes were set up to achieve the cultural change needed. All employees' progress was tracked through training modules and individual performance objectives set. Performance against objectives was regularly discussed in appraisal sessions with their line managers.

Performance was rewarded with numerous bonus and incentive schemes that are used to encourage employees to deliver good customer service and high levels of sales.

In its 2003 Speak Out survey, Argos found that amongst its employees:

- o   82 per cent believe the company wants to beat its competitors.
- o   74 per cent believe strong teamwork is a major contributor to Argos's improved performance.
- o   77 per cent believe the business is customer-focused.
- o   80 per cent of employees say they clearly understand the company's goals and objectives.
- o   89 per cent of employees say they know what is expected of them in their job.

Reward for Argos came in the shape of the Retail Week magazine award as 'Retailer of the Year – 2003'. Another reward is that Argos are able to fill 80 per cent of their management vacancies through internal appointments.

Activity 1.4

Review the internal communication that you as an employee receive from your own organization. Consider if you fully understand all the messages sent and how relevant they are to you personally.

How could both the message and the method of communication be improved?

If you work for an organization that does not communicate, consider the minimum amount of information that you would like to receive and the method of communication that should be used.

Improving customer communications

Having identified the various segments that 'customers' can fall into, we then have to consider the best methods of communicating with those groups. We must also realize that as ICT developments, such as e-mail and mobile phones, have made communication cheaper, faster and more frequent, customers are expecting to establish a dialogue as part of the buying decision-making process, to ensure the planned purchase will meet their needs.

Two-way communications

Internal communication
To encourage a two-way flow of information, organizations can choose from a variety of methods to enable managers to hear the views and opinions of employees:

- Regular staff meetings and team briefings.
- Meetings with senior managers where the overall performance of the firm and future developments are discussed.
- Performance reviews/appraisal systems that enable staff to suggest how they could be empowered to do their jobs better.
- Suggestion schemes where employees are rewarded if they suggest ideas that are implemented.
- Work councils where staff can get involved in the running of the organization.
- An organization intranet which allows targeted messages to be sent and information to be accessed by the staff.

External communication
Two-way communication can be used to provide customers with more detailed information that they may require about the products/services offered by your organization. Product options, stockists, prices and stock availability can all be communicated, allowing the customer to make a more informed decision. Two-way communication can be achieved by:

- Developing a website which is regularly updated, to which all other forms of communication then refer.
- Incorporating a frequently asked questions (FAQ) section on the website with an option to e-mail further questions, with a guaranteed response time.

       o Incorporating a digital 'red button' within television advertisements to allow more detailed information to be communicated to those customers who are interested.

       o Digital telephone systems that can ensure the customer query is either answered electronically or directed quickly to the relevant person.

The communications mix

The internal communications mix

Internal customer communications involve the effective use of memos, letters, reports, notices, e-mails, meetings, team briefings, telephone calls and presentations. Obviously, some of these communication methods can be used to communicate externally. In this coursebook, we are making the distinction that external communications are those that are used to promote and sell the organization's goods and services, which we will refer to as the *external communications mix*. For guidance on using internal customer communication methods, see Units 4 and 5.

Shared values – B&Q

B&Q is a do-it-yourself retailer employing over 22 000 people spread across 286 sites. This means that communicating a consistent message to these employees is a complex yet important task, if there is to be brand consistency.

B&Q utilizes a number of different internal communications tools to undertake this task, including e-mail, team briefs and energize sessions (early morning team work-out sessions). The company has a distinct and visible personality in that it requires employees to act as brand ambassadors. There are five main values that act as the central pillar of the organization. These are:

    o A down-to-earth approach
    o Respect for people
    o Being customer driven
    o Being positive
    o Striving to do better.

In partial fulfilment of these values, B&Q staff feature in the retailer's advertising. These show staff offering advice on tools and materials, ideas for gardening and indoor projects plus information about prices. This reflects the importance of integration because (real) staff are shown endorsing their brand and in essence challenging all customers to ask employees about a range of matters. To make this loop work, staff need to know about the product range and how products might apply to different customers. If the message transmitted by employees (the promise) is not realized and experienced by customers, then there will be disappointment, falling expectations and a failing corporate image.

B&Q recognizes that its staff are a major part of the organization's success. It also recognizes that the continuing commitment of its staff is essential, and effective internal communications are an important component in the process to gain this commitment.

Source: Fill, C. (2002) *Marketing Communications – Contexts, Strategies and Applications,* 3rd edition.

Figure 1.2 Internal communications

The external communications mix

To communicate with external customers, organizations use a range of activities that can be described as the *external communications mix*. These activities range from advertising, direct marketing and selling to public relations and the creation of a strong corporate identity. These activities are used to create brands, to inform customers about product improvements and to promote sales, and because most organizations are not interested in a one-off sale, communications are used to build an ongoing relationship with the customer. For guidance on how to use these communication activities, see Units 7 and 8.

Figure 1.3 The external communications mix

17

Summary

In this unit you have studied the following:

o   What is meant by the terms 'customer' and 'stakeholder'.
o   The range of internal and external communications that individuals and organizations use to communicate with their *customers*.
o   How internal communication and internal marketing can help achieve customer focus.

Further study

It is a good idea to supplement your reading with books other than the CIM coursebook to gain a wider view of the marketing and communications industry. The following books are recommended:

Fill, C. (2002) *Marketing Communications – Contexts, Strategies and Applications*, 3rd edition, Prentice Hall, Chapters 1 and 7.

Forsyth, P. (1999) *Communicating with Customers*, Orion Press, Chapters 3, 4 and 10.

Hints and tips

It is also beneficial to read the *Marketing Press, Marketing Week, Marketing, Campaign* and *The Grocer*, all published weekly. These can also be accessed online as can some other useful news websites:

www.brandrepublic.com
www.media.guardian.co.uk
www.thetimes100.co.uk

The Knowledge hub on the CIM website www.cim.co.uk is also available to you and within the site www.shapetheagenda.com will allow you to access debate on some contemporary marketing issues.

www.marketingonline.co.uk is also available to you as a purchaser of this book.

All of these sources will inform you of current marketing and communications thinking.

You are also able to download past exam papers and the current assignment-based assessments from the CIM website (www.cim.co.uk). Appendix 4 has an analysis of the June 2005 and December 2004 papers. As we progress through the units, the relevant exam questions for that unit will be given.

Exam hint

Be prepared to answer questions where you have to identify the stakeholders or customers in a given situation. Ensure that you are able to distinguish between internal and external customers, and able to determine the appropriate communication method and message that might be relevant in a given situation. Avoid attempting to rote learn the contents of this unit. Instead, familiarize yourself with the material so that the knowledge you have gained will give you an overview of the whole subject before you cover other topics in the book.

Bibliography

Berry, L.L. and Parasuraman, A. (1992) *Marketing Management.*

Fill, C. (2002) *Marketing Communications – Contexts, Strategies and Applications*, 3rd edition, Prentice-Hall.

Lewis, D. and Bridger, D. (2000) *The Soul of the New Consumer; Authenticity, What we Buy and Why in the New Economy*, London: Nicolas Brearley.

unit 2
buying behaviour

In this unit you will:

o Examine the differences between consumer buying behaviour and organizational buying behaviour. See syllabus section 2.1.

o Identify the factors which influence buying behaviour. See syllabus section 2.2.

o Develop an understanding of how customer behaviour determines the development of Customer Communications. See syllabus section 2.5.

o Relate communications theory to the buying process. See syllabus section 2.5.

Having completed this unit you will be able to:

o Explain the differences between consumer buying behaviour and organizational buying behaviour (2.1).

o Explain the importance of understanding buying behaviour (2.2).

o Describe the DMU and the roles of its constituents (2.3).

o Describe the decision-making process (DMP) for consumers and organizations (2.4).

o Explain the impact and effect of the DMU and the DMP on the communications mix (2.5).

This unit relates to the statements of practice

Gb.2   Support the management of customer relationships.

Key definitions

Decision-making process (DMP) – The staged process consumers and organizational buyers go through in order to decide whether to buy or not to buy.

Decision-making unit (DMU) – A group of individuals who take part in the purchasing decision-making process, usually within an organizational context but sometimes in complex family purchases.

Unique selling proposition – A unique attribute or benefit of a product or service that can be used to highlight the difference between the product/service and the competitor in the mind of the buyer. The USP can give the consumer the reason to buy.

Sustainable competitive advantage (SCA) – Where a product/service has a USP that is difficult for the competitor to copy it is possible to extend the period that these particular attributes can be used to differentiate the product/service offering.

Study Guide

This unit covers the theory of buyer behaviour in both consumer and organizational markets and examines the factors that influence those decisions. This is especially important when we go on to develop customer communications message that tap into that buying decision-making process. Unless we understand the various stages that the consumer undertakes when making the buying decision, we will not appreciate how communications can help them; for example, a consumer purchasing a car may need to know that interest-free finance is available early on in the buying process. Communicating this may result in the car being considered more seriously in the 'evaluation of alternatives stage'.

The unit will take you approximately 2 hours to work through, read and understand and a further 2 hours to complete the activities.

The purpose of communication within a marketing context

The world in which we live is an increasingly competitive environment. In both consumer and organizational markets, the range of choice is increasing daily and the differences between products and services available to us are getting smaller and less easy to define. The other elements of the marketing mix combine to produce what we hope will be a competitive offering within our individual markets but it is the Promotional P that allows us to communicate those benefits and attributes to our chosen target market(s). We can have the best product in the world but unless we send the right message to the right people to influence their purchasing decisions then it will have all been for nothing.

The ability of our competitors to quickly copy our unique selling proposition (USP) often means that the way in which we communicate to our customers and stakeholders is the only way to differentiate out products and services in the minds of the consumer. This leads to communications being responsible for delivering a sustainable competitive advantage (SCA).

Our communications need to convey a succinct intrusive message to our target audience. It is thought that, at present, as individuals we receive 30 times more messages in a day than our brains are capable of processing. Therefore, only a few actually enter our subconscious mind to be dredged up at a later point and are used to influence a buying decision.

In Unit 1 we identified and applied the DRIP factors that cover the reasons for the message. It may be that we are launching an entirely new product, which we need to *inform* our target audience about. A new competitor may have entered the market and we need to highlight the differences to enable the consumer *differentiate* between the products. We may have a seasonal product such as a hot chocolate drink which we need to *remind* our existing consumers about as the dark nights draw in. Luxury items tend to use *persuasion* to demonstrate the benefits of their products to the target group.

In Unit 1 we identified the various stakeholders that an organization needs to communicate with. The message developed needs to address the needs of as many of these groups as possible. Communication is an expensive business and we cannot develop different messages for all stakeholders. A degree of *integration* in the messages that an organization sends out will result in the whole communications appearing more widespread than it actually is. However, we must not fall into the trap of producing one message that fits all as this leads to bland and uninteresting communication that will be remembered by no one. We must clearly define the message that meets the consumer needs and convey that message using a series of audio and visual cues that deliver it in a memorable way. We must also consider the potential differences between the consumer and the user. In Unit 1 we demonstrated two ways that children could be targeted, in this case to whom is the message targeted to – the parent or the child.

Within this unit we will look at buying behaviour. In Unit 3 we look at communications theory and how we can combine theory with behaviour to develop a successful communications package. In Units 7 and 8 we move on to determine which media will be most effective at delivering the message.

Therefore, we must always consider the following when needing to communicate with any of our stakeholders.

- What is the most effective message?
- Which media can best transmit that message?

 Activity 2.1

> Identify a major purchase that you have made recently. Think about the process you went through to decide upon your final purchase. What sources of information did you investigate before making your decision? What was the deciding factor that made up your mind and where did you learn that fact? What methods of communication are you aware of that helped you to make that decision?

Influences on customer behaviour

Customers do not operate within a vacuum merely deciding what they are going to go out and buy that day. They have a range of influences and constraints imposed upon them that will affect their buying decisions. Some are external influences, economic conditions will determine how much disposable income they have. There have been various articles expressing concern on the level of consumer spending on credit but people generally consider what they can afford rather than just go out and buy. The increasing effect of technology on the home may mean a consumer is encouraged to upgrade the family PC to enable the family to access better services.

The consumer also has internal influences that will affect their buying decision. Have a look at the goods and services you purchase. For how many of those purchases were you influenced by family and friends? Peer group pressure is a strong influence and organizations should recognize that word-of-mouth recommendations are a powerful communications tool. We need to gain an understanding of these to fully appreciate what our communications message has to achieve.

The range of influences are shown in Figure 2.1, further on in this unit.

Personal and social influences

Within the Marketing Fundamentals module you will have addressed the concept of Segmentation Targeting and Positioning (STP). The first part of this process, Segmentation, is concerned with clearly defining who your target consumer is in terms of their demographic profile (age, sex, family life stage) and lifestyle choices. Lifestyle criteria are discussed further on in this unit. Social influences overlay the demographic criteria to move us towards understanding how and why our customers behave in a certain manner. We need to understand these to ensure we develop the message using the right terminology, tone and visual images. These social influences include:

o *Social class* – A consumer's income, job, educational background and status will all influence the types of goods and services they will purchase and the media that they consume. In your mind, consider a policeman – where will he go on holiday, what newspaper will he read, how would he furnish his house? Now do the same for a footballer. Yet on Saturday afternoons they might both be shopping in the same place – but with a very different attitude towards purchasing.
o *Family life cycle stage* – A mum with two young children will be purchasing different items than an 18-year-old in their first job or a 30-year-old single businessman. The mum will consider which washing powder will get the stains out of clothes without affecting the children's skin. The businessman will probably pick the first one he lays his hands on. Their level of disposable income will also vary considerably. In terms of developing messages, people often respond more favourably to messages which feature people like them or who they would like to be.
o *Culture and social groups* – The strongest cultural influences are those of religion and ethnicity. These have a core effect on some of the most basic buying decisions such as food (some religions prohibit the consumption of beef or pork). Ethnicity can influence the clothes that you wear, as in certain cultures you cannot expose your arms, legs or the majority of your face. Social groups have a less easily defined effect. These depend

on the level of influence a social group exerts upon the individual. Dibb *et al.* defined four types of social group:

1. *Primary membership groups* – Family, friends, work colleagues and neighbours. People that you tend to interact with on an informal but regular basis.
2. *Secondary membership groups* – More formal groups where less interaction takes place. There is a more formal sense of belonging (Trade Unions, Professional bodies such as the CIM, even Weight Watchers).
3. *Aspirational groups* – These groups represent who we would like to be and belong to. These groups can strongly influence some purchasers. Recent bad press about Kate Moss and her alleged cocaine use has led to many organizations such as Burberry and Chanel deciding to end their sponsorship arrangements with her so as not to promote her behaviour as aspirational.
4. *Dissociative groups* – These are groups that you don't want to belong to. 'Chavs' are a recently emerging group easily distinguishable by some of the products they purchase.

Insight

Teenagers

Teenagers have always been a regularly targeted group who place great importance on the products purchased by their friends and other social groups. Every generation has a teenage 'look' that is copied to the finest detail within that age group.

Nike and Adidas have recognized the existence of Global Youth culture where the 15-year-old in the UK, USA, Asia and Africa will aspire to buy the same product and achieve the same look.

A recently emerged group is Teenagers – especially amongst the female population where 9–12-year-olds are now making the same level of product choice previously associated with the older age group.

A growth in media opportunities has enabled the advertisers to effectively target this impressionable group, although research by Advertising Agency Ogilvy and Mather suggests that mums need to be targeted to, as often the relationship between mum and daughter is open, sharing interests and some-times purchases, especially in the cosmetics market.

And, of course, mum has the disposable income that the teenager does not.

Involvement

Consumers do not consider all purchases in the same detail and with regard to the same influences. A purchase like washing powder can be a habitual or routine purchase decision based on past experience or it can even be price-related. The decision-maker will most likely be one person on behalf of the whole family.

However, when that same purchaser comes to consider changing the family car or booking a holiday, a greater amount of care is taken in the decision and more members of the family tend to get involved (DMU). This is known as a *High Involvement Decision* whereas the routine purchase will be a *Low Involvement Decision*. The level of involvement will depend on the individual and the influences that will affect their decision-making. Some people with dairy allergies will be very involved when purchasing products such as milk, cheese and butter, whereas these are routine low-involvement purchases for the majority of the population.

Risk

With some purchases there may be a level of risk attached that will vary with each individual such as can I afford it?, will my friends like it?, have I chosen the right product to fit in my kitchen? These are all elements of risk in the buying process. Communications need to address these risks and allay people's fears about purchasing. Risk is a concept which will not be examined at this level but is interesting to consider when trying to understand the influences upon the consumer.

There are six recognized areas of risk, not all of which will relate to all purchases. They are:

1. *Performance risk* – Will the product do what it says it does? Will it do what I want it to?
2. *Financial risk* – Can I afford it? Can I get it cheaper elsewhere? Is it good value?
3. *Physical risk* – Will it fit where I need it to? Will it harm me or my family?
4. *Ego risk* – Will this make me feel good? Will my self-esteem suffer?
5. *Social risk* – What will my friends and family think?
6. *Time risk* – Have I got time to decide which to buy? Will I have time to use it?

Insight

Argos – 16-day money back guarantee

Argos was not often the consumers' first choice for some high involvement non-food purchases, as the consumer was unable to see and feel the product until after purchase. Argos's in-store processes would have become much slower and less efficient if they had to show consumers products before they decide to buy. So, Argos, although able to compete on price, was losing out on many purchases due to this problem.

Argos's response was to offer a 16-day money back guarantee on all products as long as they were returned unbroken and with the original packaging. Consumers have embraced this change, which has reduced many risk factors for them, and Argos has reaped the benefit of additional sales.

This policy was not a new idea. Argos was always willing to refund but they had not communicated that fact to the consumer. A simple message that had a significant increase on sales.

Motivation and beliefs

Motivation affects each individual in a different way. Some people are very ethical in their approach and will consider purchases made against an environmental backdrop. Many of us have busy lives and will make purchase decisions based on convenience, regardless of price. There are some product categories that none of us are motivated by, like gas, electricity and council tax. Often, these organizations try to make the payment process easier by offering discounts for direct debits and informing us of how well they do their job.

Some of these categories will be dealt with in the Lifestyle section further in this unit.

Beliefs and values can be far more deep rooted and extend from just being ecologically sound. Many beliefs arise out of religion and culture. Communication needs to ensure that a positive regard for all beliefs is considered. Personality will also affect your purchasing. Going back to risk, some people are willing to take risks and will take problems that occur in their stride. Others will be very concerned about making decisions and take a great deal of time over it, even seeking reassurance after the purchase is made.

Attitudes are an expression of people's beliefs, and values can be classified into three different categories:

1. *Cognitive* – What a person knows or has learnt
2. *Affective* – How a person feels about a product
3. *Conative* – How people behave

These can be built into a piece of communication. Some of you may be old enough to remember advertising for fresh cream cakes. The slogan or strapline was 'Naughty but Nice' and featured various celebrities tucking into a fresh cream cake. The advert acknowledged that cakes were not good for you but everyone deserved a treat every now and then. This appealed to the various attitudes stated in the following ways:

- *Cognitive* – The message stressed that the organization were not trying to convince people that cream cakes were good for you. They knew the consumer knew this was not the case.
- *Affective* – By featuring people enjoying themselves and acknowledging with the strapline 'Naughty but Nice' indicating cream cake was a treat, consumers were able to relate to feeling indulgent.
- *Conative* – Despite knowing it wasn't good for them, people ate the cakes because it made them feel good.

Lifestyle

Lifestyle encapsulates all of these individual influences and focuses on how the person as a bundle of beliefs, motivations and cultural restraints operates as an individual. Consumers today have a higher proportion of their income as disposable income, and the choice regarding which products to spend their money on has grown considerably. Some advertising agencies have developed lifestyle categories to help them get a picture of a certain consumer to help develop a promotional message. McCann Erickson have developed a different set of lifestyle categories for men and women which you will come across in more detail in your Professional Certificate studies. Here are a few examples:

- *Avant Guardian – Women*. Liberal left opinions. Trendy attitudes. But outgoing, active and sociable.
- *Lady Righteous – Women*. Traditional, right-minded opinions. Happy, complacent with strong family orientation.
- *Chameleons – Men*. Want to be contemporary to win approval. Act like barometers of social change, copiers not leaders.
- *Sleepwalkers – Men*. Contented under achiever. Do not care about most things and actively opt out. Traditional macho views.

Activity 2.2

Take another look at the purchase you were considering in Activity 2.1. Analyse which of the individual influencing factors were most prevalent in making your decision. Look at other purchases you have made – assess how often the same influences affect your decision.

Now consider an older member of your family – how different are their attitudes and beliefs to your own? Which of the influencing factors affect them more than they do you?

In putting together your communications diary from Unit 1, make sure you collect a series of adverts that are targeting towards people of different ages and lifestyles.

Case study

Kellogg's – Changing the focus to health

Like many of its packaged food rivals, Kellogg's has been working hard to promote its products as healthy to offset the negative publicity concerned with the rising levels of obesity.

Two issues have lately put Kellogg's into the spotlight. In October 2004, the Advertising Standards Authority upheld a complaint against the Frosties television commercial. It maintained that the phrase 'eat right' contained within the advertisement conferred a healthy aspect onto the product, which was misleading. Kellogg's were ordered not to use this phrase in the future.

In August 2004, the BBC were berated for its promotional tie-in with Kellogg's which gave away coupons free or discounted BBC DVDs in return for proofs of purchase of Kellogg's Cornflakes.

Kellogg's have moved on to develop a number of sports- and fitness-related initiatives. These include:

o Kellogg's Frosties Football Skills days for 7–11-year-olds.
o Funding of 135 residents of disadvantaged areas to take part in the great Manchester Run alongside 60 Kellogg's employees.
o Sponsorship of the National Breakfast Week to highlight the problems with child concentration when breakfast has been missed.
o Calories in–Calories out. A campaign to provide new labelling and exercise advice on how to incorporate Kellogg's products into a healthy balanced diet.

Kellogg's are hoping this re-focused communication will enable them to develop new communication methods with the consumer before the Government White Paper (2004) comes into effect. This will result in no unhealthy foods being able to be advertised to children before 9 p.m.

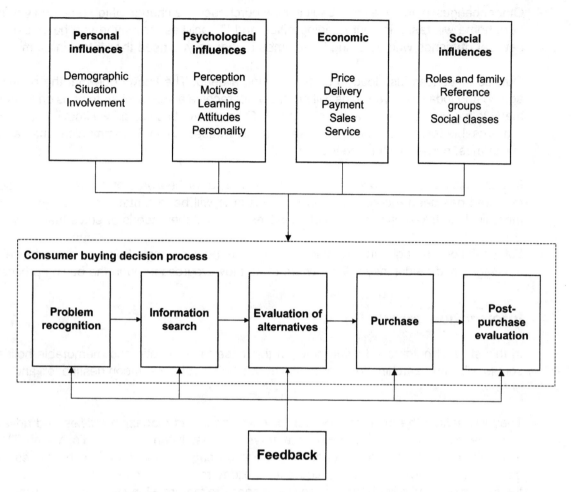

Figure 2.1 The purchase decision-making process
Source: Hughes and Fill (2004) CIM Coursebook, Marketing Communications, Elsevier Butterworth-Heinemann; see p. 10 of the revision cards

The figure above shows clearly how the personal influences feed into the decision-making process. We now need to move on to examine the stages of the consumer buying decision-making process as detailed in the lower portion of Figure 2.1.

The buying decision-making process and its links to the communication objectives

Need recognition/Problem-solving

Recognizing that as a consumer you need to purchase a product or service can arise for a number of reasons. It may be that you need to replace something you already own, which no longer fulfils your needs. A new father of twins may realize that his two-seater sports car is no longer the ideal car for him to own.

Other changes in your life may result in new purchases – a change of job requiring you to work from home will result in your needing office and IT facilities, or maybe you have just made a new set of friends who go skiing three times a year so you need the kit to join them.

Outside influences also lead to us recognizing a need. The knowledge that the population is ageing and today's 40-year-olds will probably not receive a sufficient state pension is prompting many to top up their personal pension plans. On a different scale, did we know that we needed a disposable toilet brush before we saw one advertised on TV? Communications can be the single most powerful influence if used well.

Needs arise for different reasons and different people will be aware of different needs, but once the need has been recognized then the consumer will be in a state of heightened attention, more likely to take notice of products/services that fulfil their needs or solve their problems.

Let us follow through an example of a couple booking their honeymoon, and see what messages and media they will be aware of as they progress through the buying process.

Information search

In this state of heightened awareness, in this case for an exotic and memorable holiday, the couple will start searching for information about their ideal honeymoon destination and itinerary of travel.

They will search the Internet, look out for newspaper and magazine articles and advertising, walk the high street to interrogate the travel agents, listen to the radio, watch TV travel programmes and ask their friends and work colleagues about their experiences. At this stage, the message needs to be about the holiday resort. The strapline needs to conjure up the feeling of being on holiday and the visual needs to feature a long white beach, turquoise sea and palm trees.

The media will need to be carefully chosen to reach the target group – a Bridal magazine will reach this couple but not other consumers for an exotic holiday. The media chosen needs to take both groups into account.

In Figure 2.2 (page 32) you can see how this stage of the buying process is linked to the frequently used AIDA consumer behaviour model. At this stage, the *interest* is high and the couple will soon know all they need to know about booking a honeymoon. Communication at this stage needs to *inform* and *persuade.*

Evaluation of alternatives

Having collated a plethora of information, the couple now need to sift through that information to make a considered decision. They will start considering their important criteria in order to sift the information – which country, which resort, hotel or self-catering, duration of flight, departing airport. At this stage, they will find information gaps and need to gain additional, more detailed information on certain options. Websites and the travel agent can provide this information but it needs to be easily accessible for them to retain interest in a particular holiday package. They are also looking for a USP or differentiating factor that will make their choice easier. This could be a complimentary bottle of champagne on arrival or a limo to the airport. Whichever is likely to appeal to this couple is what the holiday company needs to be finding out and communicating to them. This message is unlikely to be the banner headline for the company but in all the brochures, websites and travel agents it does need to be contained within the communication from the organization. The key objective here is to *inform* detail.

The purchase decision

In most cases it is the salesperson either in a shop or on the phone that will move the consumer towards making a final purchase decision. In the case of online purchasing, the ease of access and navigability of the site will aid the purchase transaction, but a site that shows positive customer feedback and comprehensive resort guides will help the purchaser towards the final purchase.

It is important at this stage that there are no last minute hitches to put off the purchaser. A crowded travel agent, ever-ringing phone or an unavailable website will mean the couple do not see the final purchase decision through and could lead to them reconsidering their decision.

Added value gained at the point of purchase can also sway a decision. A third week free could encourage people to lengthen their stay; free travel insurance can encourage them to consider another company. It is important that the messages received by the consumer at this stage help to confirm in their minds that they have made the right decision and they feel secure in their choice. The key objective here is to *differentiate.*

Post-purchase evaluation

We cannot forget the consumer once they have made their purchase. What happens after purchase will affect their repurchasing decisions and the feedback that they give to family and friends. There needs to be feedback devices incorporated within any communication so that problems can be detected early and acted upon. Front-line staff need to be competent in dealing with problems and complaints. The message here needs to be one of reassurance that problems will be sorted out and there are available resources to enable that to happen. Only if this occurs can customer satisfaction arise. The key objective here is to continue the *differentiation* to *remind* the couple why they made this choice.

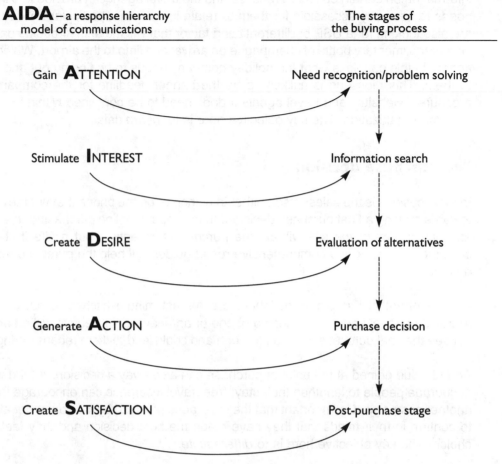

AIDA – a response hierarchy
model of communications

The stages of
the buying process

Gain **A**TTENTION → Need recognition/problem solving

Stimulate **I**NTEREST → Information search

Create **D**ESIRE → Evaluation of alternatives

Generate **A**CTION → Purchase decision

Create **S**ATISFACTION → Post-purchase stage

Figure 2.2 Relating communications objectives to the stages of the buying process
Source: Hughes and Fill (2004) CIM Coursebook, Marketing Communications, Butterworth-Heinemann

Sony Playstation Portable Launch

Dedicated computer games enthusiasts queued until midnight in the hope of getting their hands on a gadget described as the 'new iPod'.

The Sony Playstation Portable (PSP) has been described as the Walkman for the 21st century because it can also play films, access the Internet and store digital photographs.

There has always been unusual demand for the handheld console, which officially goes on sale in the UK today, with many retailers no longer taking advance orders to ensure they have enough units to sell over the counter. Sony believe that one million PSPs will be sold in the UK by Christmas. It took the iPod more than a year to sell the same quantity.

Hundreds of people flocked to HMV's flagship store on Oxford Street last night for the PSP's official launch at midnight. The shop held back 500 unreserved consoles to sell on a first-come, first-served basis.

HMV's Gennaro Castaldo said, 'These major games platforms come in cycles of three to four years. There's a real "must-have" emotional approach to it if you're a games fan.'

He predicted stocks of the PSP would be sold out by the weekend.

Tesco, which is selling the PSP in 133 stores, is expecting such interest that it has launched an online 'tracker' to help shoppers find out where the console is still on sale.

Sony's UK Publicity manager confirmed that 'We are targeting the 18–34 market, not kids. People with disposable income.'

Source – Excerpts taken from *The Independent* – 1 September 2005.

Activity 2.3

Using the AIDA model and the model that illustrates the buying process, complete the table below to indicate which promotional tool a car manufacturer might use at each stage.

The buying process	AIDA model of communication	Promotional tool
Need recognition	Gain attention	
Information search	Stimulate interest	
Evaluation of alternatives	Create desire	
Purchase decision	Generate action	
Post-purchase decision	Create satisfaction	

Influences on organizational buying behaviour

Having dealt in detail with the process of consumer buying, we also need to concentrate on the buying decisions that occur between two businesses (B2B). These are just as frequent, important and considered as consumer buying decisions. In some areas the influences can be similar when considered from a different viewpoint. Just as the message may need to change the media we can use to transmit the message also needs to change. This market tends to be much easier to segment and therefore it is easier to determine quite specifically who the target group is and how we can reach them. We will consider each of the factors in turn.

External factors

The PESTLE (Political, Environmental, Social, Technological, Legal and Economic) factors will be constantly changing and have the ability to affect the organization in several ways. Depending on the type of industry, some PESTLE factors will have more of an influence than others. Pension companies will be more influenced by Social, Legal and Political change whereas an online book retailer, such as Amazon, will be more affected by Technological and Economic change.

Political/Legal factors

The government has far-reaching powers and can cause a ripple effect on other external factors. For example, a change in corporate taxation could affect the spending power of the organization. The European Commission may also have powers which influence certain industries. Food labelling and the amount of cocoa allowed in chocolate have been two recent initiatives. Other more everyday laws and policies will be health and safety laws, employment laws and the laws regarding filing of accounts, and so on.

The communications industry is also subject to legal constraints although as an industry they also have self-regulatory bodies to ensure they act in a fair way.

Economic factors

The effect of economic factors will directly affect consumers who, if they have less disposable income, will reduce their spending in certain areas. A buoyant house market will result in an uplift in trade for DIY stores. Some industries are not subject to such significant change. For example, electricity and gas companies do not see the effect of decreased disposable income so significantly as people have to keep their homes warm, regardless of the cost, to a certain degree. New product development can be the first casualty when income becomes restricted. Communication budgets also suffer requiring the organization to find more efficient and effective methods of communicating.

Social factors

Changes in demand and fashion will result in some industries having to spend a great deal in renewing ranges of products. Switching from non-profitable lines to more profitable areas can require significant investment. The housing market is currently switching away from building large family houses to building more apartments to house wealthy older people or young singles, more dwellings per acre mean more bathrooms are needed!

Technological factors

This area has enforced significant change on many industries over the last 10 years, especially ICT has changed the way we order, supply and market goods and services. Automated systems and the rise in extranet and intranet communication has meant significant upgrades and investment in ICT-related areas.

More staff with ICT skills are also needed. Communication between organizations is not as one-to-one as it used to be with many everyday functions being carried out by ICT.

Environmental factors

Increasingly, organizations are being judged on their level of environmental conduct both by governments in controlling the levels of pollution entering the environment and also by consumers throughout all aspects of the processes the organization goes through to deliver goods and services. Corporate Social Responsibility (CSR) is an emerging contemporary marketing issue and most organizations are developing a CSR stance to depict their caring philosophy onto the consumer. However, to do this properly requires cultural change and a lot of training to ensure CSR philosophies reach every employee in the industry. Mistakes in this area can be very costly for an organization and result in very damaging PR coverage.

Case study

Shout about it or keep quiet

The Body Shop has become synonymous with ethical trading, proclaiming its beliefs on its packaging and advertising. Its ethical pronouncements have become part of its marketing strategy. Yet this can still lead to problems – whether of your own creation or not.

A decade ago, it emerged that almost every cosmetic the Body Shop sold had almost certainly been tested on animals. According to regulations in the US, the EU and Japan, no product could be sold unless it had been certified as safe. To gain such certification it would have to be tested on animals. New methods to gain safe certification had to be found and the Body Shop now carries a disclaimer on animal testing – it has added 'since 1991' to its publicity.

The issue is not whether the Body Shop intentionally or innocently misled; rather it is that the negative publicity is stronger because of the previous ethical stance.

Hennes and Mauritz (H&M) is a company that has clear moral principles, with strict rules ensuring that no sweatshop workers are used to manufacture its clothes. It also supports Wateraid.

But H&M does not publicize its moral code; it does not advertise itself as an ethical company. H&M believes that its brand values are fashionable clothing and affordable prices. It focuses on promoting that and nothing else.

When asked, it reveals what it has in place to ensure moral behaviour. But H&M does not want customers to think it is jumping on the ethics and responsibility bandwagon.

Source: *The Marketer* – January 2005.

Internal or organizational factors

The internal factors that guide the way an organization will deal with its suppliers from whom it purchases goods and services will largely depend on the culture of the organization. This can largely depend on which type of company they are or the industry in which they operate. The cultural glue and ways of working will be very different when comparing an organization in the private sector to one in the public sector. Charities will also differ in the way they do business. Whatever the culture, the main difference between consumer and organizational buying is the size of the purchase and the number of people who play a part in the buying decision process. The DMU comprises of a number of individuals, each with a different slant on the forthcoming purchase. The following are the elements of the DMU.

Members of the DMU

In this section as an example, we will use a firm that supplies computer systems to other businesses. They will need to communicate with a variety of people who may not be customers but who may influence the decision to buy and therefore need to be communicated with. These are referred to by the following names:

The purchaser

A purchasing official may have sourced a new computer system and may ultimately place the order. As far as customer communications are concerned, it is important to make the purchaser's job easy, ensuring that up-to-date product, contact and after-sales information is easy to digest and that the ordering process is easy. This person will be interested in the price, delivery timescales, guarantees and payment terms related to the purchase. They may know little about the technical specification of the system being purchased.

The initiator

The initiator or the specifier could be a member of staff, senior manager or even an external consultant, who sees the possibilities for new computer equipment to improve efficiency. The computer company must consider who these people might be and raise their awareness about its products, possibly via relevant trade press advertising, sales promotional material, exhibitions or public relations activities.

The user

The users in this example would be the staff that would use the computer system. These people may not influence the decision at the outset of the process but may be invited along to test equipment as part of a task group before the purchase decision is finalized. After the decision to purchase has been made, the good opinion of these people is vital if repeat business is to be transacted. The computer company could ensure good customer communications by providing value-added services such as training and help line support.

The influencer

Influencers could be the technical staff who affect the purchase decision by supplying information about a variety of suppliers or by setting buying specifications. Or they could be staff in the finance department who could block the purchase decision with financial constraints. Similar to the situation with initiators, these *customers* need to be supplied with sufficient information about the product/service via whatever channels are considered suitable. These people will be considering several options and therefore will need communication that *informs* them of the computer system's ability and the details of the package that *differentiate* one system from another. This information will need to be communicated before the actual need arises so that the computer company is in the influencer's 'mind set' when the actual need does become an action point.

The decision-maker

These people are the most influential in terms of making the purchase decision. They may be senior managers or the managing director. It is vital to identify who these people are within an organization. The computer company's message could be communicated directly by a sales representative who might use some form of corporate entertaining to initiate the relationship and to close the purchase decision. These people will need to be aware of top-line details and be convinced that the other members of the DMU are happy with the decision. It is therefore likely to require a regular two-way form of communication.

The gatekeeper

Gatekeepers control the flow of information through an organization and may be switchboard operators or secretaries who are responsible for dealing with incoming calls, mail shots and trade journals that arrive by post. The computer company should communicate effectively with this customer in order to be able to reach others in the DMU. Sales representatives need to be able to talk persuasively to the gatekeeper to obtain appointments or pass on information to the decision-makers or influencers. Again, this is likely to require face-to-face communication.

Type of organizational purchase

The organizational purchase can be divided into three main categories shown below. The level of involvement and risk will differ with each type of purchase in a similar way to the effect on consumer buying demonstrated earlier in the unit. The following are the three approaches:

1. *Straight rebuy* – This is the most straightforward buying DMP, involving routine repurchase of standard items. This could be as simple as a stationery order or a bulk order of tyres to go onto a car. Stacks are re-ordered when existing stocks fall below a certain level, a process often monitored and carried out by ICT. Change will occur only if a problem occurs in the standard of good sent to fulfil the order. This will require discussions with suppliers to ascertain the origin of the problem and whether it can be solved. This process can also be interrupted if a competing supplier approached the organization with a better offer causing the buyer to re-assess the suitability of the original supplier. Communication needs to be regular but not necessarily frequent – this could be face to face with sales people or via e-mail. The purpose of the communication being to deal with any small problems before they become big issues and to ensure the buyer feels valued by the supplier.

2. *Modified rebuy* – This is a similar but slightly different process to the straight rebuy in that the buyer, in this instance, requires a modification to the order. This could be concerned with the specification of the product, the quantity ordered as a batch, delivery schedules or, most commonly, price. Communication here needs to reassure the buyer and effect a renegotiation of terms that is mutually beneficial, hence the need for this to usually require a meeting or phone call. It is unlikely that a matter such as this would be resolved entirely by e-mail.

3. *New task* – This is the longest and most complicated of the three categories. The buyer will have a need for a product/service and a list of suppliers that he is prepared to approach. In a process very similar to the consumer buying DMP, he will probably be alerted to the need by the *user* in the DMU. His search for information will be extensive and he will probably refer to *gatekeepers, influencers, and other buyers* in his quest for information. He will make the purchase decision along with the *deciders and approvers* hence spreading the risk from an individual concern to an organizational one. All members of the DMU will be involved in the post-purchase evaluation stage as will other colleagues from outside the original DMU such as delivery and logistics staff.

The stages in the organizational buying decision-making process are as follows:

- o Anticipation or recognition of needs
- o Determination of product/service required
- o Specification of characteristics/quality
- o Search for potential suppliers
- o Analysis of proposals
- o Evaluation of proposals/supplier selection
- o Negotiation of contract or routine order
- o Performance feedback/evaluation

Figure 2.3 Stages in the B2B buying process
Source: Customer Communications Revision cards, p. 15

Types of organizational buyer

In the same way that we use Consumer Lifestyle analysis to guide us in developing an effective campaign we can also segment organizational buyers in the same way. Dickinson (1967) identified the following categories that existed within USA buyers:

- o *Loyal* buyers – who remain loyal to a source for considerable periods.
- o *Opportunistic* buyers – who choose between sellers on the basis of who will best further their long-term interests.
- o *Best deal* buyers – who concentrate on the best deal available at the time.
- o *Creative* buyers – who tell the seller precisely what they want in terms of the product, service and price.
- o *Advertising* buyers – who demand advertising support as part of the deal.
- o *Chisellers* buyers – who constantly demand extra discounts.
- o *Nuts and Bolts* buyers – who select products on the basis of the quality of their construction.

Communications objectives for the organizational buying process

The objectives to build and develop an effective communications package to facilitate the organizational buying process fall into two basic categories. The first objective is to gain awareness in the mind of the buyer so that you will be considered alongside other suppliers when a *new buy* situation comes along.

This may need to be a concentrated campaign over a period of time before it reaps rewards. Organizational buyers don't really tend to change suppliers that often unless they are in one of the more transactional categories as detailed above. It is also generally easier to buy very specific media that reaches the organizational buyer, an advert in the 'Sun' may not reach many of your consumer audience in percentage terms but an advert in 'The Grocer' will most probably reach a high percentage of people working in the food industry.

To gain awareness and to get into the buyers mindset requires the uses of *personal selling, direct marketing, public relations techniques such as exhibitions and corporate entertainment and industry trade press*. Word of mouth and the past experience of the buyer, maybe at a previous organization, will also be an important part of the campaign. The purpose of communication is to differentiate and inform.

Once an organization becomes an accepted supplier, the key objective is to build and develop the relationship. This will require more frequent, ongoing conversation to ensure that problems or opportunities that arise can be dealt with as soon as possible. Regular communications using *personal selling, intranets and extranets*, and *corporate entertaining* are mostly required.

Activity 2.4

Consider the differences between two organizational buyers, one an office manager for a small IT company needing air conditioning units, the other buying tyres and sound systems to be fitted into cars. Analyse the differences against the following criteria:

o   Size and frequency of order
o   Type of purchase
o   Stages of the buying process the buyer will go through
o   Communications that will affect the buyer's decision
o   Level of risk that the buyer will feel
o   Likely number of DMU members.

Key communication differences between consumer and organizational buyers

Table 2.1 Differences between consumer and B2B communications

	Consumer-oriented markets	**Business-to-business markets**
Message reception	Informal	Formal
Number of decision-makers	Single or few	Many
Balance of the promotional mix	Advertising and sales promotions dominate	Personal selling dominates
Specificity and integration	Broad use of promotional mix with a move towards integrated mixes	Specific use of below-the-line tools but with a high level of integration
Message content	Greater use of emotions and imagery	Greater use of rational, logic- and information-based messages although there is evidence of a move towards the use of imagery
Length of decision time	Normally short	Longer and more involved
Negative communications	Limited to people close to the purchaser/user	Potentially, an array of people in the organization and beyond
Target marketing and research	Greater use of sophisticated targeting and communication approaches	Limited but increasing use of targeting and segmentation approaches
Budget allocation	Majority of budget allocated to brand management	Majority of budget allocated to sales management
Evaluation and measurement	Great variety of techniques and approaches used	Limited number of techniques and approaches

Source: Fill, C. (2002) *Marketing Communications – Contexts, Strategies and Applications*, 3rd edition

Success at Dell

A company that has successfully integrated messages across the consumer and business markets is Dell Computers. Dell has accomplished this feat by using five demand generation channels:

1. The field sales force
2. Third-party business partners
3. Retailers
4. Telechannels
5. The Internet.

Dell uses its field sales force to reach major corporations, institutional customers and governmental customers, which generate 65 per cent of their total revenue. To reach small- and medium-sized businesses, Dell uses third-party business partners, telechannels and the Internet. To reach consumers, Dell uses retailers and the Internet. Dell encourages the customer to place additional orders either by telephone to inside salespeople or through a special premium Internet page that Dell sets up for the business customer. The premium Internet page allows the business customer to order merchandise not normally available via the Internet.

Dual channel marketing is a key to Dell's success. Specializing its methods of reaching consumers has led to growth in sales. At the same time, Dell maintains its image across all markets: one of being a quality provider of various computers.

Source: Clow and Baack (2002) *Integrated Advertising, Promotion & Marketing Communications.*

Summary

In this unit you have studied:

- ○ The purpose of communication.
- ○ The buying decision process for consumers and for organizations.
- ○ The differences and similarities within the buying process for consumers and for organizations.
- ○ How customer behaviour and the buying process related to customer communications.

Further study

Attempt Question 3 on the December 2004 examination paper from Appendix 4. Attempt Question 3a on the June 2005 paper; the paper and examiners' reports can be found in Appendix 4 and on the CIM website (www.cim.co.uk).

Hints and tips

Try to extend your communications diary by looking for communication that would be targeted at organizational buyers. There may be some trade press and direct marketing literature notes available for you to access at work; if not, then your local library or searching the Internet are viable alternatives.

Consider within your own organization; who are the members of the DMU? How many are there? Do people overlap roles? Try to arrange a discussion to ascertain what criteria they consider whilst making their decision. Ask also about suppliers they have rejected: Why was that? Would those suppliers be included within the possible list in the future?

It is essential that you remember that as much marketing activity is planned on a B2B basis as in consumer marketing and that you will need to be prepared to answer exam questions. Having examples within your Communications diary will provide you with up-to-date examples to use when answering questions.

Bibliography

Dickinson, R.A. (1967) *Buyer Decision Making*, Berkley, CA: Institute of Business and Economic Research, *The Marketer*, PG 7 – January 2005 edition.

Fill, C. (2002) *Marketing Communications – Contexts, Strategies and Applications*, 3rd edition, Prentice Hall.

http://www.euromonitor.com

unit 3
the communication process

In this unit you will:

- Examine the process of communication. See syllabus section 3.3.

- Recognize the barriers to successful communication. See syllabus section 4.2.

By the end of this unit you should be able to:

- Explain the structure and function of the communication process (3.3).

- Describe the communication process and explain the importance and the advantages and disadvantages of different types of communication in a variety of face-to-face situations (4.1).

- Identify barriers to communication and explain how they can be avoided and overcome (4.2).

- Explain the communications planning process to produce effective strategies for improving alternative communications formats (4.3).

Study Guide

This unit provides an overview of the communication process and an insight into how to be an effective communicator. It considers the barriers to communication that can occur. Think about situations in your own experience either at work or at home when misunderstandings have occurred and try to analyse where the breakdown or barriers to communication happened. This is important in a communications environment where ICT is enabling more two-way communication. Feedback will be valuable only if it answers the question you believe you are asking. If the message is misinterpreted then the feedback may also be valueless. It should take you about 2 hours to read through this unit and a further 2 hours to work through the activities.

The purpose of communication

Unit 1 covered the purpose of communication and the use of the DRIP factors when communicating externally and internally.

Communication needs to have impact in order to be noticed and retained by the recipient. Successful communications will occur only if the person communicating has a clear purpose or objective, which can be achieved as a result of the communication. Increased ICT applications have resulted in an increase in communications methods available.

In Unit 1 we looked at the growing importance of two-way communication. Dibb *et al.* (1991) pointed out that 'for a dialogue to occur each participant needs to understand the meaning of each others communication'. Therefore, before trying to plan efficient and effective communication, it is important to understand what actually happens when communication occurs.

The communication chain

Wilbur Schramm (1955) developed the most commonly known model of communication, which broke the process down into five clearly defined consecutive stages or dimensions (see Figure 3.1).

These are:

1. The sender has the need to communicate
2. The need is translated into a message (encoding)
3. The message is transmitted
4. The receiver gets the message (decoding)
5. The receiver interprets the message and provides feedback to the sender.

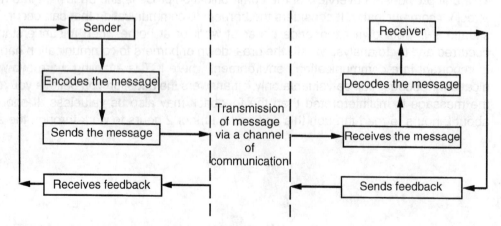

Figure 3.1 The process of communication

1. The need to communicate business messages to your internal and external markets is an essential part of the marketing process as covered in Unit 1. The DRIP factors help us to identify what kind of message, is required at which stage of the product life cycle. In deciding to send out a message we must be clear what customer needs we are meeting and the objective behind the planned communication. Once this is clear, you can then move on to plan the message content.

2. Messages may be *expressed* in a number of different ways. It is usual that in any business communication the message content and method of communication is a result of careful planning rather than an off-the-cuff remark. Most promotional messages are more sophisticated than 'this product's good, so go and buy it'. In planning the message content, the sender will consider:

    o The purpose of the communication
    o The subject to be communicated
    o The likely needs of the recipient
    o The communication methods available for use.

    It is imperative that we communicate to the recipient in a way they will easily understand and will arouse interest. This process is known as *encoding* and involves a combination of words, pictures and symbols to represent the message to be transmitted. The first step to encoding is to decide what and how much to say; if a message contains too much information it is difficult to absorb, but if you do not include enough, it will not meet with the expectation of the recipient and may leave room for misinterpretation.

3. The *medium* you choose for transmission will depend on the message to be conveyed, location of the recipient, speed, convenience and degree of formality required. The usual internal methods are memo, report, e-mail, telephone and face-to-face interaction. External methods available will be determined by the media consumption habits of the recipient. For example, one of the best ways to communicate to 16- to 19-year-olds is by advertising in cinemas or SMS messaging.

4. *Decoding* is the interpretation of the message that has been received by the recipient. If the decoding message is the same as the encoded message then the communication will have achieved its objective. However, if the recipient decodes the message in another way, it may mean that the communication is entirely wasted. The degree of misinterpretation will need to be established before the message content is adapted.

5. *Feedback* (or lack of) is the response that the recipient sends back to the sender and is a key element in the communication process because it enables the sender to *evaluate* the effectiveness of the message. Feedback may take the form of verbal (telephone call, face-to-face interaction, etc.), non-verbal communication or action (body language, etc.) or written messages. The inclusion within the message of a response mechanism to establish two-way communication will aid this feedback. Marketing research is a more formal (and expensive) way of eliciting feedback.

Feedback is the key element that creates a *cycle* in the communication chain, enabling the information that is sent to be *reviewed* when it is received back. If the feedback shows that the communications objectives have not been met then corrective action, usually changing either the message content or communication method, can be taken.

Consider the Persil Non-Bio Press advertisement below. Look at the way two-way communication is encouraged by the insertion of a careline number and the website address. Think back to the factors which can influence purchase that we covered in Unit 2 – Performance risk is being reduced by the reference to the British Skin Foundation. Beliefs and attitudes are being tapped into with the use of two babies – one black, one white, both in nice clean clothes – a real aspiration for some busy mums.

This advertisement shows that most communication carries more than one message and the more messages that can be conveyed in one 'hit' makes the communication more valuable.

Figure 3.2 Persil press advertisement

Activity 3.1

The ability to create a memorable strapline will enable a communications campaign to be more easily understood in the minds of the consumer and allows the organization to *extend and integrate* the campaign into other marketing activities. But the strapline needs to be created first. For how many of these can you identify the brand or service?

- I liked it so much I bought the company
- Your flexible friend
- Raise your hand if you are sure
- Scchh ... you know who
- Don't just book it
- Pleasure you can't measure
- Work, rest and play
- Vorsprung durch technik
- Can hate be good – can hate be great?
- Have a break have a ...
- I'm loving it.

Barriers to successful communication

Distortion

It is possible to lose the meaning of a message during the communication process. This can occur at the *encoding* stage, where the sender decides upon the best way to communicate the message. It can also occur at the *decoding* stage, where the recipient attempts to grasp the meaning of the message, but somehow takes out a different meaning than what the sender intended. The process here is said to be affected by distortion and can be caused by either the sender or the recipient.

Although there may be instances where people deliberately choose to distort the message and understand only what they want the message to say, the most common reasons for the meaning being lost in the 'handling' of the message are as follows:

- Using the wrong words
- Using jargon or technical words that are not understood
- Using a foreign language or an accent that is not understood
- Using words or pictures that have more than one meaning.

Distortion can occur with an advertising message where there is ambiguity in the message, whether intentional or not. For instance, if the people who write and design an advertisement to be used in international marketing are from one culture and the recipients of the message are from another, there may be problems in how the advertising message is interpreted. For example, Esso's advertising campaign slogan, 'To put a tiger in your tank', caused problems in Taiwan where people attach a religious significance to tigers and therefore had a different understanding of the message being conveyed. HSBC have used this communication ambiguity to their advantage in demonstrating some of the differences that can occur, and how their prior knowledge of these issues make them a more understanding organization.

The communication method chosen can also cause distortion, in that the method chosen can hinder the non-verbal communication. It is difficult to convey the message that 'Daz washes whiter' unless we can see the evidence. Using radio to communicate the same message may well cause message distortion.

Noise

Noise, such as distractions or the interference that occurs as the communication is being encoded, transmitted and decoded, can obstruct the transmission of the message. There are many different types of noise that can render the message inaccurate, unclear or even mean that it is not received at all.

Technical noise
Technical noise can occur while the message is being transmitted; for example, a poor telephone connection means the caller's voice cannot be heard or the break down of a fax machine.

Physical noise
Physical noise can occur while the message is being transmitted; for example, people talking, traffic or noisy machinery could render a speaker's voice inaudible during a presentation.

Social noise
Social noise creates interference in the transmission and decoding of messages. It is caused when people are prejudiced against others because they are of a different age, gender or social class. For example, a young woman delivering a presentation on corporate funding to older businessmen may be perceived to lack credibility by some of the audience who are prejudiced because of her age and gender. Social noise can also be used to retain interest or differentiate the whole message. Think of the Diet Coke – 11.30 a.m. advertisement.

Psychological noise
A person's emotional state or attitude could interfere with message transmission. A person's anger or hostile attitude can create psychological noise. For example, a customer whose goods have not been delivered may be unable to hear the reason why the goods have been delayed because he is so angry about the situation.

Other barriers

Perceptual bias – Can occur where the recipient of a message makes assumptions and selects what they want to hear. This can result in the wrong message being received. For example, if a doctor has told a patient that their condition is not serious as long as they change their diet, the patient might choose to hear only part of the message and not take in the message about changing their diet. With promotional messages, we often need to find what a customer's perception of a product/service is before developing a message to change this to a more favourable one.

Information overload – Can occur if the recipient of the message receives too much information or information that is too technical. The result is that the key messages are not conveyed or understood. For example, when a new member of staff is given a very detailed demonstration of how several pieces of equipment work in a short span of time, it is likely that they will become confused and remember very little about what was actually said. This problem can often be avoided by developing a simple message that carries with it a signpost to more detailed information, if the recipient requires it; website addresses are often used in this way.

Contradictory non-verbal – Contradictory messages can occur if the person encoding a message says one thing but their body language says something else. For example, if a person wears casual clothes and a baseball cap to a job interview in a formal business environment and says that they think they would fit into the organization, they are conveying mixed messages to the interviewer. Body language is also important; it is difficult to trust the message spoken by a salesperson who cannot retain eye contact.

Language – Can act as a barrier if two people speak different languages and cannot understand each other. This causes problems with people not only from different countries, but also across different areas of the country and different age groups where commonly used colloquialisms can be used.

Contradictory verbal messages – Using an inappropriate tone and pitch of your voice can result in the message being misunderstood. Try saying something like 'you are really annoying me' in a tone of voice you would use for saying 'Thank you for doing that for me' and see how the recipient responds. If they are listening intently they will be confused, if they are not they will probably respond 'that's okay'. Confusing, isn't it?

Pace of speech, either too slow or too fast, can result in the message being misunderstood. Too slow a pace can also make the recipient feel insulted that we feel they don't understand. Why do some people speak English slowly to people of other nationalities?

The use of jargon can also be confusing. We should not assume that our receiver is cognizant of all the day-to-day terms that we use frequently. Checking if people can understand the jargon can also be misread as an insult so it's better to avoid jargon overall.

Any inflections in speech should be appropriate to the message in the sentence. '*This* is very important' is different in meaning to 'This is *very important*'.

Activity 3.2

Look again at the elements you have collected in your communications diary. Think about the likely demographic profile of the intended recipient. Now think about how the message would need to change if the recipient's demographic profile changed considerably. Think about the pictures, symbols and method of communication as well as the wording used. Does the emphasis of the message change? Try and incorporate some examples of this into your communications diary.

Case history

UK factory hosts Japanese delegation visit

A UK manufacturing company hosted a delegation from an associate company in Japan. The marketing manager was given the task of arranging the first day's activities, which were to include a 2-hour long presentation about the history, structure and objectives of the firm, a tour of the main manufacturing site and lunch followed by a brainstorming session on how the two companies could forge closer links and benefit from future joint projects. However, little consideration was given to the communication barriers that arose during the visit:

- ○ Cultural differences in the way Japanese people greet others, their degree of formality and taste in food.
- ○ The language barrier in that many of the delegation did not speak English and none of the host company spoke Japanese.
- ○ The unfamiliar technical environment and organization of the company, which meant that the jargon and abbreviations specific to the host company that were used in the presentation, made the presentation incomprehensible to most of the delegation.
- ○ The noisy manufacturing site meant that during the tour most of the visitors could not hear what was being said to them.
- ○ The lengthy presentation meant that the visitors who understood English had 'information overload'. Most lost concentration and could not take in the overall message that was being conveyed.
- ○ The delegation did not feel confident or comfortable with contributing to the brainstorming session.

For future visits, the marketing manager thought of a number of ways to eliminate the communication barriers:

- ○ Employing an interpreter.
- ○ Researching cultural differences and using this information to provide appropriate refreshments and use appropriate greetings, seating arrangements and so on.
- ○ Ensuring that no jargon or colloquialisms are used by speakers.
- ○ Using small groups to tour the factory at a quiet time so that visitors can hear what the guide is saying.
- ○ Using a shorter presentation to prevent boredom and information overload.
- ○ Using a different presentation approach, with visual media, such as slides or video and Powerpoint software.
- ○ Increasing interaction with the audience with question and answer techniques to check understanding.
- ○ Providing a pack of information in English and Japanese, containing key points about the company, such as its structure, objectives and current operations.
- ○ Avoiding the brainstorming session as it is probably too ambitious an exercise. Replacing it with a more social event where individual host managers can be 'partnered' with visiting managers, and interpreters used to help exchange views in a less threatening context.

Insight

The Hong Kong and Shanghai Bank – HSBC – is one of the UK's four big banks that also has a significant global presence. Their advertising campaign over the last 2 years looks at this difference in 'cultural' communication to support their well-recognized strapline 'The World's Local Bank'.

The creative treatment features on elements of behaviour and body language which have different meanings across the world. Here are a few examples they have used:

Showing the soles of your feet is highly insulting in some Asian countries.

The okay signal people make using their thumb and index finger has an entirely different meaning in Brazil.

Clearing your plate of food is considered polite in UK but is taken as a sign that you want more food in Japan.

How to avoid barriers to communication

Communication barriers cause mistakes and can damage the business relationship with external customers. With internal customers, communication barriers can lead to conflict (at worst) and irritation (at best), neither of which are a good recipe for internal marketing and customer care.

To overcome possible communication barriers, careful thought needs to be put into the encoding process so that the full message is conveyed in a way that the recipient has the best possible chance of decoding the correct message. Gaps in messages are usually caused when assumptions about how people will 'decode' the message are made.

Target audience

It is important to understand the profile of your target audience, as this is the key to avoiding barriers to communication. If the message is to be decoded correctly, an understanding of your target audience's need is essential and should mean that you are able to have the same 'mental image' about a product or service that your customers have. This understanding results in greater accuracy and precision at the encoding stage, hence more effective communication.

Training

Where staff are placed in face-to-face situations, they are often responsible for the content and message delivery to the external customer. Training in effective communication is required to ensure that staff can eradicate as many barriers as possible, and to avoid making assumptions about customers or by reacting inappropriately when customers make complaints.

Simplify the message

When communicating with customers it is essential not to create information overload and to be aware that only part of the message may be heard. You may have to repeat a message many times before it is fully heard.

Staff can be trained to ask 'checking questions' and information sources such as brochures, telephone helplines and websites can be provided for detailed information provision. It is important not to over-simplify the message, as the content can be lost completely.

Source credibility

It is also important to establish credibility so that customers feel you and your message are trustworthy and both internal and external customers believe in what you say.

Many internal messages regarding pay and conditions carry more importance if they are in the written form. Many promotional messages use specialists or celebrities to add weight to the message. Ariel used Carol Vordeman, presenter of BBC's Tomorrow's World programme, in their advertisement to add weight to the scientific message that was being conveyed. Unfortunately, the BBC saw this as an abuse of her position and terminated her contract. However, many car-related products use Jeremy Clarkson's voice to infer a celebrity approval of the product, linking it to the success of the Top Gear TV programme he presents.

Sainsbury's have similarly used Jamie Oliver's school meal success to change their use of him within their advertising, to promote healthier alternatives available in store.

Listening

Within a two-way communication scenario it is possible that decoding is unsuccessful due to the recipient simply not listening properly. They then send out a similarly badly encoded message in return and communication breaks down. Disagreements often arise when the recipient picks up a different meaning to the message sent out and then sends an angry message back. Although it is difficult to ensure our external customers listen properly, by trying to remove as many of the above barriers we can improve the chances of the communication being heard. Staff who deal with external customers need to be trained to listen effectively and not interrupt customers before the whole message has been relayed.

When communicating with the internal audience it is important that time is allowed for the message to be conveyed and understood. In today's business environment, time is often our biggest barrier to effective communication and we need to counteract this barrier through planning time to communicate in the workplace, for example meetings, coffee breaks, debrief sessions and so on.

By taking some time to consider how a communication might be received, you are more likely to shape a message that will not be misinterpreted or misunderstood. In other words, by carefully shaping your message and considering the effect it might create, it is more likely that the communication will be successful.

Likeability

As we demonstrated in Activity 3.1, a memorable strapline is a useful communications device to have at your disposal. Advertisements that are liked get remembered and talked about, jingles get sung, phrases get repeated. Currently, the BBC series 'Little Britain' which seems to have a plethora of phrases attached to its sketches, seem to be repeated across UK by parents and children of all ages. Likeability is related to a personal meaningful feeling that an advertisement invokes within the message recipient. Each time they hear the message that feeling is also evoked so if it is a pleasurable feeling it will result in the brand/service being viewed pleasurably.

For this reason advertising agencies, when deciding how to convey a particular message, think long and hard about the type of people and the activities shown within an advertising treatment. Careful consideration of the profile of the target audience and their everyday experiences are analysed to find a likeable formula that the target audience will be able to relate to. Consider how many advertisements you encounter where you end up knowing just how that person feels and can empathise with them. This level of involvement will make the message easier for the receiver to remember and recall at an appropriate time.

This involvement is usually created by using messages of either an emotional or rational message. The commonly used elements of appeal are shown in Table 3.1.

Table 3.1 Types of appeal

Emotional appeal	Rational appeal
Fear or anger	Price/Value comparisons
Sex, love, social interaction	Quality levels
Security, reassurance	Past experience
Aspiration/ego	
Humour	

Insight

Brent Spar – A series of missed messages

When Shell decided to sink the Brent Spar oil platform in the North Sea, its actions were widely condemned. Sinking the platform was the cheap option, critics claimed, and Shell was accused of putting profits over safety.

But Shell was acting responsibly. It had carefully considered the available options. Breaking up the rig in situ and bringing the pieces back to land to be disposed of was the safest option if the operation could be successfully completed. However, there was a high risk factor attached to this option. If the dangerous procedure had not gone according to plan, there was a high risk of human injury or fatality.

By sinking the oil platform into the sea there was minimum risk to human life. The damage to marine life, it was estimated by independent consultants, was significant in the short term, but the local ecology would return to normal within a few decades.

So Shell took this option. Some pressure groups claimed this was a manoeuvre that would cause 'significant damage to marine life' – arguably using Shell's own report out of context – and pointed to the fact that bringing it ashore was a much more expensive option than sinking it at sea.

In the end when negative publicity reached a critical mass, Shell decided that the best risk management strategy was now to apologize for its mistake. Better PR and a more robust communication of the fact that Shell had considered all the options and balanced safety – both of human and marine life – against cost would have made the public much more sympathetic to Shell's complicated problem.

Source: Crisis and Risk Management, Kogan Page, 1997.

Planning the business message

Professional communicators decide the purpose of their communication at the outset. By being clear about their intention, they then know if they have achieved their objective at the end of their communication.

Business communications tend to be planned, formal, impersonal and succinct. The degree of planning involved in the communication depends on the purpose and context of the communication. For example, you may carefully plan a sales call to a prospect, since you may need to deal with any objections that the customer may raise. However, you are unlikely to do this when you want to arrange lunch with a colleague, even though there may be several important matters you wish to discuss with him. In this situation, you may not make detailed notes of the issues but your planning may extend to making a mental note of them.

A planning framework – The PASS mnemonic

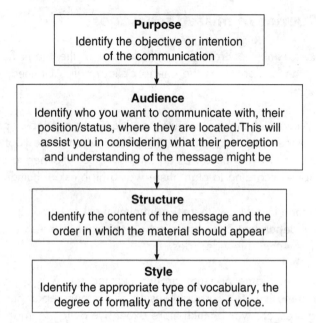

Figure 3.3 A planning framework

The PASS framework is an easy to remember mnemonic that you may be familiar with. To assist yourself in the planning of messages, you should also consider the communication *mode* you intend to use, as the communication format and media you use will be important in determining the structure and style you adopt.

Purpose

There are an infinite number of reasons why you might communicate in business. Generally, in internal communication situations you will be informing colleagues, line managers or subordinates about something, responding to a previous communication, obtaining a decision or requesting action. In external markets you may be trying to raise awareness in the media, persuading customers to buy or stimulating some other response, such as ordering a catalogue or ringing for more information.

Barker (1999) recommends that you do not confuse your document's purpose with its subject. He says that if you were writing about a new piece of equipment, you could write about it in many ways. The way you choose will depend on your purpose and what you want your document to do.

According to Barker, possible objectives of a product include:

o   Justifying the cost of buying it
o   Comparing it with similar products
o   Telling the reader how to operate it
o   Listing the options for using it
o   Detailing its technical specifications
o   Explaining how it fits into an existing network or system.

It is possible to closely align Barker's objectives to the DRIP mnemonic used in Unit 1 in the following way when writing about that new piece of equipment.

- o *Differentiate* – Comparing to similar products. Listing the options for using it.
- o *Remind* – Not used as these are concerned with a piece of new equipment but the benefits of use may be used in subsequent documents.
- o *Inform* – Telling the reader how to operate it. Detailing its technical specifications.
- o *Persuade* – Justifying the cost of buying it. Explaining how it fits into an existing network or system.

Each purpose will generate a completely different document. The document will only be useful if it addresses the purposes required clearly. Where the document has more than one objective it is essential to ensure all objectives are met.

Audience

For internal communications, the position of the person you are communicating with and how well you know them will determine the style of communication you adopt in terms of the detail, complexity and words used. In addition, the purpose of the communication and the urgency of the matter will determine which communication format and media you will use.

In order to tell a colleague that you will not be available for lunch for another hour, you may either visit them their office or telephone them. In contrast to this, you may write a memo or send an e-mail to inform staff about a change in the time and place of the weekly sales meeting.

In writing a press release to announce some important news about the company you work for, you may draft two versions of the press release. One may be tailored for the national press and one may be targeted at the trade press. However, if you had a particular contact in the broadcast media whom you wanted to inform, you may consider using the personal touch and actually telephoning the contact with the information.

In developing advertising to your target market, you will need to consider the characteristics of the target audience in terms of their age, gender, education, social background and lifestyle when composing the words and deciding on the visual approach and the media you will use.

Structure

Having identified why you are communicating and with whom, you need then to consider what you are going to say and how you are going to organize the content of the message.

Business communications should be succinct, so you should be selective with the content you choose to include. Use relevant, accurate information and make sure that you do not overload the recipient with too much information.

Having selected the material for your message, you need to decide how you will organize it. The way you group material together and how you sequence it determines the shape of the message.

It may help you to structure the message if you identify the most important point and then follow with the supplementary information you need to include. If you are dealing with particularly complex material, it may be helpful to present the simple information first and build up to the more complex argument or points you wish to make. You may feel it is important to present information in a chronological order, particularly if you are dealing with a series of events or a complaint about a number of issues.

Whatever structure you adopt, you should note that it is easier to read an argument that follows a logical progression and quicker for people to absorb information that is grouped together in chunks with relevant headings.

Style

The style you adopt in any message is governed by the words you use, the way you structure sentences and the tone of voice you adopt.

The way you use vocabulary is a personal choice. The English language is very rich and you may often have several words to choose from that will convey the same meaning. However, you should consider your audience and their familiarity with the words you use. It is not always appropriate to avoid jargon or technical words, especially when you know your audience is familiar with them and where it is important for you to establish credibility and common ground with your audience.

By changing the structure of sentences you can place emphasis on certain words and by altering the order of words you can produce greater fluency or flow.

The tone of any communication conveys the overall effect. You can create an overall impression of friendliness and informality with the greeting you use, simple wording and colloquial expressions. For example, the following sentence has a friendly, informal tone: 'Thanks for lunch yesterday. It was useful to go through the client list and I will make appointments to see each of them a.s.a.p.'

Alternatively, you can convey a formal tone by giving instructions, using technical wording and an impersonal tone. For example: 'The figures indicate that sales staff need to cut the cost of expenses by x per cent. Consequently all journeys over x miles should be agreed by the Sales Manager.'

By emphasizing points, by appealing to the recipient's emotions, repeating selling points, using reassuring terms and asking questions that lead the recipient to a series of benefits, you can create a persuasive message. For example, the following statement has a persuasive tone: 'How can Home Care help you? With Home Care you can be assured of quality care in the comfort of your own home. No more struggling with the cooking and cleaning.'

 Activity 3.3

> Consider the use of jargon in your own areas of work. Imagine you had a new member of staff joining and you had been asked to write a 'Glossary of Terms' for their use, identifying and explaining each term and mnemonic frequently used.

Mode of communication

The PASS mnemonic is used for planning the message content. When using PASS it is necessary to consider the way in which the message is being transmitted to the recipient. The mode or method of communication is as important as the content, as it must be capable of transmitting the message clearly to the right recipient in order that the communication objectives be met.

The communication format (whether that is a written report or an oral presentation at a meeting) or the media (whether that is the telephone or any electronic means or some form of advertising media) that you use to transmit your message will influence its structure and style. Television advertisements are usually 30 seconds long and expensive to use – not ideal for transmitting a long and complex message.

When communicating internally, you will need to consider the purpose of the communication and the audience you wish to communicate with, in order to decide the correct communication format. For example, there will be some occasions when it is suitable to put a notice on the notice board to communicate with colleagues and at other times it will be more appropriate to send a memo or organize a face-to-face meeting.

The level of formality and confidentiality can affect the mode of communication – it is more confidential to send an e-mail, rather than a fax. You will need to confirm a verbal offer of a job in writing, setting out the various terms and conditions that form the contract.

Where you need to raise awareness about an issue or a new product, your choice of media will influence the style you will adopt.

Activity 3.4

For example, if you were trying to raise awareness about the dangers of driving without seatbelts, you could use either a press campaign or a radio campaign to communicate your message. However, the treatment of the message would be different in each case. For radio, you could use sound to communicate an emotional message of a family talking about the death of a loved one. For the print advertisement, you could go into more detail, as you would not have the same time constraints as a short radio commercial. So you could include more facts and figures about the number of car accidents caused by not wearing a seatbelt. Such a detailed message would be totally inappropriate if it was read out loud in a radio commercial but could be absorbed by people reading it in their own time and at their own pace. The suitability of each mode will be considered in detail in Units 4–6.

Two memorable emotional messages are as follows:

Lemsip TV commercial featured a woman who has just returned home from work struggling with flu symptoms and feeling awful. She gets a Lemsip and sits down in an armchair to drink it. As she comes to the end of the drink her face becomes more relaxed. She rests back into her armchair and the armchair becomes bigger and softer curling itself around her. She's feeling better already!

Cancer Research – These adverts show various family photos where one member becomes hazy and disappears leaving a gap in the photo – the scene then shifts to a mum helping to get her son warmly dressed for school, they are both looking in the mirror and as the boy looks at his mum, she disappears. He is alone in the hall. For £2 per month you can help Cancer Research.

Ronseal Woodstain – Very rational message delivered in a very loud strident tone – verging on the aggressive. The advert shows a can of Ronseal woodstain with a newly stained fence behind it. A man's hand strikes the top of the can with a bang. His voice informs us 'Ronseal – does what it says on the can'.

Figure 3.4 A print advertisement can contain more detail than a radio or poster advertisement

How the PASS framework can help in planning messages

If you needed to raise awareness among teenage girls in one city in your country about the dangers of smoking, the PASS framework could be your starting point to help you decide what you want to say and how you should frame your message.

For example, by considering the 'purpose' of the communication task, you would be clear about the message you needed to convey, that is to warn of the dangers of smoking.

By considering the 'audience' you would ensure that you concentrated on teenage girls. This may influence the language you use, that is not technical or medical language. For instance, sending text messages is very popular amongst teenagers so you could use that type of language to give your message impact and credibility. As the style and structure of a message are greatly influenced by the communication method you are going to use, you would consider this aspect next. Assuming you were restricted to a tight budget, you may consider that posters or outdoor advertising could be an economical medium to use. However, you would also need to consider where you would place your posters. Relevant places could be community and sports centres that young people use. Or outdoor poster sites at cinemas and shopping centres or transport advertising on buses and underground trains or at 'Adshel' bus stop sites could be used.

The next consideration would be the 'style' of the message that would suit your target audience. You would have to ensure that your style was not patronizing. You could even use a celebrity who appeals to this age group. You would need to consider the restrictions of the poster format and the best design of the poster in terms of layout, typeface, colours and imagery that could be used.

The structure would be the final consideration. This would mean looking at how you are going to convey your message. You would have to be selective with words and group the material in a sequence that is logical. In other words, you would have to focus on the most important point and make that first. This could be a fairly straightforward task when determining a short poster-style message.

Thus the PASS framework can help in planning messages.

Activity 3.5

Suggest an appropriate communication style and mode of communication for each of the following situations:

1. You work for the city council and wish to use an advertising campaign to inform motorists that tolls will be introduced on routes into the town centre.
2. You work in the marketing department of a washing powder manufacturer; it has become evident that the new product launched by your competitor contains chemicals so strong that it is causing clothes to rot. The marketing director has asked you to inform the sales force so that they can inform the trade.
3. You are the distribution manager at a chemical company. There have been problems with deliveries from the warehouse to a number of distributors. You have collated your findings about the problems and now need to communicate them to the sales and marketing director.

Insight

Dove Soap – for Real Women

The current campaign for Dove soap has generated an extraordinary amount of free publicity for the brand.

The advertisements feature a series of unconventionally attractive women of all shapes, sizes and age. The 'campaign for real beauty' slogan is used to infer that this is what beauty is all about – normal everyday women around the world leading their lives everyday. It is not about unrealistically beautiful models.

The campaign does not actually espouse any of the brand benefits, it does not claim to transform the world or take 10 years off. It's just soap.

Dove is the latest brand to utilize this 'brand belief' approach. Nike pioneered the approach in the 1990s. Unlike their competitors, Nike did not make advertisements about trainer technology. Instead they espoused an ideology of self-improvement through willpower with the 'Just do it' campaign.

Similarly, Apple sold Imacs not on the basis of their superior computing power but by expressing a belief in the power of maverick creativity using 'Think different'.

The brand-belief approach to advertising has clearly come of age. There are a couple of underlying reasons why we will be seeing more of it in the future. First, it's getting tougher to talk about product benefits. Advertising regulations that govern the claims they can make are becoming more stringent.

Second, we are becoming a society that looks increasingly to brands to tell us what to believe in.

And it's working for Dove. After the first stage of the campaign, sales were up 700 per cent, on a brand that was growing at 20 per cent per annum already. It is estimated it will reach a turnover of $2 billion within a couple of years.

Source: Media Guardian – 12/01/05.

Summary

In this unit you have studied:

  o The purpose of communication
  o How communication occurs
  o How and why barriers to communication occur
  o How to overcome communication barriers.

Further study

Attempt Question 6a from the June 2005 examination paper by downloading the paper from Appendix 4 or from the CIM Learning Zone (go to www.cim.co.uk). You can also access the specimen answers and Senior Examiner's advice for this exam question from the website (www.cim.co.uk).

Hints and tips

By now your communications diary should be getting quite thick. If you have not been adding to it or have not even started then it is essential that you catch up at this stage. It is impossible to develop a real appreciation of how powerful a tool communication is, if you do not spend time analysing the wealth of examples out there in the real world. As we move on to the more nuts and bolts aspects of communication in Units 4 and 5, you will be able to refer to your communications diary to access live examples of how skills learnt in verbal and written communication can be used in the marketing world. Go on – catch up – it is not too late!

Bibliography

Fill, C. (2002) *Marketing Communications – Contexts, Strategies and Applications*, 3rd edition, Prentice Hall.

unit 4
verbal communications – theory and methods

In this unit you will:

o Use non-verbal communication effectively. See syllabus section 4.4.

o Become a better listener in face-to-face situations and on the telephone. See syllabus section 4.4.

o Arrange, manage and lead meetings effectively. See syllabus sections 4.4, 4.6.

o Prepare the appropriate meeting documentation. See syllabus sections 4.6, 4.7.

o Understand the role of interviews in communicating with others. See syllabus section 4.4.

By the end of this unit you will be able to:

o Explain the importance of effective body language, tone, verbal and listening skills in communication and strategies for developing and improving verbal, non-verbal and listening skills (4.4).

o Interpret, summarize and present, oral, written and graphical information (4.5).

o Explain key communication factors to consider in meetings, including arranging and convening a meeting, documentation involved and strategies for conducting a meeting (4.6).

o Plan, prepare and deliver a presentation using appropriate and effective visual aids and media (4.7).

This unit relates to standards of practice

Cb.2   Develop direct or indirect communications.

Study Guide

In Unit 1 we identified the different groups that we need to communicate with. In Unit 2 we looked at how buyers behave when in the purchase mode and how communication can affect them. In Unit 3 we examined the theory supporting communications. We can now move on to examine each method of communication and the advantages and disadvantages of each in communicating internally and externally. Units 4 and 5 will deal with each under the categories of:

- ○ Verbal communications
- ○ Written communications.

Face-to-face communication

Effective verbal, non-verbal and listening skills are an essential part of every day life. Within business life these skills are just as important but within marketing we have the extra dimension of having to communicate with customers in an increasingly competitive environment.

This unit will deal with face-to-face communication in terms of verbal and non-verbal techniques that we can use when communicating internally and externally. The use of these techniques in message encoding will be examined.

The importance of listening will be examined especially in relation to face-to-face situations.

As an extension to verbal communication we will also be examining how the telephone can be used as an effective tool for both internal and external communication.

Verbal communication

When speaking with customers, whether face-to-face or on the telephone, it is important that what you say is perceived as helpful, welcoming and appropriate to the situation. In a face-to-face situation, the chart on the next page demonstrates that it is not just what we say that is important, but more about *how* we say it and our *body language* being consistent with the message being sent. Obviously, body language will not take an active part in telephone communication but that will put additional emphasis on the tone of voice used and other non-verbal cues such as speed of answering and ability to gain the required response.

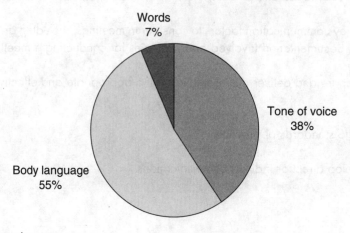

Figure 4.1 How we receive messages

It is sometimes ironic that the people who interact most frequently with the group of greatest importance to every organization – *customers* – are sometimes the least well trained and lowest paid. Having spent a great deal of time and money on promotional messages and persuading the customer to purchase, the actual transaction will take place only if the customer is dealt with in a welcoming way and the interaction leaves them feeling valued.

Activity 4.1

Change the following phrases so that they demonstrate a helpful attitude to the customer.

1. 'I don't work in that department.'
2. 'Hang on I'll need to check.'
3. 'I don't know if we will be having more of those in.'
4. 'You're ten minutes late for your appointment. You will have to wait two weeks now.'

Pitch and tone – how you say things

The tone that you use can be, either intentionally or unintentionally, inappropriate and can infuriate customers. An apathetic, droning or listless tone of voice can convey the message that you don't care or are not interested in the customer and their problem/query.

A rushed tone can make you sound impatient with the customer. In fact, different tones of voice can change the meaning of the same words. By changing the inflection in your voice, you can say the words 'Your statement is ready now' in an angry way, sarcastically, apologetically, shyly and even in a humorous way.

Customers obviously want to be greeted or spoken to by someone whose tone of voice sounds interested, helpful and patient. If they have been treated unfairly or a mistake has been made they will expect an apologetic and sincere tone to be used. It helps to smile whilst you are talking even when you are on the phone you will be surprised how doing this simple thing lifts the tone of your voice.

Consider the expression 'Oh, that's just great'. A different message can be conveyed depending on how the voice is used to express the words. For example, said in a friendly tone of voice when someone has received something they are pleased with, it conveys a friendly, grateful message. If the same expression is shouted at someone, it could be a sarcastic message that in fact they are not pleased with something and things are not in fact 'great'.

Pitch is also used to change the emphasis of the message. Consider your tutor for this module. If they were to speak in a very quite voice that you could hardly hear, you would probably feel they were not confident in what they were saying to you. If they were to shout, you would feel that they were treating you as an inferior person, not respecting the role you can play in the learning process. A well-modulated pitch, at a level that all can hear, is what we expect.

So the tone of voice, volume and pitch that are used can affect the message being conveyed.

Enabling two-way communications

In most situations it is essential to establish two-way communications. It is not usual that we encounter a situation where we are simply required to talk at people with total disregard for their opinion on what we are saying. Some basic pointers to enabling this are:

Talk with people not at them – This can be more difficult when speaking on the phone. Sometimes it helps to have a mental picture of the person in your mind so that you can start to build a rapport.

Enable a two-way flow of conversation – Do not interrupt but ensure they are aware you are listening by using non-verbal cues such as maintaining eye contact and nodding when communicating face to face. On the telephone, verbal cues such as 'Yes' and 'Hmm' help this. Conversely create gaps in your own conversation so that the other person can respond.

Don't jump to conclusions – You may think you know what the other person is going to say but you cannot be sure until the message is delivered. By anticipating bad news and showing via your body language that you are on the defensive, you can change the whole atmosphere of the interaction before it is even started.

Interrupting people before they have finished what they are saying may result in your gaining the wrong impression completely and responding in an inappropriate way.

Non-verbal communication skills

Non-verbal communication consists of:

o   The body language you use, such as eye contact, facial expression, posture, gesture and physical space.
o   The impression/atmosphere you create by your punctuality, hospitality, manners and personal appearance.

Non-verbal communication can convey messages without words or add meaning to whatever words are being used.

Eye contact
The look in someone's eyes can have a variety of meanings. In a romantic scene, the way an actor looks into the leading lady's eyes conveys a very different meaning to the way a person can stare in defiance or in a challenging way. In a business context, avoiding eye contact can convey disinterest or shiftiness but making positive eye contact while you are delivering a presentation shows that you are relating to and connecting with your audience. Therefore, in order for the message you are conveying to be taken as 'trustful', it is important that eye contact be maintained. In two-way communication, the fact that someone cannot meet your gaze may mean they are uncomfortable with what you are saying and you may wish to change the message content in light of this.

Facial expression
Your facial expression and coloration can convey various meanings. A flushed face can indicate embarrassment or shyness, while the colour draining out of your face can indicate shock. Pursed lips can reveal your irritation at something, a frown can show disapproval and a smile can indicate happiness, approval or a welcome.

The expression must be appropriate to the situation. People working closely with customers are often told to 'keep smiling'. However, if the customer is in the process of making a serious complaint, a fixed smile will only infuriate them further.

Posture

If you adopt an upright posture, it can show that you are attentive and the opposite can show that you are disinterested. If you were lounging in your seat when your managing director walks past, it could indicate that you do not respect the individual and you are probably not working that hard either.

It is important to adopt an open posture when dealing with customers, folded arms will put people off whereas leaning towards them will indicate listening. Other postures/gestures can be used to send out non-verbal messages – consider how you would feel if the person you are speaking to started drumming their fingers.

We now know from a series of studies on human and animal behaviour that we tend to mirror the body language of the person we are communicating with if we feel empathy with that person and their point of view.

Physical space

Physical space also refers to the invisible line that surrounds people and is referred to as *personal space*. By breaching someone's personal space you can intimidate him or her and be perceived as overbearing and insensitive.

An accepted move into someone's physical space in Britain is the friendly handshake. In Europe and other countries, kissing on the cheek may be acceptable. Different countries and cultures have different norms. In China, the size of acceptable physical space is much smaller than in Britain because their population density is much greater.

Physical space can also be about how people are seated whilst communicating. Sitting on a big chair behind a big desk so that people who enter your office have to sit on a lower chair opposite you, with the desk as a barrier, can communicate your authority and the level of formality you expect from others. Alternatively, you can achieve informality in meetings by using a horseshoe-shape layout.

The impression/atmosphere

You can create a favourable impression in a business situation with a smart appearance in terms of your clothes and personal grooming. If you are punctual and use the appropriate greeting, for example a formal handshake, particularly when meeting new business contacts, this can influence whether you are seen to be acceptable by conforming to the norms of business behaviour.

It is important in order that the person you are interacting with feels comfortable in the situation they find themselves and so feels able to communicate with you effectively. Much of what is covered here is basic in its approach and you may feel it is stating the obvious – however, consider how many of the issues raised here have happened to you when visiting other organizations, and how communication was affected.

Similarly, your hospitality can be judged not just by the words you express but if you are seen to be helpful and considerate to visitors. This can include taking their coats, checking that they are warm/cool enough, whether they need a drink and ensuring that your body language is positive, for example smiling rather than looking at your watch as if you are in a hurry to get rid of them.

67

It is important that when people come to see you they are not kept waiting in a draughty reception for longer than absolutely necessary. You should also go to meet them rather than expecting them to find you. The availability of visitors' parking spaces, signposted toilets and an easily identifiable reception area also remove visitors' anxiety and communicate that they are welcome to your organization.

The atmosphere may be affected by external noise outside of your control. In this instance it is best to acknowledge the problems and to work at finding the best way around them with the co-operation of the person with whom you are communicating.

International body language

Even though body language is common to everyone, there are still cultural differences and language sub-groups, which, if you operate in the global marketplace, you should learn. One of these is the size of personal space across the world. Other examples include:

- Even if your gaze is meant to be sincere, avoid staring into a Japanese person's eyes. In Japan, long stares are regarded as bad manners and people prefer to keep their gaze fixed on the neck.
- Never wink at anyone in Hong Kong, as it is considered to be impolite.
- In the Middle East and Far East, always present things to people with the right hand and do not use your left hand for eating as it is regarded as 'unclean'.
- Japanese people bow rather than shake hands.
- Nodding your head means 'no' in parts of Greece, Yugoslavia and Turkey and shaking your head means 'yes'.
- Never show the sole of your shoe when you are in an Arab country as this is considered to be a grave insult. However, eye contact is important in the Arab world.
- Do not blow your nose at a business meeting with Japanese people and always present your business card with both hands.

Activity 4.2

In Unit 3 we considered HSBC's use of non-verbal communication across the globe. Look within your communications diary and consider how the creative treatment of messages would differ across the world.

Listening skills

Good listening skills are important in marketing, simply because you will use them during meetings, interviews, negotiations, other people's presentations and when you are in a selling or briefing situation. As detailed in Unit 3, effective two-way communications is dependent on both parties listening properly.

You need to work at your listening skills so that you possess all the necessary and relevant information, avoid wasting time and maintain good relations with both internal and external customers. Listening skills are particularly important if you are dealing with a customer who is trying to air grievances.

Many people imagine that listening is something that just happens. However, it is important that you distinguish between hearing and listening. *Hearing* is what might happen when you have the radio playing in the background whilst you do something else. *Listening* means engaging your mind and your memory, and you are active in selecting information, organizing, interpreting and storing it.

Listening skills are a vital part of customer care. By using effective listening skills you can obtain all the necessary and relevant information you need to find out what customers need, or what is making them unhappy. Listening is an active, not a passive activity. By checking what a customer has said and paraphrasing it, you can check that you have understood exactly what they mean. This avoids confusion and wastage of time. Writing down information can also reassure the customer that you have listened to their problem and are more likely to respond in a positive way.

In many situations where you are dealing with unhappy customers, listening skills are very important to understand the problem. Often customers will go into great detail about a number of things that they are not happy with. However, it is usually one thing in particular that they want rectified. A good listener can select the most relevant information and decide what can be done about the situation. It is important not to interrupt but to let the customer 'get things off their chest' and then begin a dialogue, which summarizes their problems and begins to show your willingness to deal with them.

It is also important to use the correct body language when listening, and maintaining eye contact with the other person is essential if they are to be convinced that you are listening. Positioning your body towards the other person also gives the impression that you are interested in what they say and will devote the time for effective listening.

Barriers to listening

Your thought processes operate four times faster than most people speak, and as a listener you may become bored and allow your mind to wander. You may regard what is being said as dull or irrelevant and close your mind, thus missing vital pieces of information.

You may have prejudices or fixed ideas about things and, if you are listening to something with which you disagree, you may react by pretending to listen but actually 'tuning out' to the message or becoming angry and distracted from the message that is being communicated.

You may be listening to someone who is talking about something technical that you do not understand, with the result that you stop following the conversation and may become too embarrassed to ask questions. If you are the customer in this situation then it will be safe to assume you probably won't be making a purchase.

You may be listening to a great number of facts and figures and lose track of what is being said because of information overload, or the method of communication used.

How can we be better listeners?

- o Be an active listener
    - Concentrate
    - Make notes
    - Check out understanding through questioning and paraphrasing
    - Use body language to show you are listening and have empathy.

 ○ Be a patient listener
  – Don't interrupt – listen to the whole story
  – Don't argue – try to be helpful and look for solutions not excuses.

 Activity 4.3

Your friend has recently taken a job as a receptionist at a Doctor's surgery. The people that she regularly encounters can often be difficult to understand either due to age, infirmity or because they are distressed by a medical emergency. She is aware that she needs to listen carefully so that she can accurately assess their needs and ensure that she understands the names of drugs of treatments they are requesting. Suggest four ways in which she can become an effective listener.

Using verbal communications skills

Having looked at the theory and best practice attached to the use of verbal communication, we will now move on to look at each of the communication methods available to us that utilize these skills. These methods include:

 ○ Telephone conversations
 ○ Presentations
 ○ Meetings
 ○ Interviews.

The emphasis within the coursebook will be on the use of these methods within a business context – internal and external customers. However, most of the points covered would also be relevant to social interaction.

Study tip

As we progress through this unit and Units 5 and 6, we will look at the advantages and disadvantages of many methods of communication plus the application of the PASS mnemonic to those methods. This will be helpful to you within both exams and assignments where you are often required to recommend suitable communications methods and to justify that choice.

Using the telephone

With all the various methods of communication available to people, the telephone remains a popular tool. Figure 4.2 shows how the greatest importance is attached to the tone of voice rather than the words.

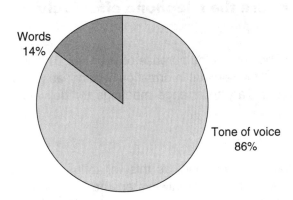

Figure 4.2 How we receive messages by telephone

The tone of voice you use in telephone conversations becomes so important, because your body language cannot be seen. You can overcome the barrier of not being seen by adopting the tone of voice that is relevant to the message being communicated (see voice characteristics in the section on verbal communication skills in this unit). You should also vary the tone of voice you use, as a relentless monotone can give the impression either that you are boring or that you are bored with the conversation. Verbal cues such as 'yes' and 'hmm' along with the use of checking questions can be used to replace body language to communicate to the other person that you are listening to.

The recent lowering cost of mobile 'camera' phones has resulted in a visual now being possible; however, technology is still in its infancy and the subtleties of body language are still not easily transferred via this medium.

Advantages and disadvantages of using the telephone

Advantages	Disadvantages
Cheap, quick, easy access – global coverage	No body language possible – lack of visual can lead to mistrust developing
Two-way communication possible – all issues can be covered at time of call	Not ideal if a visual is required – for example, to approve a piece of advertising copy. Camera phones can go some way to addressing this problem
Gatekeepers can field calls and take messages – better use of time possible	Telephone tennis – lots of calls don't reach the recipient first time
Automated message facility available showing date and time with remote access possible	Difficult to gauge if the recipient is really not available – or just avoiding you
Easier to hide emotions and deal with sensitive or personal issues and no eye contact required. The introduction of videophones will remove this benefit	There is no permanent record of what is discussed – often need to be followed with written communication
Easier to terminate a telephone call than a face-to-face meeting	

Using PASS to use the telephone effectively

Purpose

Plan your call and be sure of the purpose of your call. This will guide you in deciding what you have to say. Have all the relevant information at hand; as well as the correct telephone number. You may need your diary to arrange meetings, or delivery notes if you are chasing a late delivery.

Audience

Consider who you are contacting, as this will influence what you say and how you say it. Whatever the reason, you should always ensure you are polite and friendly. Think about the best time to call; many organizations are inundated first thing Monday morning. Two hours later you may get through more easily and find a less stressed person on the other end. Likewise, some issues are best raised in the morning to enable a solution to be found that day itself.

Structure

In planning your message it may be helpful to make a checklist of points you wish to make as a reminder for use during the telephone conversation. If you also note down actions agreed upon, these notes could form the basis of any written confirmation you may need to produce later.

A call should always begin by greeting the person who answers: giving your name, company name and asking for the person you wish to speak to. At this point, you may have to give a brief outline of the purpose of your call.

Having made sure that you are speaking to the right person, continue your call in a courteous, clear and concise way. Make sure all your points are covered.

If the person you need to speak to is not available, you may need to leave a message – this will need to be short and concise, detailing the action required. It is not always suitable to leave a detailed message if you are dealing with sensitive issues, in this instance you should politely ask for the recipient of the call to ring you back.

Style

You should be confident when making a business telephone call, or at least sound confident. Smiling as you speak can help to achieve this. One of the advantages of telephones (at least those that are not videophones) is that the recipient of the call cannot see you. However, using gestures whilst you are speaking on the phone can help you to put the correct inflection and emphasis into your speech. Remember to consider the pace of speech, when someone is slightly nervous on the telephone, they sound hurried and use careless speech. Consequently, you should speak slightly more slowly than your usual pace. This is also important because the recipient of the call cannot lip read, so it is important that you pronounce words clearly.

Some words or numbers may need to be repeated or clarified in a more succinct way – the number 15 can become 'one five', clarifying something like a postcode is helped if we use accepted symbol words to confirm which letters you mean – that is 4OD becomes 4 Oscar Delta.

It is important to remain business-like during a telephone call and avoid slang or words that are over-familiar, such as 'OK' 'yeah', 'ta ra then'. Likewise avoid jargon, you cannot see the message receiver to observe from their body language if they are understanding you or not. As you get to know people that you call regularly then a certain level of informality may be possible but business etiquette still applies.

Guidelines for receiving calls

Most organizations have their own documented procedures for answering the telephone, but whatever procedures are set down for staff to follow, it is essential that a friendly and efficient image be conveyed to anyone who contacts the organization.

Obviously, callers should not be left waiting while the telephone rings. Many organizations stipulate how quickly the telephone should be answered. Guidelines should also be in place to handle:

- o Answering calls
- o Putting calls on hold
- o Transferring calls
- o Taking messages.

Answering calls

It is usually considered acceptable to answer a call within three to five rings. The opening greeting should be friendly and appropriate to the situation. It is always helpful to have pen and paper at hand to take messages and an internal directory to transfer calls.

- o *Answering on behalf of the company* – Caller needs company name, maybe your name and a greeting, for example 'Good Morning, AW Plumbing, Adam speaking, how can I help you?'
- o *Answering on behalf of the department* – Caller needs the name of the department and your name, for example 'Good morning, Bathroom Supplies, John speaking, how can I help you?'
- o *Answering your telephone extension* – After progressing through the company, the caller just needs to know it is you who is answering. Therefore, 'Good morning, Steve Wood speaking, how can I help you?'
- o *Answering some one else's extension* – Extensions should never be kept ringing. When the customer has got this far it is infuriating to fall at the last fence. Therefore you should answer but make it clear you are not the intended recipient, for example 'Good morning, Steve Wood's extension, Helen speaking, can I help you?'

It is important that whatever the required greeting it should be delivered clearly, concisely and slowly. It may be the hundredth time you have answered the telephone but it is the first time for the caller so a hurried sing-song response can sometimes be totally incomprehensible.

Putting a customer on hold

It is important that callers are put on hold for the shortest time possible. Their permission should always be sought before being put on hold and an explanation of why it is necessary. If you cannot put the call through quickly or obtain the information required, it is best to take the caller's details and call them back rather than keep them waiting.

Callers are rarely asked if they mind being put on hold. What usually happens is that before the caller draws breath at the end of a sentence, they are summarily sent to telephone limbo and forced to listen to music, while the person on the other end of the line tries to transfer them or consults their files.

Transferring a call

It is not surprising that customers become intolerant when they are transferred over and over again, having to explain their situation several times over.

- The best approach, is to explain why the call needs to be transferred and to whom. You should ask if the customer minds being transferred. Before you hang up, make sure there is someone to pick up the call. Before the customer talks to the person they have been transferred to, you should briefly outline the nature of the call, so that the caller does not have to repeat details again. If the intended recipient is not available then it may be appropriate to give the caller a name, department or extension number to enable them to pursue the matter if they need to call back at a later date/time.

Taking messages

It is very important to get the details of a message right the first time. This is where your listening skills will be very useful. Take details of the caller's name, company, telephone number, the nature of the call and the action required. You should repeat the details back to the caller. It is good practice to write the message down along with your name and the date and time of the call.

Many messages are now automated, taken by machine or voice mail. You should ensure the message on either is appropriate to the situation and updated daily. Messages should be cleared and dealt with daily. If that is not possible (e.g. you are on holiday) then this responsibility should be given to someone else in the organization to deal with in your absence.

Developments and trends

Mobile phones

The cost of mobile phone communication is becoming so low globally that often we are able to contact the person we require directly and cheaply, at any time of the day. The mobile phone has become responsible for extending the working day and we, as demanding customers, often get frustrated when a contact is not available when we need them.

It is unfair to expect business contacts to be available all day, every day, so a good personalized message facility (voice or text) should be available and responded to, in business hours, at the earliest opportunity. We should be aware of mobile phone etiquette at all times, turning phones off during meetings, resisting the tendency to shout into them in public places and to make the ringing device as unobtrusive as possible. Organizations expecting their staff to use mobile phones should ensure they have hands-free set for use whilst driving, as this is now a legal requirement.

Mobile phones can now allow documentary evidence in the form of SMS messages although the use is limited to short messages only.

When making international calls, we must always be aware of the effect of different time zones and the working practices of the country being called; much of Europe still operates a siesta period during the summer.

The addition of camera and video technology in the third generation (3G) of mobile phones can help to remove some of the disadvantages (and advantages) of using the telephone. The cost of these has fallen considerably in the last 6 months and it will be interesting to see how the use of this facility develops in the next year.

Some mobile phones incorporate personal data, diary facilities and e-mail access. One of these, called 'Blackberry', enables all of these functions in a handset that is less cumbersome to handle than the average calculator.

Samsung have pushed to the forefront of innovation within the mobile communications industry. Their stated forthcoming updates include voice-recognition technology to convert speech into text messages and the ability to scan in personal data from a colleague's business card.

Conference calls

The technology exists to have several different people in different locations talking to each other at the same time. While these conversations lack the impact of a face-to-face meeting, they can be a convenient and relatively inexpensive method of getting people together for instant feedback, especially when people are spread over a wide geographic area.

Paperwork required for the meeting can be sent out in advance of the call, and the members prepare for the call in the same way as for any meeting.

However, it can be difficult to avoid situations where everyone speaks at once and the conversation flow is often inhibited by the lack of non-verbal cues.

This can be helped by having a chairperson who has a similar role to the chair in a formal meeting (see further on in this unit) and members have to address the chair before speaking, and the chair can invite comment from members who have not had much input. This is a newly required skill within an organization and one which can be very beneficial in being able to arrange meetings in a shorter time span and cutting costs and lost time, spent travelling to and from meetings.

Activity 4.4

Effective use of telephones

You are the marketing manager of a medium-sized electronics company. The department's administrative assistant has recently been replaced due to maternity leave. The new employee is very young and inexperienced and does not really understand how to use the phone properly – her greatest sin is leaving the phone on the desk and shouting across the office to gain the attention of the person for whom the call is intended. As many customer calls come through to the department, you are worried about the impression this is giving to your customers and suppliers. Construct an e-mail to advise her of how you would like her to deal with calls in the future.

Presentations

Types of presentations

For most marketers it is an inevitable part of their professional career to give speeches or presentations. In the early part of your career you could be asked to give an informal briefing to colleagues on a recent training course or a demonstration on how a piece of equipment works. As you become more established you may find yourself going through the results of a campaign to a group of managers, giving colleagues a progress update on a project, putting forward your proposals to a client or even delivering a sales pitch. In short, the number and seniority of the people that you are presenting to will tend to increase as you progress through your marketing career perhaps culminating in being asked to be a conference speaker to a few hundred industry figures.

Study tip

Start assessing the strengths and weaknesses of any presentations that you attend, thinking specifically about how you feel it could have been improved. It may help to prepare an evaluation template to assess how closely the presentation met its objectives.

If you find yourself doing a presentation (and perhaps you should volunteer) then ask someone to evaluate your performance and arrange a feedback discussion after the event.

Using PASS to plan an effective speech or presentation

Purpose
The planning of the presentation begins with objectives. Consider the purpose of the presentation, why you are delivering it and what you hope to achieve. At the end of the presentation you should be able to determine if you have achieved your objectives. Supporting documentation may need to be circulated before the presentation to ensure all attendees can play an active part and enable any decisions that are required. It is a good idea to start your presentation with your interpretation of the purpose so that everyone is on board with the reasons for attending.

Audience
The profile and size of the intended audience will help you to determine the level of formality, likely interaction, and level of industry jargon, which can be used. If the audience is travelling to attend the presentation then you may need to consider their needs in relation to refreshments, the room the presentation takes place in and the start/finish time.

The likelihood and frequency of questions will need to be considered in terms of the structure and timing. Some audiences will be listening intently whereas others may have lots to contribute which can bring its own problems.

The level of prior knowledge and where that knowledge needs to move to will be critical to the content and length of the presentation. This will also affect the structure below.

Structure
Knowing what your purpose is and what your audience's requirements are will help you decide on the structure of your presentation. You should decide on the key points, the order that they should go and how you will link the material together.

You are probably aware of the well-known quote, 'Tell them what you are going to tell them, tell them and then tell them what you have told them'. In essence, this gives the presentation a beginning, middle and end, which prepares the audience and revisits the core message to ensure their understanding. In order to achieve this, mind mapping can be a beneficial technique to develop to determine content and flow. The sample below shows the content and flow of a presentation to inform the board of a DIY chain the details of a new store opening.

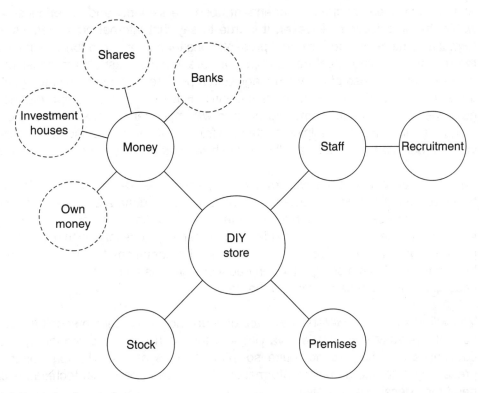

Figure 4.3 Example of a mind map

By starting the map with the main topic area and then drawing in branches to represent key areas and their relation and interrelation, it is possible to plan the flow and to develop speaker notes to include all the relevant points.

The structure should also take into account the needs of the audience. If you have a great deal of detailed information to impart, it may be best to intersperse the 'solid' information with lighter subjects rather than deal with it all at once.

The time and length of the presentation will also determine the structure. Many people are aware of the pitfalls of a presentation filled with facts and figures in the after-lunch slot; if the content cannot be varied then it may be better to change to a morning slot.

It is important to have a realistic idea of the presentation timings to ensure that you get through the whole content and the correct amount of time is spent on the subjects that are most important. Time must be built in for refreshments, questions, comfort breaks and so on. It is the job of the presenter to ensure that these are adhered to and that any discussions keep to the objective of the presentation and that the group do not waste time going off at a tangent.

Style

To determine the style of the presentation, you will have to decide the level of formality and involvement that is appropriate. For a small group, you could deliver a presentation on a complex matter in a fairly informal way with a high level of participation from the audience. For a larger group, the increased participation may result in time being wasted.

The type and style of visual aids to be used will change the impact and structure of the presentation. Are they being used to prompt discussion or to convey information? A good presenter will speak confidently and easily using slides as a backdrop, whereas an inexperienced presenter will often 'read' slides adding very little additional information to the words shown.

Style is a very personal thing dependent upon the seniority and experience of the presenter within the organization. However, it is true to say that internal presentations tend to be less formal and interactive and external presentations tend to be more formal with a specific slot for the questions arising. Gestures and posture are important aspects to consider when giving a presentation. The use of body language and a posture that communicates you are glad to be there and giving your full attention is essential. However, it is also important not to overdo the gestures. A rigid upright unmoving posture will imply nervousness whereas overuse of body language will deflect the recipients attention from what you are saying. It is a good idea to video yourself doing a trial run. This will quickly show what areas you need to concentrate on.

The importance and sensitivity of the subject will be key, a presentation of the creative treatment for the next TV advertisement is likely to generate more audience participation than a market research presentation on the whole market. It is important to let your audience know when questions are appropriate; interspersing questions within the main body of the presentation can give a livelier interactive feel. Presentations to large numbers of people can lead to too much time being spent on questions and the focus of the content being lost, in this case questions may be best left to the end.

You will need to vary the tone and pace of your voice. It is usual to speak a little slower than in normal everyday conversation; varying the tone can break the monotony, especially when covering areas that are not quite so interesting as others. This can often happen when presenting data and graphical information. Good use of graphical techniques can reduce the need for extensive explanation.

Preparing for the presentation

When planning a presentation there are a few other areas that need to be considered so that the total message is delivered in a professional and businesslike-manner. These areas include:

- o Room preparation
- o Visual aids
- o Tone of voice
- o The effect of body language.

Room preparation

It is important to plan, organize and check the layout of the room to be used for the presentation and the other facilities required such as cloakrooms, refreshments, heating and lighting and so on. It is important to the well-being of your audience and their ability to take in the information being communicated. The following checklist can be used:

- o The layout of the chairs and tables (for a small group, a horseshoe shape is often better than lining people in rows).
- o That there are enough chairs and tables for the audience.
- o That you will be visible from where you are going to stand.
- o That there is a lectern or table for your paperwork.
- o That the equipment for visual aids works.
- o That the lighting is adequate.
- o That the room is tidy and has adequate heating/ventilation.

Visual aids

Visual aids, such as overhead projector slides or acetates, pictures, slides of still photography or flip charts, can be used to give variety and impact to a presentation. However, in the modern office environment, these have mostly been superseded by more technologically advanced methods of presenting. Visual aids, such as computer generated graphs and charts, enable complicated information to be presented in a format easier for the audience to understand. Specialized software such as PowerPoint, video walls, electronic whiteboards, and acoustic equipment can be used to enhance a presentation, adding clarity and impact. It is essential to remember that technology is an aid, not a crutch, and will only enhance a presentation if the content is relevant to the subject and the audience. Any visual aids should be produced to a high standard and the presenter should ensure they are proficient in using the software before the presentation takes place.

When you use visual aids, do not stand in front of them and obstruct the audience's view. Do not read from them verbatim – it is better to talk around the issues that the visual aid encapsulates.

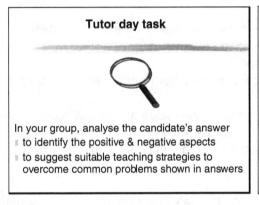

Tutor day task	We need 7 groups – so if 20 people could be 6 groups of 3 and 1 group of 4.
In your group, analyse the candidate's answer ▪ to identify the positive & negative aspects ▪ to suggest suitable teaching strategies to overcome common problems shown in answers	You have 30 minutes to look at a question, so if you are group 1a, analyse the candidate's answer to q1a on last session's paper and identify the positive and negative aspects of the answer and suggest suitable teaching strategies to overcome the problems shown in the answer. I'd like to stress that these are fairly common answers… Could you use flip chart paper to put down your main points and appoint one person to be scribe and another to present on behalf of your group. After the half hour is up we will come back for a plenary session to see what all the groups have to say.

Figure 4.4 A slide and the speaker's notes

The use of video walls at conferences is growing, as companies want their brands and the people speaking on their behalf to appear larger than life. Unfortunately for presenters, it means that every movement is seen in close-up. They can also have an unfortunate effect on people's clothing. Clothing with big patterns, very bright colours and glittering jewellery can blur and produce a strobe effect. The presenter can also blend into the background, if the colour of their clothing is the same as the background.

Always assume that the technology you plan to use for your presentation is going to fail. Be prepared to present blind of technological aids if required. It is unlikely that the audience will be receptive to convening at another time, just because the PowerPoint projector refuses to work. If your speech does not stand up on its own without the technology, you should question whether the script is good enough.

Tone of voice/verbal skills

Except in specific circumstances where you might need to use an authoritative tone, you would normally use a friendly tone to deliver a presentation.

You should consider practising your talk to calculate how long it takes you to get through it. Often nervousness can lead to presenters speaking very quickly, talking at, rather than to, the audience. It is essential to slow down and be aware of the audience's responses. You can use pauses not only to slow down the pace but also to place emphasis on important points. You also need to give people time to absorb the information in any visual aids you use.

You need to connect with your audience, so use vocabulary that fits in with them. Consider how people listen and take in information. People tend to take in information at the beginning and at the end and only snippets throughout, so it helps to use punchy sentences and avoid unnecessary jargon.

The pitch and tone of your voice will also need to vary in order for you to keep the audience interested. Consider using humour (carefully), rhetorical questions and repetition to break up the content. Use of a fast relentless monotone is guaranteed to send the audience straight to sleep.

Remember above all the more relaxed you feel, the more the audience will relax and tune into the message being conveyed, rather than stare fixedly at a nervous presenter.

Body language

The nerves that some people feel before delivering a presentation are usually connected with having to stand up in front of an audience that is totally focused on you. You should try not to be seen to be nervous by having control of your body language. You should aim to do the following:

- Don't look tense – smile, but not fixed and not when delivering bad news.
- Stand upright with your shoulders relaxed.
- Do not fold your arms across your chest.
- Don't hunch up/bend your head down to read from your notes – just refer to them occasionally.
- Maintain eye contact with the entire group – don't stare at one individual or one section of the group. This can be difficult if you arrange the group in a horseshoe shape.
- Avoid gesticulating wildly or other distracting mannerisms, such as jangling the change in your pocket or scratching.

It can be quite useful to video a practice session to analyse the gestures and mannerisms that you have so that you can concentrate on minimizing these during the 'real thing'.

 ## Activity 4.5

Your colleague has been preparing a presentation she is to give to the marketing team at the next departmental meeting. The visual aids have been prepared, copies made, room booked and refreshments arranged. Her only concern now is how to deal with questions, and she has come to you for advice. Make some notes for her to consider before the presentation.

Meetings

Meetings are an assembly of people for the purpose of discussion, with regard to agreement of actions required and decisions to be reached. They occur face to face or remotely by using satellite communications or video conferencing. Meetings are an extremely useful means of communication but while they present good opportunities for obtaining immediate verbal feedback and demonstrating or observing non-verbal feedback, they can present problems if they are not organized and planned.

Advantages of meetings	Disadvantages of meetings
Enable information exchange and two-way communication	Much time can be wasted on social chat as people 'catch up' on other business and non-business issues
Discussion allows ideas to be developed amongst all interested parties	Can be difficult to get everyone at the same time, then decisions can be left hanging
Decisions agreed and responsibility for action allocated	Badly organized meetings can lack focus and direction, wasting the time of those attending
Can be motivational in that people feel part of a team	Organizations/managers can get into 'meeting paralysis' where everyone spends most of their time in meetings talking about doing things but never getting around to doing them
Sensitive and confidential information can be discussed	Difficult to arrange with much time spent on documenting agreed items and action points
Non-verbal communication and feedback possible	

Within this unit, we will deal with meetings by categorizing them as follows:

- o *Formal meetings* – such as board meetings, branch meetings.
- o *Informal meetings* – departmental meetings, client and supplier meetings.
- o *Interviews* – generally between two parties, appraisals, selection interviews.

Using PASS to plan effective meetings

Purpose
Meetings take place for a variety of reasons. They can involve just two people or many, from a variety of organizations. Meetings usually fall into one of the following categories, which are related to their original purpose. The purpose/type of meeting required will then affect all other sections of the PASS model.

Formal meetings
These tend to be required to take place for constitutional or legal reasons, for example, Annual General Meeting. They have a pre-determined audience, many of which have specific roles such as chairperson and secretary. They have formal agenda and minutes, which will be covered later in the unit.

Formal meetings require *proposals* to be put before the meeting in order that they can be discussed and relevant decisions made. If the motion is approved or *carried* by the meeting, it then becomes a *resolution* or decision. The procedure for dealing with a motion means that the *proposer* must speak first on the matter, followed by the *seconder*.

Rules concerning motions mean that they should be feasible and not *ultra vires*, that is, outside the power or scope of the meeting. Motions need to be worded so that ambiguities do not exist. For example, a motion stating 'That a ban on smoking be introduced' is too vague because it does not state exactly where the ban extends to and when it should take effect.

This type of meeting often requires a degree of supporting documentation such as a formal agenda and minutes – these will be covered in depth later in this unit.

Informal meetings

These can range from a regular or previously arranged meeting to an informal get-together. In marketing, these will typically include departmental meetings and meeting with clients or suppliers such as advertising agencies. They can either be just two people getting together in the normal course of their work to discuss a particular issue or a pre-arranged meeting involving many parties. As a rule of thumb, the larger the meeting, the more important it becomes that all relevant people are invited and should only go ahead if all decision-makers are available. These meetings can be categorized further as follows:

  o *Interviews* – These could include customer interviews to assess their future needs. Recruitment interviews to employ a new marketing assistant or interviews with current staff for appraisal or disciplinary reasons. Interviews usually involve only two or three people and will have objectives and will usually include some kind of agreement between the parties concerned. Any agreement can be documented in a formal or informal manner depending upon the objectives.
  o *Negotiations* – These usually occur with customers and suppliers, and require more planning and discussion on detailed information. An outcome, which meets the needs of both parties, is required but often not possible, so both parties need to work towards an acceptable compromise. Negotiations will be covered in greater detail within personal selling (Unit 8).

Whatever the type of meeting, they always require careful planning and organization. Problems can occur if people arrive at a meeting with differing objectives about what is to be achieved. It is essential that the objectives are communicated to all those attending and are reiterated at the beginning of the meeting. It is also good practice to review how far the objectives have been met at the end of the meeting.

Circulation of relevant information may be required before the meeting to ensure that the meeting runs in a timely manner and that no one feels their time has been wasted or is stuck in a meeting for longer than was originally planned.

Any additional information necessary for the meeting should be prepared before the meeting starts, to maximize the use of time.

Interviews

The purpose of an interview will be very much more specific with a very measurable outcome. As interviews mostly involve two people then it is important that both parties are fully aware of the meeting's objectives and the level of preparation required.

In summary, before arranging a meeting it should be considered whether that meeting really needs to be held and also establish clear objectives that need to be met.

Audience
Formal meetings

With formal meetings there will be a list of who should be invited and the roles that those people take within the meeting. There may be a minimum amount of people required for a quorum to exist; that is, a certain number of people are required in order that decisions taken are judged to be representative of the total group. Formal meetings require the preparation of a notice to advise those who need to attend. These can be communicated by personal written communication such as a letter or an invitation or, if numbers are large, may be posted on a notice board or advertised in the national newspapers. The minutes of the last, meeting should be provided or the attendee directed to where they can be found.

NOTICE OF ANNUAL GENERAL MEETING

Notice is hereby given that the Annual General Meeting of Anyone Limited will be held at the Anyplace Hotel, Anywhere Road, Anywhere on 10 June 200X at 10.30 a.m. for the following purposes:

1. To receive and adopt the Reports of the Directors and Auditors and the Accounts for the period ended 31 March 200X.
2. To declare a final dividend.
3. To re-elect Mr J. Sugree as a Managing Director of the company.
4. To transact any other business.

By order of the Board
Mr B Keating
Company Secretary

Figure 4.5 Notice of a formal AGM

Informal meetings

The person who initiates the meeting should decide upon the audience for less formal meetings. They should consider what is a suitable number for discussion to be effective and who needs to attend from which organizations. The people are invited who may also want others from their own organization to attend, and the meeting initiator should decide on this. A balance of people from different organizations needs to be maintained as it would be unfair for a sole representative of one organization (say the advertising agency) to have to cope with six or seven people from the client organization.

It is important that the meeting does not grow too large or it will be difficult for everyone to contribute and communicate effectively. If people do not get a chance to contribute, they may then feel undervalued and that their time has been wasted. If some attendees are required only for a proportion of the meeting, it may be better to have a flow of people in and out at appropriate times if this can be arranged.

Communication to arrange and confirm the meeting could be initially by telephone to assess availability, with confirmation in writing by business letter, memo or e-mail.

MEMORANDUM

TO: The Marketing Task Group.

FROM: Roy Keane

DATE: 19 September 200X

The next Marketing meeting will take place on Thursday 25 September 200X at 2:30 p.m. in the board room at head office.

As usual meeting will be reviewing current marketing projects and will also be discussing matters relating to developing the company's marketing plan, so please forward dates to me in advance of the meeting which indicate when you can be away from normal office duties for a 3 days block. In addition, if you have any other items you would like putting on the agenda please contact me on 0161 448 7212 no later than Monday 21 September 200X.

Figure 4.6 Notice for an informal meeting

Interviews

The audience for an interview will be specifically dependent upon the objectives and is likely to be restricted to fewer people than in other types of meetings. For an appraisal, the interview is likely to be restricted to the person being appraised and their line manager. It may also be company policy for a member of the Human Resource department to be present.

For interviews with customers, the salesperson and the customer will definitely be involved, other people could include the sales manager and a support person from the customer's organization.

Structure

For anything other than an impromptu meeting that colleagues may arrange informally all meetings require a degree of planning and organization. The person who initiates the meeting or is assigned to organize it should ensure a suitable time for everyone required to attend, in a suitably located venue. Within each type of meeting, the structure will take account of

- ○ *Agenda* – or content to be covered
- ○ *Procedures* – to ensure the objectives are covered
- ○ *Minutes* – to document points agreed upon and actions.

Formal meetings

In communicating to those attending (again either by letter, e-mail or memo), the objectives of the meeting should be explained and any preparation that is required should be fully briefed. When there is more than one issue to discuss, the meeting may require an agenda showing the order in which issues will be dealt with and who will lead the discussion on that item.

Agenda

Agendas for formal meetings are prepared by the elected secretary who has the responsibility to enable all participants to propose items for discussion. The chairperson then has a chance to review the suitability of the items on the agenda before it is issued to all participants. Copies of the agenda can be sent out with the notice of the meeting or distributed on the day. The secretary is also responsible for providing a more detailed agenda for the chairperson to ensure they are fully briefed on all matters to be covered.

Agendas normally contain the following items:

1. Apologies for absence – announced by the chairperson once the meeting has been officially opened and the time and date recorded by the secretary.
2. Minutes of the previous meeting – the chairperson will ask members whether the minutes represent an accurate record of the previous meeting and if so, he/she will sign them as such.
3. Matters arising give an opportunity for participants to declare views or report back on developments since the last meeting.
4. Details of correspondence from parties outside the meeting that may be pertinent to items to be discussed.
5. The main agenda items – in order of discussion.
6. Any other business.
7. Date of next meeting – to be arranged before people leave.

Snack Attack

The Quality Sandwich Delivery Service

MARKETING MEETING
AGENDA

19 September 200X at 2:30 p.m.
in the boardroom at head office.

1. Apologies for absence.
2. Minutes of the last meeting.
3. Matters arising.
4. Evaluation of radio advertising campaign.
5. Update of database software.
6. Discuss product development for Winter hot soup range.
7. Motion: 'That the company purchases two new delivery vans before the Christmas period'. Proposed: Paul Rapaporte Seconded: David Surinam.
8. Company marketing plan arrangements.
9. Any other business.
10. Date of next meeting.

Figure 4.7 An agenda

Procedures

Procedures for formal meetings are also quite clearly defined. The *chairperson* is responsible for running the meeting and ensuring that the meeting runs to time. Formal meetings are required to discuss those issues that are on the *agenda* or not *ultra vires*, which is outside the powers of the meeting. People speaking within the meeting should do so by *addressing the chair*, which means that all remarks are directed towards the chairperson, allowing them to keep control of the items discussed and the time allocated. These specific procedures are known as *points of order*, and are in place to ensure that regulations are being adhered to.

Within formal meetings decisions are made through voting, usually by a show of hands (open voting), or by a general voice vote, where it is judged whether yes or no is said the loudest or even by secret ballot.

The results of voting may be declared in the following way:

○ Passed *unanimously* – everyone voted in favour.
○ Passed *nem con* – no one voted against but only a few have voted for the proposal with the majority abstaining.
○ *Lost* – the majority voted against.
○ *Casting vote* – the chairperson is given an additional vote to break the deadlock of an equal number voting for and against a proposal.

At the end of the meeting, the chairperson will officially declare the meeting closed.

Minutes

These are a written record of the transactions that took place and should be as accurate as possible, reflecting the duration and general tone of the meeting.

For formal meetings the secretary, who will word process and distribute them as quickly as possible after the meeting, usually takes the minutes. Minutes are an important channel of communication and source of reference.

Their style tends to reflect the style of the meeting and for formal meeting tends to include the following:

- ○ *Resolution minutes* – where the resolutions are recorded and therefore do not reflect the tone of the meeting or specific points made leading to the resolution.
- ○ *Narrative minutes* – a brief summary of the meeting which led up to the resolution (decisions) and include the comments made by the participants, which have gone on record as their judgement of the arguments preceding the resolution.
- ○ *Action minutes* – detailing the specific courses of action that have been agreed to.

Research and Development Group
Minutes

Minutes of the Meeting held in the 'Panelled Room' at 'Building Headquarters', Bromley, Kent on October 15th 20XX at 4 p.m.

Present: T. Stones (Chair), A. Peters (Secretary), L. Simons, K. Andrews, J. Clarke

1. Apologies for absence.
    Apologies for absence were received from J. Thyme, L. Young and P. Ankers.

2. Minutes of the last meeting.
    The minutes of the last meeting were taken as read and signed as a true record.

3. Matters arising.
    Further to item 2, the Chairman has received a report of the new innovation currently in prototype stage and will circulate a copy to all members before the next meeting.

4. Proposal to cut the budget by £I million to be phased in over a period of three years.
    All members present argued for a strong statement to be issued to the M.D. on the consequences for new and existing projects as a result of this budget cut, and seek clarification if jobs are also to be lost in this process.

5. New product development.
    Len Simons and Ken Andrews presented a visual report on the new products to be commercialized by the end of the financial year.

6. AOB.
    Jane Clarke raised the need for a new laser printer. Angela Peters will receive literature and circulate this to members of the group before the next meeting.

7. Date of next meeting.
    The next meeting of the R&D group was scheduled for January 10th 20XX at Building H.Q.

Signed X   T. Stones (Chair) Director R&D. Date November 10th 20XX

Figure 4.8 Resolution minutes

Informal meetings
Agenda

Agendas for less formal meetings often follow the same kind of format to a formal meeting but more often appear like a list of issues to be discussed.

The meeting initiator should be responsible for canvassing the attendees for items they wish to discuss and will probably add or delete items as they see fit, very much like a formal chairperson. Agendas are still required for informal meetings for the benefits they can deliver.

Procedures

These are also still required but less clearly defined and formal. It is good practice for any meeting to have a chairperson or lead person to ensure that the meeting is run in a timely and efficient manner. This lead person will again be responsible for making sure all items are covered, objectives met and that everyone within the meeting has had a chance to contribute.

Other attendees will take a much larger role in an informal meeting and will be able to speak and interject more freely than at formal meetings. Often certain people will take the lead on different subject areas for which they will have prepared and certain areas of discussion will be divided.

It should be decided at the start of the meeting if there are any additional items to be discussed and who will take the minutes. It is unusual for an informal meeting to include a vote, but during discussions it may be relevant to ask for a *show of hands* to gauge the feelings of those attending.

Minutes

The same rules apply but the minutes taken tend to be more concerned with what was discussed (narrative) and the actions agreed (action). As at formal meetings, it is essential that these be distributed quickly after the meeting so those people who have actions to undertake feel fully informed.

It is usual that the lead person brings the meeting to a close and summarizes what has occurred. Any outstanding points can be clarified before people leave.

ITEM 7: The task group discussed the proposal to purchase two extra delivery vans.

JD felt that the business development work in the two new industrial estates in the East of the city had resulted in several new contracts that would be coming on stream in the next few weeks and this would put undue pressure on the current vans.

HG also admitted that the run up to Christmas would be very busy and extra resources would be needed.

GW complained about the extra cost and suggested buying one van as an interim measure. By a majority of 5:1, it was agreed that two additional vehicles should be purchased by the end of the month.

Figure 4.9 Narrative minutes

Item No.	Topic	Action
7.	Proposed purchase of two additional vans.It was agreed that the purchasing manager should look into the costs of leasing compared with purchase.	SW to cost options.

Figure 4.10 Action minutes

Interviews

It is not usual to have an agenda for an interview although it is acceptable to either discuss or communicate in writing before the interview to ensure that both parties are aware of the purpose of the interview and the items that will be covered.

Many organizations have set procedures in place for specific interviews such as appraisal and selection. This may include an informal first interview and a more formal second interview. These procedures may have some paperwork attached to them, which can guide both the interviewer and the interviewee on how the interview should proceed.

Minutes are usually not formal but in a more informal written format like a letter, memo or e-mail, and exist to keep a record of what was discussed at the meeting and actions agreed.

Style

Before considering the style of each type of meeting, it may help to consider in more detail the theory behind the use of questions within the meeting scenario. One consideration across all scenarios is the style of questioning that is used.

- o Open-ended questions allow interviewees to express themselves in detail, expressing and explaining their opinions and feelings. The response is entirely determined by the respondent, for example what do you think about our new chocolate bar that is being launched this week?
- o Closed questions require short responses which are largely determined by the person asking the question. Answers such as yes, no, or don't know, are frequent, for example have you received our latest catalogue?
- o Probing questions often combine a closed question followed by an open question to gain more detail, for example have you received our latest catalogue? What do you think of the new product range? These are often used to get the interviewees to justify the answer to the first question or to checkout levels of understanding.
- o Restatement questions are often used to ensure that the interviewee has fully under-stood the information given, for example you said you have not ordered anything from us in 3 months. Is that right?

Formal meetings

As their name suggests, formal meetings are just that. They are run on clear guidelines and are subject to the *constitution* of the organization or club, with any changes having to be discussed and passed as a resolution.

There is an expectation that attendees come prepared for the meeting having completed any tasks actioned against them at the last meeting. There is a whole raft of meeting terminology most of which has been covered in this section. The paperwork also has to be produced in a given format to a given timetable.

Discussion is only interrupted by *points of order* (discussed within structure), comments are addressed *through the chair*, and finishing in a timely manner with all items discussed and objectives met is a measure of the success of that meeting. In order for this to happen, the crucial point of the planning process is when the agenda is prepared as that determines the number and scope of issues discussed. If the agenda is badly prepared then it is likely that the meeting will not be an effective use of time.

Questioning will usually be probing after someone has presented information at the meeting and restatement questions used to clarify points before agreeing the minuted point.

Room layout is important to ensure everyone can see either the chairperson or visual aids being used. The room layout will often be *conference style* – rows and row of chairs facing the focal point of the room or smaller numbers lead to the use of *theatre style*, where chairs and tables are arranged in a U shape facing inwards with the chairperson's seat and table being slightly distanced from the others on the fourth side. This setting apart highlights the different function they fulfil within the meeting, and ensures everyone can see the *chair* they are *addressing*.

Informal meetings

The style of the meeting will be determined by the size and composition of the audience. A small internal meeting is likely to be more informal than a large meeting involving people from a number of organizations.

The style will be largely determined by the person who has called the meeting, as they are usually the ones who speak at the beginning of the meeting to gain everyone's attention and focus them on the reason for being there.

Informal meetings can lose focus very much quicker than formal meetings, especially if there is no agenda and that is why it is wise to have a lead-person in place to keep the discussion on the intended subjects. Interjections and interruptions are tactics often used at informal meetings where comments do not have to be addressed *through the chair*. Again it is necessary for someone to take the role of moving the meeting on and ensuring that everyone has a chance to put their point across but no one person is able to 'take over'.

All kinds of questions will be used as people express opinions and check out their understanding by asking closed and restatement questions. The room will usually be laid out in *board-room style* with a large table with everyone sitting around. If there is a lead-person, they can become the focal point and it is beneficial if they are seated halfway along the long side of the table. The size of the room should be appropriate to the number of people attending the meeting, with everyone having a seat and a piece of table for their use.

Interviews

Face-to-face interviews are good for improving working relationships between clients and suppliers; hence the phrase 'It is nice to put a face to the voice.' Interviews provide opportunities to develop the social side of business communication that makes doing business easier and more pleasant. Internal interviews such as appraisals and disciplinary interviews may be the only quality time that the parties involved get to interact uninterrupted.

In this respect, there are fewer opportunities for misunderstandings or for communication barriers to exist than in other situations. It is usually easier to appreciate the underlying message being communicated because it is possible to read body language in face-to-face interviews.

Interviews involve complex communication processes and require both interviewers and interviewees to demonstrate good communication skills, but there are plenty of opportunities for interviews to be less effective than they might be. Common problems relate to insufficient planning, inappropriate body language, not controlling the content, the pace, the tone. These issues are the responsibility of the interviewer to consider and plan for.

It is important that both parties are clear about what is to be discussed before the meeting takes place and feel adequately prepared. In a disciplinary interview there are clear guidelines to follow to ensure correct legal procedures are adhered to.

In an interview, you can use various questioning styles to gain a better understanding of what is being said, more open questions are used to establish 'a rapport' and to elicit people's thoughts and opinions, that are important to establish in interview situations. Probing questions to delve deeper and replacement to clarify what is meant are also used. Closed questions tend to stop rapport developing and free-flowing questions.

The room layout is also very important. In business or formal interviews, it is usual to have a table between the two parties, which very much feeds the 'two sided' discussion that is to take place. In job interview and appraisals, having no table can help to make the situation more relaxed and friendly and encourage the interviewee to open up more about their thoughts and feelings.

The end of the meeting tends to become more formal as a summary of what has been agreed can be used to move forward and plan the future actions required.

Activity 4.6

You have been asked to participate in your company's management training programme. Prepare for the first topic 'Effective Interviews' by drafting explanatory notes based on the PASS model. You are required to prepare people to plan and manage the following types of interviews:

- Job selection interviews
- Appraisal interviews
- Disciplinary
- Customer complaints.

You should include comments upon the types of questioning and room layout required for each type of meeting.

Developments and trends in verbal communications

Having dealt with developments in telephone communications earlier in this unit, there is one remaining area of development more specific to meetings as a method of verbal communication.

Video conferencing and conference calling offers a realistic and cheaper way of running meetings involving participants from widespread geographical locations. Although the technology to enable video conferencing still requires significant investment, the global organization can still reap benefits from conducting meetings in this way, reducing time and expense spent on travelling to and attending meetings. No investment is required for conference calls so the increased use of this method of meeting has somewhat outstripped video conferencing at present and will probably continue to do so.

Video conferencing and conference calling requires precise planning from ensuring the facilities are available at a given time (time zone shifts can make agreeing a time difficult) through to ensuring all personnel have the required information and documentation available, usually via e-mail and ISDN facilities.

Someone is required to take the role of the chairperson to ensure the meeting runs smoothly and everyone has a chance to contribute. This can be more difficult with video conferencing. The time delay between speech emanating and being heard (think of an international phone call) can put people off leading them to jump in with comments of their own leading to people speaking over each other. The attendees need to get used to waiting until they are sure the person has stopped speaking and then starting their own speech with an introductory comment such as 'I would like to make the point'. In this way if there is an overlap, important information need not be lost or repeated. The chairperson must introduce some rules of engagement asking people to speak in order, or to use a visual sign or agreed verbal cue to indicate when they wish to speak.

In meetings, we use many non-verbal cues to signify that we wish to speak, such as moving forward in our chair or adjusting our seating position. Some of these do not transfer so easily in video conferencing as they are not so noticeable, hence the need for a new set of cues to be developed.

One other consideration is to avoid certain styles of clothing. Striped or patterned shirts when filmed in front of a video wall can cause a glare or distortion that can be very hard to carry on looking at. It is more pleasing to the eye if plain neutral colours are worn which do not detract attention from the speaker's facial expressions.

It does not take long to adapt one's communication skills to the use of this method of conducting meetings. If an organization intends to utilize the technology on a regular basis, it is essential that the attendees get prior training and a few 'dummy runs' before entering a real meeting situation.

Summary

In this unit you have studied:

- o Why and how meetings are used in marketing.
- o When documentation is needed and how it is used in meetings.
- o How to lead and manage meetings effectively.
- o How and why interviews and negotiations are used in marketing.
- o How to improve your interview technique.
- o How to be a successful negotiator.

Further study

Attempt Questions 4 and 7b from the June 2005 examination paper and Questions 4b and Q6 from the December 2004 paper. Access the learning zone on www.cim.co.uk to also access Specimen Answers for these exam questions.

Hints and tips

Within an exam situation you will be asked for recommendations on the use of verbal communications. You need to know whether a meeting or informal discussion is required in a given situation. If it is the former, you may be asked to explain the steps that need to be taken to plan and hold the meeting. It is therefore important that you are conversant with all aspects of meetings, notably the issuing of a notice, setting the agenda and producing minutes. You may be given a fictitious scenario and out of this asked to set an agenda and/or issue a suitable notice – all settings will have a marketing context and you may need to rely on your knowledge from other parts of the Certificate course to place suitable details in these documents. You will be expected to know the general rules and guidelines in the planning of interviews and to explain these in the examination. You need to be aware of the different types of interview that can take place in business and how to plan and contribute effectively to negotiations in marketing. You should be aware of the different types of questions that can help you to solicit the required information. You should also expect to comment on any body language, speech and listening skills as important tools in meetings, interviews and negotiations for successful communication.

Bibliography

Forsyth, P. (1999) *Communicating with Customers*, London: Orion Business.

unit 5
written communication formats

In this unit you will:

- Examine the variety of written communication formats. See syllabus section 4.8.

- Understand the correct layout and presentation format for different types of communication. See syllabus sections 4.5 and 4.8.

- Communicate effectively using a range of communication formats. See syllabus sections 4.5 and 4.8.

By the end of this unit you should be able to:

- Interpret, summarize and present oral, written and graphical information (4.5).

- Use a variety of formats to communicate with internal and external customers, including telephone, letters, memoranda, notices, reports and e-mails (4.8).

This unit relates to statements of practice

Cb.2 Deliver direct or indirect communications.

Study Guide

This unit covers 4.5 and 4.8 of the syllabus in greater depth. It provides you with the knowledge and understanding necessary to enable you to use a variety of written formats to communicate with internal and external customers. These formats are letters, memos, e-mails, notices, reports and articles. It will take you 3 hours to read through this unit and a further 3 hours to work through the activities.

Study tip

Spend some time evaluating the written communications that you are exposed to in your personal and working life. Select a good and bad example of each of the following:

- o Letters
- o Memos
- o Notices
- o Reports
- o E-mails.

For each example, note down why/why not it is effective. Consider the communication that you are involved in, in a variety of situations. Undertake this exercise at regular intervals. Can you see an improvement in the way that you are communicating?

Why study communication formats?

Written communication is still important in marketing even in these days of sophisticated information communications technology. Written communication, whether it be a letter or e-mail, can form a lasting recollection of an agreement made.

You may use your writing skills in letters, memos, e-mails and reports regularly, in which case you may wish to proceed directly to the activities and past examination questions to check how well prepared you are to be tested in this area. On the other hand, you may find that, because of your role or the type of organization you work in, all letters and memos are produced by someone else (such as a departmental secretary). Or it may be that you are not yet in a position that requires you to use all the communication formats tested in the exam (such as reports). Whatever the case, you should be aware of how to use the various communication formats, and you may need to spend some time looking at how you could develop your writing skills.

This is especially important for those of you choosing the assignment assessment option as you will be required in many cases to write a report or prepare a presentation – something that you may not have had to do before.

If you work in an organization where there is a 'house style' for reports and letters, then this style can be used in the examination situation, but if this is not the case, then you may find you can use and adapt the templates and examples provided in this unit.

Written communication skills in marketing

For any situation, whether you are writing a letter, memo or report, the following structure should be adopted:

- o *The beginning* – where you get to the point of why you are writing, whatever you are writing
- o *The middle* – where you communicate your message
- o *The end* – if appropriate, where you summarize the main points (especially for reports) or where you state any action required (more for memos and letters).

The PASS (purpose, audience, structure, style) mnemonic can prove to be a useful guide when you are writing (see Unit 4 for more details) or be a useful way to cross-check when you review your writing. In essence, planning the communication will help you to produce an effective communication message. You should consider (alongside the PASS model) the following three stages to planning a communication:

1. Make note about the content and tone. What details are absolutely necessary?
2. Consider the logical sequence of the message to aid the reader's understanding.
3. Draft the communication first. Then read it to decide how it can be improved. It would help to get a colleague to read the final draft.

ICT has made this process much easier than the days when secretaries used to use type-writers and Tippex correction fluid, but the ease of changing copy and structure on word processing packages, such as Microsoft Word, has lead to more people preparing their own documents. This is very empowering and cuts cost but we must ensure we plan our communication properly – a skill we need to develop. Many people just sit down in front of a monitor and rattle something off without checking content, structure, punctuation or spelling.

It is essential that all communication is planned and checked properly before distribution. People's time and resources can be wasted by ineffective communication.

General communication issues

As you progress through this unit you will notice some written formats that you do not use. Some are rapidly becoming outdated. Memos have been almost completely replaced by e-mail technology and intranets within an organization. Communication between some members of the Micro environment has also evolved to replace paper-based communication with electronic communication through e-mail and extranets. This will be dealt with in more detail in Unit 9.

But not all of the formats that you may not have encountered are out of date; report writing and letters of recommendation tend to be heavily paper-based in their format and so those skills are required in today's commercial world.

Most business documents should be clear and concise and have a logical structure to them. Start new paragraphs when you move on to new ideas. Arrange your thoughts in a logical sequence so that ideas and information flow from one paragraph to another in a clear and easy-to-understand way.

To keep letters, memos and reports brief, it is best to keep to short sentences, simple expressions (avoid analogies) and words that people can understand. Marketing is an industry full of jargon, and the communications industry extends the use of even more jargon. You should be careful about the use of words that your audience may be unfamiliar with and all abbreviations should be explained by giving their meaning in full, the first time they are used.

Use terms that are unambiguous. For instance, the words 'quickly', 'as soon as possible' and 'large' could be interpreted in different ways by different people. Generally, it is better to be specific, giving an amount or a date instead of using words that could be misinterpreted.

For letters, in particular, you should avoid the kind of official and cliché-sounding terms that can lead to readers not understanding exactly what you are trying to say. For instance, instead of 'Re: your correspondence dated', you could say, 'Thank you for your letter of', and the phrase 'The contract should be submitted to the undersigned upon completion' could be more simply written as 'Please return the contract when you have completed it'.

In general, you should avoid passive phrases, such as 'should be sent to' and use the active form, 'please send to'.

You should try to avoid negative terms when writing to customers. For example, 'I am unable to make a booking until you pay a 25 per cent deposit' could be phrased in a positive way as 'When you pay a 25 per cent deposit, your booking will be completed and confirmation sent to you within three days.'

You will get a better response to the letters and memos you send if you use a courteous 'please', 'thank you' or 'I would be grateful if you could' instead of using a brusque or directive tone. This form of courtesy is often forgotten in e-mails which, although often used as a business communication, often omit to utilize the same structure or protocol.

If you are writing a memo or an e-mail which does not require a specific action, then you should include the phrase 'for information only'.

If you are writing a report, you should avoid sexual bias in your writing. By using 'he' or the masculine form of a noun, you could cause offence. Either use non-gender specific terms such as 'staff', 'employees', 'individuals' or 'people', or change the sentence. For example, the sentence, 'The number of air stewardesses will have to be increased on each flight' could be changed to 'The number of air crew will have to be increased on each flight'.

In summary, we should always remember the mnemonic K.I.S.S – Keep It Short and Simple. That way more people have more chance of improving their understanding of the purpose of the communication.

When to use letters

Whatever type of organization that you work in, if you are in an office, you are likely to write and receive letters. However, if you work in marketing then communication is likely to be a vital part of your job and therefore letter writing will be too.

Although letter writing is not the quickest way to communicate, there are many different types of letters and occasions when letters are the suitable format for communication.

Letters provide a permanent record of a message, which could be useful if you are confirming details of an exhibition stand booking or enquiring about late payment and need proof at a later date that a letter has indeed been sent. Letters also have a legal dimension inbuilt within them and are an essential part of the law of contract.

Letters are also quite formal, which means they are an excellent way of sending important information. For example, you would want to send a formal letter if you were informing someone that they were successful in a job interview, if you were giving someone notice about a disciplinary matter or if you needed to send a covering letter with a cheque payment.

Letters are suitable for long, complex messages that can be read and re-read over a period of time. Consequently, they are often used for direct marketing purposes (mail shots) where the 'offer' has a number of benefits that need to be read in detail. They are often used where the product is quite complex as they can be read again when the person has had more time to think about the offer.

Letters are suitable for communicating personal information directly to the individual concerned. The use of computers in even the smallest firms means that professionally presented letters can be produced easily by most staff, not just trained secretaries.

The use of mail-merge facilities means that standard letters can be produced, saving time and money. This means an organization can decide to communicate with some or even all of its customers by linking letter production to an updated customer database.

One of the disadvantages of letters is the timing of delivery; however, if speed is of the essence then letters can usually be faxed or sent as an e-mail attachment.

Letters are generally sent to external customers (in their widest sense), although in very formal situations (such as confirmation of terms and conditions, requests for leave or with disciplinary matters) letters may be sent internally within an organization.

The layout of a business letter

Undoubtedly you would already have been involved in writing business letters as millions are composed, produced and delivered daily. Every organization has its own style (which is important in reflecting image and efficiency) but there is a set of basic rules of layout that all will follow. Firgure 5.1 shows both blocked and semi-blocked layouts.

Business letters are made up of the following parts:

- *Letterhead and/or logo* – Communicates the corporate image through its graphic style and usually also contains address, telephone, telex, fax and e-mail details
- *Letter references* – Initials of the typist and author
- *Date* – Usually, the month is placed first, fully written (not numerals), followed by the day
- *Details of recipient* – title, name and address
- *Salutation* – For example, Dear Sir, Dear Madam or Dear Mrs Jones
- *Subject heading* – This is usually indented and underlined, for example, Conference on Marketing Communication, 25 September 20XX, Queen Elizabeth's Hall, London
- *Body of the letter* – Short paragraphs centred on the page
- *Complimentary close* – 'Yours sincerely' for named recipients, (i.e. Dear Mr Brown); 'Yours faithfully' for formally addressed recipients (i.e. Dear Sir(s), Dear Madam)
- *Signature* – Usually in the sender's own handwriting
- Position/title of sender
- References to enclosure and copies.

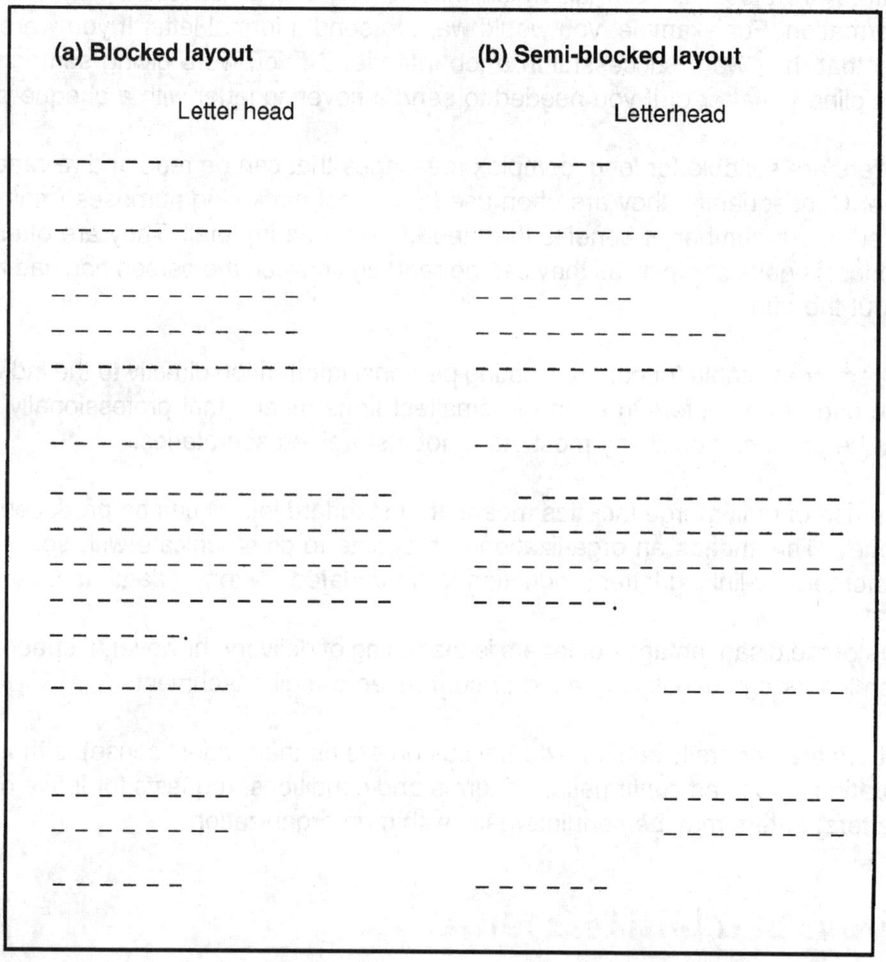

(a) Blocked layout

Letter head

(b) Semi-blocked layout

Letterhead

Figure 5.1 Layouts for business letters: (a) blocked; (b) semi-blocked

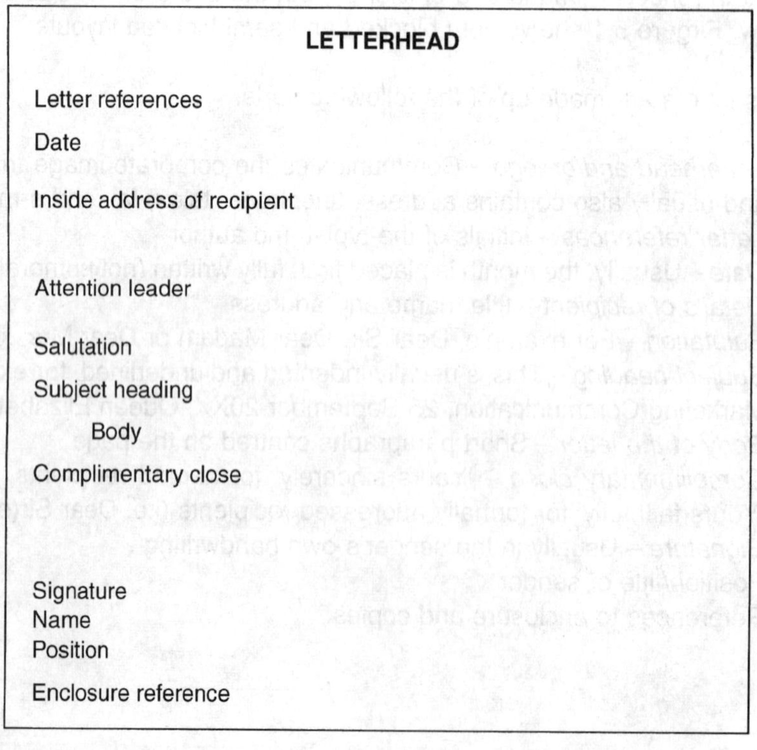

LETTERHEAD

Letter references

Date

Inside address of recipient

Attention leader

Salutation

Subject heading

Body

Complimentary close

Signature
Name
Position

Enclosure reference

Figure 5.2 A template for a business letter

Types of letters

Letters in marketing can be about any topic. Here are some examples of different types of letters:

- o Letters giving information to customers
- o Letters confirming negotiations or a booking
- o Sales letters
- o Letters requesting information
- o Letters requesting a meeting or an appointment
- o Complaint letters
- o Letters of adjustment
- o Letters requesting payment
- o Covering letters to go with payment, maps or leaflets
- o Letters querying an invoice.

Writing customer letters

These can deal with any topic and you have to be clear about the message you are trying to convey as well as what you want the customer to do.

Midshire Bank Plc

High street
Assington
Berkshire AS1 6EL

Mr Joe Davies
17 Goldthorpe Way
Assbury
Berkshire AS2 4WQ

12 April 200X

Dear Mr Davies

At Midshire Bank we try to provide banking facilities of the highest quality in order to accurately meet our customer's needs. To do this it is essential that we listen to what our customers have to say. We would like you to help us by giving us your opinion of Midshire Bank's services.

We are asking an independent market research company, TMI Limited, to interview a number of customers over the next few weeks. TMI Limited is a reputable company and your individual responses will be completely confidential to them, according to the Market Research Society's Code of Conduct.

They will be conducting the interviews by telephone and so an interviewer may telephone you at some point over the next few weeks.

Because TMI Limited will choose who to interview, you might not be contacted in this instance. If you are, we would value your contribution and hope you will be able to help us if asked.

Yours sincerely

CGowers

Charles Gowers
Branch Manager

Figure 5.3 A sample customer letter

Writing order letters

Letters are rarely used for placing orders because pre-printed order forms are usually more convenient and efficient. However, if you need to write an order letter, state your needs clearly by presenting the information in column form, with double-spacing and totalling the balance of prices at the end, explaining as to which account the balance should be charged. State the delivery address (it may be different from the address on the letterhead) and the mode of transport which should be used.

MAKE-IT BUILDING SUPPLIERS
Churchyard Grove
Pickwick
Lancashire LUI 5TF
Tel: 0123 668791

Our ref: HBJ/abc

October 1st 20XX

The Timber Merchants Ltd
Station Road
Ripon
Yorkshire YU8 TR3

For the attention of Deborah Jones

Dear Ms Jones,

Account Number: 5690   Special order under invoice 123

Further to our last order, would you supply the following additional items:

1	20 metres of extra hard-wearing timber for fencing.	£5.95 per metre excl. VAT = £119
2	5 litres of creosote liquid in natural colour.	£2.75 per litres excl. VAT = £ 13.75
3	24 litres of indoor wood varnish in antique pine.	£1.44 per litres excl. VAT = £ 34.56

Balance	£167.31
VAT on items	£ 29.28
Total balance	**£196.59**

The balance should be started on the above invoice and charged to our existing account. I would appreciate delivery by November 15th, latest.

Yours sincerely,

Harold Jenkins
Purchasing Manager

Figure 5.4 An order letter

Letters of enquiry or request

These can deal with a variety of questions, such as asking readers to supply certain information or make a presentation or inviting them to attend a function. Such letters almost always require a reply and some action to be taken, therefore they should be sent out in advance of the action date and be well written and tactful.

ULTIMATE COMPUTER COMPANY Ltd
3 The Gateway
Hounslow
Middlesex TW15 6TU
Tel: 0181 967 6345

TRJ/abc
October 1st 20XX

Mr Andrew Collins
Marketing Communications Consultants
'The Nook'
Twinkle Lane
Beaconsfield
BUCKS DU18 74R

Dear Mr Collins

Ref: 'Computers of the World' Exhibition, London, 20XX
I had the pleasure of using your professional services in helping us to prepare and present at the above last year.
We are now in the process of planning to exhibit our new product range again this year and would like to know whether you would offer us your services. I am pleased to enclose our latest catalogue.
Please contact me at the end of next week to arrange for a meeting at our offices.
I look forward to hearing from you.

Yours sincerely,

Timothy R. Jones
Marketing Manager

Enc. Catalogue of product range X.

Figure 5.5 A letter of enquiry

The opening paragraph should state the nature of the enquiry or request clearly and simply, with a personal tone that will make the reader want to respond.

If further explanation or justification is needed, explain the importance of the information required and the situation which prompted the inquiry or request and, if appropriate, the benefits to the reader. Next, specify the desired action in a positive manner.

Close the letter with a courteous statement and explain the type of action needed, the deadline by which a reply should be made and assure the reader that the information will be treated as confidential (if appropriate).

Activity 5.1

You work for a UK-based holiday accommodation agency. Owners of premium holiday accommodation appear in your directory, which is then sent out to customers who apply for a brochure by phone or online. You have built up a bank of accommodation across all regions of the country and the brochure is now quite thick, costing a lot to produce and distribute. You need to encourage more people to use online access and remove those who no longer wish to receive the brochure.

Draft a letter to send to customers to ask if they wish to continue receiving the brochure, and checking their contact details on the database.

Writing sales or persuasive letters

(Also see the section on Direct Marketing in Unit 7).

You could use the AIDA formula:

Grab the reader's *attention* by putting the focus on the reader and their situation.

- o Know who you are writing to. One way to grab the reader's attention is to use their name and to personalize the letter by using 'you', 'your' and 'yours'.
- o Ensure you know what need your 'offer' is fulfilling. You must write from the reader's viewpoint in relation to their needs and wants.
- o Know all the benefits, particularly the most important one.
- o Attract the reader's attention with a headline, picture and colour.

Create *interest* in your product or service by stating how the reader may benefit.

- o Convert features into advantages and benefits for the reader. Keep sentences short and simple.
- o Use subheadings, white space, double spacing, underlining, italics, emboldening, and graphics to keep the reader's eye moving.
- o Use the word 'you' often.
- o Use facts.

Stimulate *desire* by using persuasive language, where possible.

- o Make the reader desire your product/service by telling them how it will improve their life.
- o Make it sound easy to obtain.
- o Repeat your offer/best benefit using new wording.
- o Be credible.
- o Use the present tense as if the reader already owns the product/service.
- o Use testimonials with signatures and pictures of people.

Engender *action* by explaining what the reader needs to do next.

- Put a closing date on your offer.
- Offer a bonus for quick reply.
- Use reply-paid envelope or free-phone number.
- Make it easy to reply, for example using a coupon or order form which is easy to complete and cut out.
- Show the telephone number prominently.

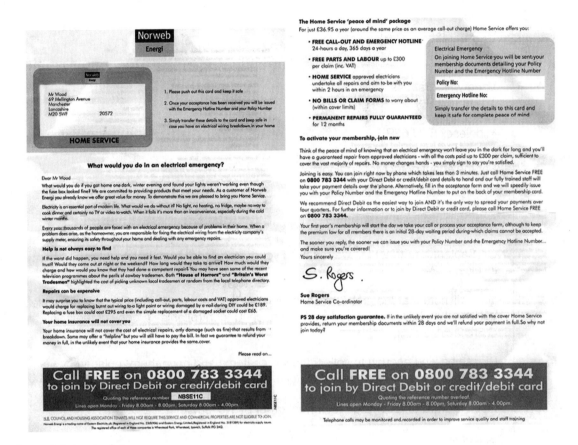

Figure 5.6 A sales letter

Writing complaint letters

In marketing, complaint letters are likely to deal with faulty, mishandled or lost merchandise and other types of customer complaint.

If you are writing a letter of complaint, your motive for communicating is to have the claim sorted out and therefore written documentation is better than verbal communication as there is evidence of action you have taken.

In writing a complaint letter, you should include the following:

1. Opening paragraph with a clear statement of the problem
2. Further information that will verify the claim or adjustment needed
3. Closing statement with a polite, non-threatening request for action, emphasizing that the business relationship need not be affected if the matter is resolved satisfactorily.

BEAUTY POTIONS LTD
2–6 Staines Road
Windsor
Berkshire BK7 9LE
Tel: 01753 576423

JK/abc
October 1st 20XX

Variety Fragrances
10 Harrow Road
Wembley
Middlesex 8TU 65R

<u>For the attention of Mr Gardiner</u>

Dear Mr Gardiner,

On September 5th 20XX, we received your order 1112, together with the invoice, 2224.

Your will note that the first item on the invoice is listed as 50. Fragrance 'Irresistible', but unfortunately we received 50. Fragrance 'Uncontrollable'. A copy of the invoice is attached.

Please be kind enough to collect the wrong items and have them replaced by 50. Fragrance 'Irresistible' at the same time.

I look forward to receiving the correct order by November 1st 20XX.

Sincerely,

Joanna Kemp
Sales and Purchasing Manager

Enc. copy of invoice 2224

Figure 5.7 A letter of complaint

Answering complaint letters (letters of adjustment)

If you are replying to a complaint letter you should not delay your response, even if all you do is confirm receipt of the letter and explain that you need to investigate the matter, if it is a serious complaint. You should show empathy and concern for the customer and if you can make an adjustment, you should apologize and do so.

If the matter is not a legitimate complaint then you should explain your reasons why there will be no compensation or adjustment. In this situation, the following layout should be used:

1. An opening statement with reference to the claim or adjustment but with a notable point on which both parties might agree.
2. An explanation which is tactful and maintains the goodwill of the organization, whilst ensuring that the claimant accepts (some) responsibility for the nature of the claim.
3. The refusal, possibly with the suggestion of an alternative course of action.
4. A pleasant close.

Activity 5.2

You are the manager of a local department store who receives a letter from a customer complaining about the quality of service and the rudeness of one member of staff in the Mother and Baby department. You have investigated the complaint and have found it to be genuine. Write a reply letter to the complainant.

Writing letters of credit

In most organizations today, the process of buying and selling goods and services is facilitated by credit. The credit manager has the responsibility for accepting or rejecting an application for credit, which is based on an assessment regarding the person's or organization's financial viability and outstanding debts, in relation to the type and value of credit required.

Approving credit
1. A pleasant opening paragraph which grants the credit request.
2. Details of the terms and conditions under which credit is granted, addressing any specific points that may not be in line with company policy, but which have been raised.
3. A courteous close.

Refusing credit
1. An opening statement appreciating the request for credit. Make the refusal, but with a notable point that both parties may agree.
2. Details for the refusal in positive terms which are specific to the reader, whilst maintaining a tactful tone to ensure goodwill.
3. A courteous close, with a sales pitch in relation to the correspondence, if appropriate.

CATERING WHOLESALERS LTD
35 Redruth Avenue
Tunbridge
Kent TN15 UCI
Tel: 01932 57311

HB/abc

October 1st 20XX

Mr R. Anderson
The Manager
'The Restaurant'
76 Sevenoaks Road
Sevenoaks
KENT

Dear Mr Anderson,

Thank you very much for your recent application for credit. I am pleased to inform you that this has been approved.

Our terms and conditions are as follows:

1.   A credit limit of £2000 is available for your establishment.
2.   Invoices must be settled within 15 days of the date of issue, after which an interest charge of 5 percent will be levied on outstanding balances.

Yours sincerely,

Harry Bains
Credit Manager

Figure 5.8 A letter approving credit

Writing letters of recommendation

Letters of recommendation convey information about people, their characteristics and suitability for the position. Figure 5.9 gives an example of a letter of recommendation. These are usually confidential and must contain the following:

1.   The name of the person
2.   The position that the candidate is seeking
3.   The nature of the relationship between you and the candidate
4.   Relevant details to the position being sought by the candidate
5.   Evaluation of the candidate by the correspondent.

If you feel unable to provide a letter of recommendation, be brief and factual in your reasons.

```
                    FINANCE and INSURANCE Co
                          The Causeway
                    Newcastle upon Tyne NN4 65T
                         Tel: 0191 35202


   SB/abc

   October 1st 20XX



   The Membership Secretary
   Chartered Institute of Marketing
   Moor Hall
   Cookham
   Berks


   Dear Sir/Madam,

   Re: Caroline Taylor

   I am pleased to support Ms Taylor's application for membership of the Chartered
   Institute of Marketing.

   Ms Taylor has been in our employment for 6 years working in the area of Direct
   Marketing.

   I understand that she has passed all her CIM examinations and will be pleased to
   receive further benefit as a member of the CIM.

   Yours faithfully,



   Sheila Brown
   Marketing Director
```

Figure 5.9 Letter of recommendation

Using PASS to plan the effective use of letters

Purpose

Usually, to gain information, relay information or to confirm details of an agreement or action taken. Letters have legal standing and can be used to ensure that misunderstandings do not occur at a later stage. Any action that is required will need to be detailed within the main body of the letter and reiterated at the end to give greater emphasis. Often the purpose can be highlighted as a heading to the letter with the use of underlining and bold techniques.

Audience

The intended recipient of the letter will be instrumental in the way the letter is put together and the language used within that letter. A letter confirming terms and conditions of working with your advertising agency can use a great deal of jargon as you can be assured of the recipient being able to understand. A letter responding to a customer complaint will be conciliatory in style. It is sometimes necessary to copy people into a letter for information or because they are required to do something detailed within the letter. This is shown by the use of c.c A.N. Other at the bottom of the letter. If a copy is being sent to keep someone informed, it is etiquette to use the term 'blind copy' or 'c.f.i'.

Structure

Similar to a presentation, a letter has a beginning, middle and end as highlighted at the start of the letter section. The letter will begin using the recipient's name or suitable alternative. The use of a heading as detailed previously should also be considered to gain the attention of the reader. The letter is usually divided into paragraphs to introduce the subject, divide the content into relevant sections and to conclude the letter.

After the introduction, the letter will go on to describe the main purpose of the communication and to introduce issues that require action, or need confirmation or clarification. Where action is required it is usual to restate this to ensure the recipient fully appreciates what is required.

The letter should end with the use of a concluding paragraph, confirming relevant details and dates.

Style

The style will be dependent on the formality of the content and the relationship between the sender and the recipient. A complaint letter will be formal, the salutation will be Sir/Madam or the formal version of their name, and the complimentary close will be faithfully or sincerely dependent upon the salutation.

A letter confirming the approval of advertising expenditure to a well-known contact at the advertising agency will use a personal salutation and probably end with an informal complimentary close such as 'with regards'.

Style is the most important part of the PASS mnemonic to get just right. An informal letter sent in a formal situation is bad business practice and can lead to the purpose of the communication being completely misinterpreted.

Memoranda

Memoranda (or memos) are not as widely used by organizations as they once were, having been replaced in the main by e-mail. Where they are used, it is mainly for internal correspondence to convey short specific information. They could be written for any of the following reasons:

- ○ To arrange a schedule of meetings
- ○ To give the results of research
- ○ To book a meeting room
- ○ To organize training
- ○ To organize attendance at an exhibition
- ○ To ask for staff cover.

Of course, this list is not comprehensive as the reasons for sending a memo are almost unlimited. What can be stated is that memos can be stored for future reference and follow composition principles similar to that for writing business letters.

Memo paper is often pre-printed on A4 or A5, in the following format:

MEMO To: From: Date: Subject:

The sender and recipient of the memo are usually addressed by job title (e.g. sales manager), but their full name may also be included. It may be necessary to circulate the memo to other interested parties, and this should be indicated on the memo.

The subject title should be clear and concise and tell the recipient exactly what the memo is about.

The body of the memorandum should be in short paragraphs, with summary headings if appropriate.

MEMO
Medical Software Ltd

To: Carole Francis (Sales and Marketing Director)
From: Clare White (Marketing Manager)
Copy to: Hannah Craven (secretary)
Date: October 1st 20XX
Subject: Software 20XX Exhibition, Amsterdam, December 1st – 3rd

We have 8 weeks before the exhibition takes place and need to finalize the details of the follow-up campaign, particularly the role of our sales force.

Further to our meeting last week, we also need to discuss the sales promotion initiatives to push our products following the exhibition.

Please confirm that a meeting on October 5th at 3 p.m. in my office will be convenient.

Figure 5.10 A memo

E-mail

Having superseded memos in many organizations, e-mail is a quick and simple way to communicate internally and with external contacts that are connected to the Internet. There are no rules about layout and the medium is usually used to send short messages with longer documents, such as letters and reports, attached by selecting the Insert, File Attachment option.

The best way to experiment with e-mail is to send and receive some and you will soon become adept at recognizing when an e-mail is appropriate and when it is better to telephone someone, write a formal letter or send a memorandum.

As a rule of thumb, if you need an urgent reply, the telephone is the best way to actually check details with a colleague or an external contact. This is because you will know if you have got through to the person or not by telephone whereas you cannot be sure that your e-mail message has been read, which can lead to uncertainty when you want an instant response. You can attach a 'High importance' rating onto urgent e-mails and add the read receipt function to your message to let you know when the message is read. But this only works once the intended recipient logs into their e-mail account. Telephone calls are more intrusive and immediate.

For more formal communications it is better to send a letter to external customers or a memorandum to colleagues.

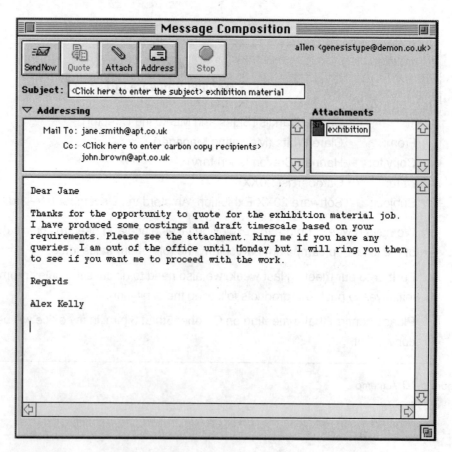

Figure 5.11 An example of an e-mail message

How to write effective e-mail

Because most e-mail messages are simply text files, the usual conventions connected with letter writing, such as letterheads, typesizes, typestyles, justification, layout, paper quality and signatures are often, incorrectly, ignored. This lack of convention encourages people to be less formal than they would be if they were writing a memo or letter on headed paper. Some people do not use normal punctuation, such as capital letters and full stops, but this can lead to confusing messages and is best avoided as it is often too easy to send an e-mail which is like an unstructured written conversation.

Although you do not really need to think about layout in conjunction with an e-mail, it is better to avoid sending e-mails that are one long block of text. They are much easier to read if you use spaces between paragraphs.

Your message will be one of many that a recipient might receive in a day. Therefore, your subject line should be concise but give an indication of the context of the message.

There is no set rule about using a salutation, such as Dear John or Dear Sir. If you are unsure of what to do, it is better to err on the side of caution and include a greeting as the absence of one could make you appear rude. Generally though, e-mails do not require formal greetings in the way that letters do. Similarly, you do not need to use a formal close such as 'Yours sincerely' or 'Yours faithfully' unless you have opted for a formal greeting. Most people sign off with a closing term such as 'regards' followed by their first and last name if they do not know the person even though it is usually clear who is the sender of an e-mail message. If you do include a formal greeting you may want to include your job title and company website details. This can be pre-prepared in the form of an electronic signature.

You should ensure that you are sending your message to the right recipients and if appropriate you can use the Bcc (blind carbon copy) line to send the message to other recipients without others knowing. Again the ease of sending e-mails to multiple recipients has led to many of us being copied in on e-mails which have little to do with our area of work. E-mail overload is becoming a real business issue both in terms of time wasted on reading and replying and the disk space used to store them.

If you expect anyone on the cc list to take specific action as a result of receiving your message, then you should make it clear in the message. Otherwise, recipients in the cc list might assume that the message is 'for information only'.

If you are sending attachments you should say so in the main body of the e-mail; people often forget to attach attachments and this will only come to light if the recipient is aware that there should be one there. If you are worried about other people being able to access the document, you can password protect the document so that it can be opened only using the password. You could then contact the recipient by another method and provide them with the password so that they can open the document. Attaching other criteria such as receipt and high importance status can also make your e-mail more effective.

E-mail etiquette

It is generally accepted that e-mails are an informal way of communicating. However, it is important to remember that the organization's e-mail system should be used only for work-based messages. Many organizations are clamping down on the use of e-mail as they are concerned about the time and disk space that is being wasted on e-mails that have no work-related purpose at all. You should be aware that your employer owns e-mail messages sent from your workplace and has the right to monitor the e-mail you send using their computers. This is also pertinent for Internet use as people use work time to search for their next holiday.

The medium also encourages brevity, which can make you more productive in dealing with and sending messages. However, it can mean that messages sound curt to the extent of rudeness, if you are not careful. Please and thank you should still be used as well as a summary sentence or paragraph to end the message content.

Just because you have sent an e-mail does not mean it has been received. If an e-mail contains important information that you are relying on the recipient to act upon then you should attach an electronic receipt which they send back upon opening. Many people's defence against an uncompleted task is 'I sent an e-mail telling them it was 10 o'clock', when the e-mail lies unopened either due to holidays or access problems.

For the same reason, you should always post an out-of-office notice when you are on holiday so that people are aware of your absence.

Legal firms advise companies nowadays that they should guard against e-mail abuse by writing to staff about the perils associated with e-mails:

o Instruct staff not to include any statements or other material that could be held to be abusive, racist, constitute sexual harassment or be threatening or defamatory.
o Point out that someone other than the intended recipient may receive the message and that both individuals and the company could be held liable for anything contained in it.
o Advise them to use password-protected documents for confidential information.

Many firms also attach a legal disclaimer to the bottom of every e-mail sent out from the firm.

Intranet

An intranet allows you to communicate on the Internet in a local network that is not publicly accessible. Many organizations use intranets to distribute internal documents.

However, it can be used outside the organization to allow nominated people to share documents, expertise or opinions anywhere in the world. The network would be protected to ensure that only nominated people could access information, thus keeping the network secure.

The most common form of intranet is where corporate information is published on an internal website, with hypertext links to related documents, enabling enormous amounts of time to be saved searching for information.

For example, a law practice that merged with another firm in a town forty miles away, used the intranet to create an internal 'who's who' of staff, including photographs. It then developed to include internal phone directories, which could be updated without continual re-printing costs, practice guides on word-processing house styles, the staff handbook, and even what was being served in the staff restaurant that week.

Eventually, it went on to be used to produce practice-wide know-how material and legal precedents. In other words, it became a giant internal library with easy access to staff from inside the firm.

The benefits of intranets

- Reduced costs in printing and distributing documents
- Publishing information without delay
- No physical filing – saving time and space
- Ability to find information quickly.

Extranet

An extranet is an intranet extended to key players involved in your everyday business processes in order to achieve total collaboration. This may include dealers, suppliers or business partners. The extranet allows e-business to take place as business transactions such as order placing linked to stock levels, delivery schedules subject to storage available, even the issue and payment of invoices can all take place electronically with little human intervention. This has huge advantages in terms of cost and time as routine clerical tasks are carried out by electronic triggers built into stock and order systems.

For example, when General Motors started using their extranet to enable purchase orders to be made by their dealers using an electronic form process, the cost of the transaction went down from £35 to less than 10p.

 Activity 5.3

Your organization has recently merged with another operating in the same industry sector – taxation and accountancy services – but servicing different areas of the world. You have a stronghold in the UK whereas their strengths lie in the US and Canada.

Many cultural differences have been ironed out via conferences, meetings and employee briefings and there is a renewed sense of optimism and team spirit. Working together appears not to be an issue. However, communication between the key sites needs to be seamless for all business opportunities to be maximized.

Write a memo to the sales managers at each of the offices advising them on the importance of keeping the lines of communication open with their colleagues in each of the sales regions. Outline the disadvantages of relying on writing letters and explain the advantages of using existing IT and telecommunications facilities such as e-mail, fax and voice mail.

Notices

Notices can play an important role in disseminating information to a large number of people who share a common interest. Effective notices should follow these rules:

1. The size of the paper should correspond to the amount of information to be conveyed and its effect when displayed on the noticeboard and possibly viewed from several feet away.
2. The AIDA principle can again be used with a large, bold heading to capture attention, detail which holds the reader's interest and creates desire, and clear instructions as to the action which should be taken.
3. The message should be simple and concise.

SAFETY FIRST!

A Special First-Aid Course designed to give you basic introduction will be available free to all employees on the following dates.

October 1st 5–6 p.m.
November 1st 5–6 p.m.
December 1st 5–6 p.m.

The number of places is limited to 20 per class so early booking is advisable.

Contact: Jane Slater, ext. 123

Figure 5.12 A notice

Reports

Reports can be used internally and externally in a range of contexts either to give information or to make proposals with justifications.

Progress reports may be of a routine nature to provide an update on a particular job or project. Special one-off reports can be requested or prepared voluntarily to interpret data, inform and/or influence recipients – for example, to analyse market research data, give information about sales trends or to propose a change of company policy.

Reports are used for a variety of purposes and can be short (such as progress reports) or long (such as investigative reports or the annual report), formal or informal, routine, occasional or specially commissioned. Before any report can be prepared, decisions about the exact nature and purpose of the report, the recipient, distribution and likely reaction all need to be addressed because these factors will determine the structure, length and style (i.e. the degree of formality) of the report.

In marketing, a formal report could be written on the current state of the market in a particular sector, or a short memorandum report could provide a range of quotes from printers for a new catalogue. Somewhere between these two extremes, an informal report could be written, proposing the use of video conferencing in a firm, for example, or outlining sponsorship opportunities or reporting back from training or the success of an exhibition stand.

How to write reports

A report should not be written in a personal style highlighting the report writer's personal view if it has been commissioned to uncover facts and/or highlight the views of several people. A report should therefore be factual and written in an unbiased style. If necessary, it should show a range of opinions and conclude with the majority or most accurate viewpoint.

The report will sound more objective and professional if impersonal sentence constructions are used, such as:

- o 'It was found that'
- o 'It was evident that'
- o 'The statistics revealed that'
- o 'The investigations showed that'
- o 'It seems that'
- o 'It appears that'.

Your report will be more balanced and objective if you avoid emotional sounding phrases, such as 'a desperate situation' or 'This must be done at all costs'.

How to structure a report

The guidance given in the first part of the unit also applies to reports – they should have a beginning, a middle and an end. However, you can also organize the material schematically, using a system of numbers and/or letters. This approach not only makes the material easier to read and follow but is also useful for referencing purposes.

In addition to using a numbering system to organize a report's contents, you could use different types of headings. These are used with the three main different types of reports: formal reports, informal reports and memorandum reports.

Formal reports

Formal reports are designed to achieve a number of goals but mainly to provide information and arguments based on investigating a problem or opportunity.

For a formal report, it is usual to have the following headings/sections and structure:

- o Report title (this should be brief, specific and informative)
- o Recipient's name
- o Author's name
- o Date
- o Contents table (including headings and page numbers), if the report size warrants this
- o Terms of reference (which should outline the scope of the report and the reason why it is being written)

- o Procedure or research method/methodology (should identify how the information in the report was obtained)
- o Findings (relevant facts and findings in order of importance, chronological order or just grouped together in relevant categories)
- o Conclusion (should summarize the main findings and should not introduce new findings)
- o Recommendations (not always required and used only if there are solutions to a problem which has been identified and if these solutions have emerged from a detailed analysis in the report)
- o Appendices (where there is a large amount of factual data, tables and diagrams that could interrupt the flow of the document and cause confusion). Appendices appear at the end of the report and their presence should be highlighted in the report. Each appendix should be numbered.

REPORT

TO: Denise Wood, Marketing Manager

FROM: Amy Mills, Marketing Assistant

DATE: 6 December 200X

GO EASY – THE CASE FOR A WEBSITE & ON-LINE BOOKING SERVICE

1. Introduction

The aim of this report is to identify reasons why our company, Go Easy, should invest in a web site and on-line booking service. This will be demonstrated by looking at the current state of the Internet market, predicted trends and competitor Internet activity.

2. Findings

a. The On-line Market

Recent studies by Business Research (December 2000) have looked at the US and UK on-line markets. Their information shows that in the US a third of all households with the Internet have shopped on-line in the past six months. Similarly, the figures for the UK are high, with 22 per cent of internet users making a purchase on-line within the past three months.

Their data indicates that in the UK, travel is the third most popular on-line purchase after PC's and books, with 15 per cent of on-line expenditure being spent on travel.

In the US, expenditure for on-line travel is set to grow from 0.5$ billion to over 7$ billion.

b. Competitor Activity

easyJet, one of our competitors, has made significant headway in this area since launching their web site and booking service in October of last year.

A recent report by 'Promotions and Incentives' magazines shows that 4 per cent of all their bookings are currently made on-line. easy Jet's aims to increase this to 30 per cent equating to £60 million worth of revenue.

easyJet have linked up with the *Times* to offer discounted flights to customers who book on-line.

c. Benefits of on-line booking

The information given in the Promotion and Incentives report shows that easyJet can handle up to 200 bookings at a time over the Internet, but only 90 at a time by telephone. Thus Internet booking gives a more efficient service to their customers.

Benefits to easyJet itself are they do not have to pay 80p commission to the telephonists, who would normally handle the incoming calls.

3. Conclusions

On-line sales are continually growing, with huge numbers of individuals potentially purchasing from the travel sector. Go Easy flights should have access to this market.

Our competition are establishing a firm foothold in this valuable market, using huge promotion and above-the-line advertising activity to do so.

On-line purchasing has advantages for both the consumer and the company.

4. Recommendations

In order not to miss out on the ever-growing on-line market, Go Easy must introduce a web site with a suitable and efficient on-line purchasing capability.

Figure 5.13 An example of a formal report

Study tip

You are required to write reports in many of the assignment-based assessments that are set by the CIM. This format is also utilized within the examination. The favoured style is the Informal style as detailed below. This is illustrated in the examples shown in Appendices 2 and 3 at the back of this coursebook.

Informal reports

For an *informal* report, it is usual to use the following headings:

- Introduction
- Findings
- Conclusion.

or

- Purpose and scope of report
- Background information
- Findings
- Conclusions and recommendations.

PRINTMAN PRINTING COMPANY

Report on Office Telecommunications Facilities

To: Mark Scrivens, Managing Director

From: Jo Goodwin, Sales and Marketing Manager

Date: 2 December 200X

Introduction

As a small printing company trying to succeed in a competitive market, we need to be able to use various office equipment to improve our efficiency and effectiveness when communicating with customers and internally. This report sets out to identify where we could upgrade our current systems and equipment to improve how sales representatives and account managers operate.

Findings

Voice Mail

During busy periods customers often have problems getting through to the switchboard with our current telephone system. With a voice mail system connected to a computer, customers could use an interactive menu system which would mean they could ring up and choose to be connected to any one of a number of our account managers without having to go through the switchboard. Customers could also leave messages when a person is not at their desk, which saves colleagues spending time taking down messages.

Networked Laptop Computers

Laptop computers could be used by our account managers and sales team while they are out visiting clients. It means they could access information here at the office and give clients quotes on print jobs immediately. In addition they could show clients examples of relevant jobs we have done on their laptops rather than carrying round a large portfolio or briefcase of printed materials. Also when it is not worth staff coming back to the office because their last client visit was near to their home, it makes sense to give them the means to finish off work, such as, quotes, reports and design briefs, in their own time at home.

An Extranet

As we have now got a computer system with Internet access, it would be good to upgrade the system to incorporate an extranet so that customers can access their accounts and check the progress on their various print jobs with us. This would reduce the number of 'checking' calls that account managers deal with and free them up to develop new business and cross-sell our services to clients more effectively.

Conclusions

These are the three main systems and pieces of equipment that we could use at the moment to improve how we operate in sales and marketing. If these proposals are of interest, then it would be a simple task to collate various information about different systems and do a price check against different products in the market.

Figure 5.14 An example of an informal report

Memorandum report

For memorandum reports, it is usual to use a memo format and to group relevant information together under different headings and categories.

Memorandum

To: Bob, Bloggs, Sales Manager

From: Marcia Merchant, Sales and Marketing Assistant

Subject: Report on Negotiation Skills Course

This memorandum report outlines the value and effectiveness of the recent Negotiation Skills course attended on 4 December 200X run by Total Training at the Willow Bank Hotel.

<u>Course Details</u>

It was a one-day course and cost £150 per delegate. Delegates who attended were from a variety of sectors but all were working in sales and marketing jobs.

<u>Course Content</u>

The course was delivered with a mixture of input, case studies and interaction with the audience. The course was well organized and the trainer was well organized and interesting.

Topics covered included preparing for negotiations, building rapport, trading concessions, maintaining advantage and controlling interpersonal behaviour.

The course was delivered from a 'buying and selling' perspective and provided comprehensive coverage of theory, practical and suggestions and skills testing.

<u>Conclusion</u>

The course runs again early next year and I recommend that others in the department attend it.

Figure 5.15 An example of a memorandum report

Articles

If you work in the marketing department of a firm that produces a staff newsletter with the aim of improving internal communication, you could occasionally be asked to contribute, or you might even be responsible for all aspects of it, such as writing, designing and arranging the printing. However, you might never be asked to write an article or an advertorial (like a press release but in the form of a newspaper or magazine article) because it is not part of your job. Nevertheless, an article is a communication format that is occasionally tested on the examination paper.

The way to approach writing an article is to use the writing skills you have honed when you have written letters and reports and to combine that with your skill in producing press releases. When you are writing an article for an advertorial or for a company newsletter, you must try to adopt an independent, unbiased tone – in other words, the 'sell' should be very subtle.

Figure 5.16 is an example of an advertorial article, written by a partner in a small labelling and sign company for a newspaper, about why logos, letterhead design and graphical symbols are important for companies' internal and external communications.

Design Works

Labelling and Signage Designs know that good design is essential for firms that need to communicate with their staff, customers and suppliers.

Essential safety notices in the workplace need to stand out so people take notice of them – in a way that words alone cannot manage. Graphical symbols can show hazards and directional symbols can indicate specific areas, e.g. toilets, disabled access, fire exits, litter bins, etc. At Labelling and Signage Designs these can be tailor-made for any individual work environment. Just visualize the 'Keep Britain Tidy' logo or the Olympic Games symbol or even a 'No smoking' symbol to understand the power of images in communicating with people.

To communicate instantly with members of the public who are unfamiliar with an area or environment, it is important to use signs which indicate where dressing rooms, pay points and exit doors are located.

However, all imagery in the corporate environment should be consistent with the image and identity the company wants to communicate to its staff and public.

Consequently, handwritten, poorly designed signs and images would portray an amateur, uncaring and unprofessional image. A professional signage company knows how important the right typeface, shape and colour is to presenting the correct image and conveying the message effectively.

Corporate Identity

The Corporate image that is communicated in a company's logo is seen on its letterheads, business cards, lorries, shop or office front, sales promotion literature and packaging or carrier bags, depending on the firm's type of business.

The designers at Labelling and Signage Designs can use graphical symbols, visual cimmunication and typefaces to give a company an appropriate image. A particular typeface can convey a certain personality or culture, e.g. formality, long-established or modern and technical. A logo which stands out can create recognition and differentiate the firm from its competitors. The right logo can link the various products and services of one organization into a single, consistent identity. Think about the distinctive type style of the Coca-Cola logo, the use of the black horse symbol that distinguishes Lloyds Bank; Kodak's outstanding black and yellow packaging certainly makes its products stand out. These well-known logos and symbols actually provide customers with reassurance that they are dealing with the best.

The logo can even indicate a firm's field of activity: an international worldwide firm might even include a globe; a people-oriented firm might show linked hands.

It is difficult with a new firm, or a company with a new product, to find a name that has not been used before. But the right acronym such as Esso or Persil could mean a product is easy to pronounce and has a distinctive name. In a similar vein, the right slogan can help customers remember a firm or its products.

Figure 5.16 An advertorial

Summary

In this unit you have studied:

o Why you need to be familiar with a range of communication formats.
o How various communication formats are structured.
o How and when to write effective letters, memos, notices, e-mails, reports and articles.

Further study and examination preparation

If you wish to gain more exam practice refer to Questions 1(a), and 2b from the June 2005 examination paper, Questions 1a and 5 from the December 2004 paper. These are accessible in Appendix 4 or on www.cim.co.uk along with Specimen Answers and Senior Examiner's advice for these exam questions.

Hints and tips

You need to be familiar with all the communication formats used in this unit as they will be tested throughout the examination paper. You will find that most questions in fact require candidates to write their answer in the format of a letter, report, memo or e-mail. Question 1 usually includes a report which is often awarded a maximum possible 40 marks and so this is obviously an important area for you to study.

You should become more aware generally of communication in all formats. The sequence of a message can often distort messages because subjects raised at the front end of the message can also have an inferred connection later on in the message even though that was not the original intention.

Bibliography

Forsyth, P. (1999) *Communicating with Customers*, London: Orion Business.

unit 6

using statistical data and visual information

In this unit you will:

o See the relevance of interpreting, analysing and presenting data in marketing. See syllabus section 4.7.

o Understand how to interpret and summarize data. See syllabus section 4.5.

o Appreciate the value of using graphs, tables and charts in the visual communication of marketing information. See syllabus section 4.5.

o Study a range of graphs, tables and charts and understand when they should be used. See syllabus section 4.7.

By the end of this unit you will be able to:

o Interpret, summarize and present oral, written and graphical information (4.5).

o Plan, prepare and deliver presentation using appropriate and effective visual aids and media (4.7).

This unit relates to the statements of practice

Cb.2 Deliver Indirect and Direct Communications.

Study Guide

This unit provides you with the underlying knowledge and understanding to be able to deal with data that occurs in the compulsory question in Part A of the Customer Communications paper and covers section 4.5 and has uses in Syllabus area 4.7.

In this unit you will examine how to analyse and interpret information and look at the ways in which information can be communicated using a variety of visual presentation techniques. This unit will help you when you tackle examination questions. The compulsory case study (Part A) regularly requires candidates to read narrative material and examine statistical data or visual data. They are then asked to interpret the data and are often asked to convey the key points in some communication format or other (often a report). In addition, they are often asked to use some part of the information on which to base a chart or graph.

It will take you a minimum of 2 hours to read through this unit and a further 2 hours to do the activities.

Study tip

To put this area of the syllabus and this unit into context, you need to appreciate why it is an important aspect of your marketing studies.

As a starting point, write a list of the types of visual and number or statistical information that you have come across in your personal and working life in the last month.

For instance, you may have watched the news on television and seen a feature about employment figures, crime rates or trends in tourism. If you had, you would probably have noticed that the presenter did not go into great detail, explaining every possible figure and percentage that the report was based on. It is much more likely that he or she would have given you a 'snapshot' view with some key, pertinent points that summarized the overall situation. Any figures would not have been shown in a long list of numbers but would probably have been presented in a visually appealing and easy to understand format, using graphs, charts, maps and possibly including graphical symbols in a pictogram format or even moving images to attract your attention.

Similarly, in your working life, you may have attended a sales and marketing presentation or meeting where market share and sales turnover figures were discussed. The presenter would probably have manipulated the data so that it could be presented in a user-friendly format such as handouts, slides or a PowerPoint presentation.

These are just two examples. Now, using your own experience before you start reading the unit, you should be in the correct 'mindset' to read this unit and appreciate why this is an area of significance when you are studying Customer Communications.

Why is data relevant to marketing?

If you work in marketing, you will find that you often have to use information to make decisions and may need to convey it to internal and potential or actual external customers. The information you deal with could range from market size, the number of brands in a range, to pricing and distribution information, or information about promotion activities, media spend, sales levels or market share.

The information can be in one of the following 'formats':

- o In a raw 'data' format (facts that are not organized in any particular way), such as market research data or sales figures.
- o In an 'information' format, where the information has been selected and sorted or analysed for a purpose, such as showing sales of one brand compared with that of another.
- o In an 'intelligence' format, where the information has been interpreted and analysed, for instance where figures show that sales have increased compared with competitor brands over the period of a special promotion.

Data can be in the form of narrative prose or consist of a series of numbers or percentages. It can be very detailed and there can be too much of it to make sense of in a short time. In situations like this, it is necessary to be able to select the most important data, summarize the key points and, where appropriate, use visual presentation techniques to make the information user-friendly.

Numerical and statistical information is used in a variety of ways in business:

- For record keeping
- To provide progress updates on advertising and promotion campaigns
- For budgeting to compare actual with forecast figures
- As evidence to support proposals
- To show trends in sales revenue for different brands or to indicate labour turnover or absenteeism
- To demonstrate proportion and show market share.

Interpreting, selecting and summarizing information

When you communicate information, you rarely convey all the facts and details that you have. For example, if you are asked the question 'What happened in the Manchester United game against Bayern Munich?', your answer would probably be to give the final score but not a detailed account of every pass of the ball and attempt on goal.

Similarly, when dealing with marketing information and communicating with colleagues and customers, you need to be able to select the relevant information given in the circumstances and to make some sense of it. For instance, in the football game example, rather than listing every single attempt on goal and every foul, you might want to sort the raw data to make the information easier to digest. For example, you might want to say that there were four fouls and two yellow cards given to Bayern Munich players and five attempts each on goal. You might also want to summarize what happened in the general flow of play, for example, Bayern Munich attacked well although their defending left a lot to be desired, but Manchester United played with flair and were unlucky not to score another goal.

Now, look at these survey findings and note the process used for summarizing this information for part of a brief market research report.

300 out of the 500 female customers questioned in a postal survey said they would be interested in the x company home shopping service. Their catalogue was judged to be appealing and to feature the kind of products that shoppers find difficult to track down, especially when parents had young children to accompany them on shopping trips.

Due to the large numbers of people who were interested in the home shopping service, the x company is looking into the possibility of expanding its retail operations to include a home shopping service.

- Firstly, the original material is read thoroughly to identify the main facts and how the ideas are developed.
- Then the information in the whole report is grouped into different categories under main headings.
- The main points in each paragraph are selected and this key information is interpreted to give it meaning. If necessary, it is expressed differently to give it impact and/or make it more understandable.

○ The material should be expressed in the third person, that is 'it has been shown' or 'the figures show that'.

○ Now look at how the information has been summarized for the report:

Sixty per cent of female customers who responded to the survey said they would be interested in a mail order service provided by x company. Because the majority of customers would use such a service, the mail order option will be further investigated.

○ Any summary of information should be checked to ensure the main points are covered and that the key points link together with some continuity.

 Activity 6.1

You have recently joined Robinsons, a grocery chain with 96 outlets in the north of England. Following a survey which was carried out by the magazine *Food Retailer*, you are required to analyse the information given below and deliver a presentation to senior management. With use of an overhead projector, draft out the visual information you would include on three acetates/slides.

Prepare a brief report on the main findings from the perspective of the senior management at the Robinsons grocery chain, to be handed out at your presentation. (For more information on report formats, go to Unit 5.) You should be selective with the information you use and summarize the main findings. Ensure that you interpret the statistical data where you can.

Table 1 How often do you shop for groceries, not including the times when you have forgotten something?

	%
More than twice a week	7
Twice a week	17
Once a week	60
Every two weeks	11
Every three weeks	1
Less often	2
Miscellaneous	1
No response	1

Table 2 On what day or days of the week do you usually do most of your grocery shopping?

	%
Monday	12
Tuesday	4
Wednesday	8
Thursday	24
Friday	40
Saturday	31
Sunday	6

* Results add up to more than 100 per cent because respondents could choose more than one day.

Table 3 What is the main reason you do your grocery shopping on that day?

	%
Most convenient time	45
Fits in with pay-day	30
Good day for special offers	26
Habit	19
Not crowded	8
Stock up for the weekend	7
Leaves weekend free	6
Run out of food on that day	6
Better selection of groceries	3
Miscellaneous	13

Table 4 At which one store do you shop for groceries most often?

Top UK retailers	%
Sainsbury	11.2
Tesco	10.4
Co-op	6.9
Asda	5.7
Safeway	4.7
Robinsons	4.5
Fine Fare	4.5
Gateway	4.4
Spar	4.2
Kwiksave	3.2
Others	40.3

Table 5 What are the reasons for shopping at [name of the shop] most often?

	%
Convenient location	42
Special offers/low prices	38
Good meat	25
Carry all brands	22
Friendly assistants	20
Quality of fresh produce	17
Good display	14
Adequate parking	12
From habit/miscellaneous	47

Table 6 What are your reasons for not shopping at the other stores?

	%
Prices too high	45
Too far to travel	27
Slow checkout	22
Prefer the shop I go to	17
Very few special offers	17
Poor selection	15
Unattractive store	7
Too small	7
Too overcrowded	5
No particular reason	3
Miscellaneous	28

Table 7 On your major grocery shopping trips, how often do you buy advertised special offers?

	%
Frequently	35
Occasionally	15
Seldom	10
Never	38
No response	2

Table 8 Which of the following are your best source of special offers? Which second and which third?

	Source		
	First	Second	Third
Newspapers	40 %	10 %	21 %
Store leaflets	25 %	24 %	15 %
Leaflet drops	15 %	31 %	19 %

Table 9 Please look at these advertisements and tell me the reference number of the one you like best

	%
Safeway	20
Fine Fare	16
Asda	14
Gateway	13
Kwiksave	10
Tesco	9
Sainsbury	8
Co-op	6
Robinsons	2
Aldi	1
No response	1

Table 10 Why do you like the advertisement you picked?

	%
Special offers are easy to find	42
Eye catching	38
Easy to read/large print	27
Easy to find specific brands	19
More bargains	17
Good variety of items	15
Other replies, none more than 8 %	45
No response	3

Why use visual information?

Visual presentations including pictures, diagrams, icons, logos, charts and graphs can be quickly assimilated and can make information much easier to comprehend. People are adept at speed-reading visual messages and find it easier to interpret figures shown pictorially.

You can use graphics to explain relationships and actions that would be difficult to convey concisely in words. For example, you could use a pie chart to show market share more effectively than a list of percentages or you could use a bar chart to show rising sales figures over a 5-year period rather than explaining the year-on-year increases.

You can use visual messages to create impact and attract the attention of an audience. If you present information visually, it is also more likely to be retained in your target audience's memory.

You can choose from a variety of ways to display data visually:

o   Tables can be used for recording and displaying a wide range of numerical data
o   Bar charts help to compare changes in relative quantity
o   Line graphs help to show trends and moving averages over time, so are useful for planning and forecasting
o   Pie charts help you see proportions of a whole
o   Pictograms show pictorial symbols of statistics to simplify messages
o   Organograms show reporting relationships between people in organizations
o   Gantt charts help with project planning.

How to present visual information

Nowadays, it is much easier to generate graphs and charts with a professional appearance on a computer using a spreadsheet or database software. (See Figure 6.1 for examples of how computers can produce three-dimensional and other visual techniques to represent data.)

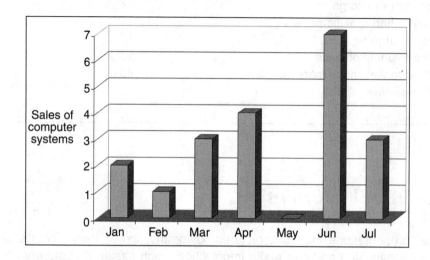

Figure 6.1

However, you should be aware of how each of the main display options can be used and should be able to produce them without the aid of a computer.

As a general rule it is best to keep charts and graphs simple. Visually it is better if the chart takes up the full axis space available. Use of colour or a three-dimensional aspect can create impact. All graphs and charts should have a title indicating the content – for example, 'marketing spend for product *x*' – and sometimes this is used to indicate the values being shown, for instance, whether it is £'000 or per cent. There should be two axes on each graph, a horizontal axis (the *x*-axis) and a vertical axis (the *y*-axis). It is best to orient the data so that values on the horizontal axis are those where there has been a choice, such as, when to measure or where to measure (this is known as the independent variable). Values on the vertical axis will depend upon the corresponding position on the horizontal axis (they are therefore known as the dependent variable). For example, when showing the change in sales revenue over the course of a year, the independent variable is time since we can choose when to measure sales revenue. The dependent variable is sales revenue since it will change according to the time at which it was measured.

The key or the legend relates the shading or pattern used on a chart to what it represents. In addition to or in place of a legend, labels can be used to mark what each bar, segment or line represents. All bars and charts should display the source of information. It is also advisable to cross reference all graphs and charts within the text, such as 'see figure x' or 'see attached appendix y'.

Tables

Tables can be useful for presentation purposes to sort complex data. However, the information presented in this way can often be used as the basis for further analysis because while the information is in this format, it is often difficult to read or follow trends.

Salesperson	Product line sales turnover (£000s) 2000–2001					Total (£)
	A	B	C	D	E	
Helen Jenkins	13	15	8	12	10	58
Jane Atkinson	8	10	9	6	5	38
Andrew Salter	16	12	10	12	14	64
Luigi Romero	23	26	13	28	22	112
Karen Mann	33	34	24	22	30	143
Sunil Singh	12	16	11	17	15	71
George Vassiliades	4	7	3	8	11	33
Alan Bennet	11	12	12	12	11	58
Tony Taylor	15	7	7	9	8	46
Christine James	22	13	21	10	15	81
Total	157	152	118	136	141	704

Figure 6.2 A table showing product line sales per representative

Bar charts

Column/bar charts demonstrate relationships and differences in variables by the respective heights of the columns/bars, which can be displayed vertically or horizontally, with the data on or near the bars. They are particularly useful when you want to:

1. Compare the size of several variables in one presentation
2. Demonstrate important differences between the variables
3. Demonstrate changes over a period of time
4. Demonstrate the composition of variables.

There are three types of column/bar chart that can be presented:

1. Simple column/bar charts
2. Multiple column/bar charts
3. Component (stacked) column/bar charts.

Guidelines for producing simple column/bar charts

Simple column/bar charts demonstrate the value of one piece of data by the respective length of the column/bar(s) on the chart. Where the horizontal axis cannot have values midway between each measurement (bar), such as between two brands or between two countries, then a bar chart should be used. Where the horizontal axis has values which can gradually change, then a line graph is best, since it shows the possible points midway between each measurement.

1. The chart must be titled and each axis of the graph must be labelled.
2. There must be a scale to indicate values on each axis (see Figure 6.3 where market share percentages are shown on the *y*-axis).
3. The vertical axis must always start at 0, so that the relative values can be accurately demonstrated, or indicate with a staggered line that the data does not begin at 0.

4. If possible, the data should be presented in some order of value, that is lowest to highest or vice versa; this is usually not possible if time comparisons are made.
5. Use spaces between columns/bars for ease of interpretation.
6. Use shading to highlight the columns/bars, making them easier to view. Figure 6.4 demonstrates how to draw a simple column/bar chart based on the data below.

1995	1996	1997	1998	1999	2000	2001
0.4%	0.7%	1.9%	2.6%	3.0%	3.0%	2.8%

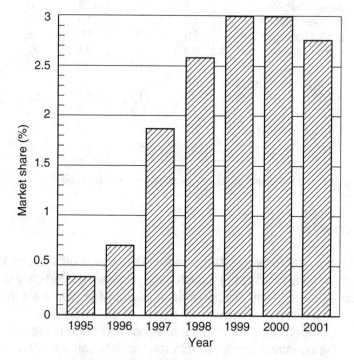

Figure 6.3 Market share for Brand 'A' for the years 1995–2001

Multiple column/bar charts

Multiple column/bar charts use several columns/bars for each variable, each column/bar demonstrating a particular aspect of the overall data.

Guidelines for producing multiple column/bar charts
1. Two or more columns/bars are used to present aspects/divisions of the data.
2. Shading must be used to distinguish the columns/bars representing different data.
3. Use spaces appropriately to draw attention to similarities, differences or trends, either in the columns/bars separately or groups of data.
4. Columns/bars can be drawn horizontally or vertically.

Table 6.1

	1999 ('000s)	2000 ('000s)	2001 ('000s)
B1	150	180	225
B2	230	245	205
B3	340	560	480

The multiple column bar chart example shown in Figure 6.4 has been based on the information in Table 6.1.

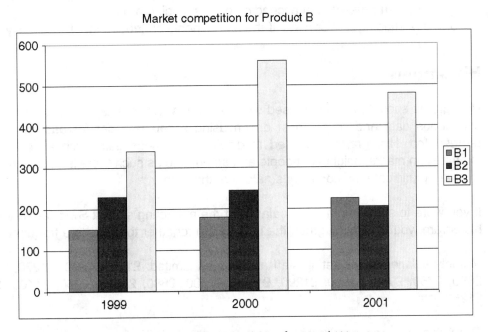

Figure 6.4 A multiple column/bar chart of market competition for Brand 'A'

Component (stacked) column/bar charts

Component (stacked) column/bar charts can be segmented or broken lengthwise to show the relative size of components of an overall total. An example is presented in Figure 6.5.

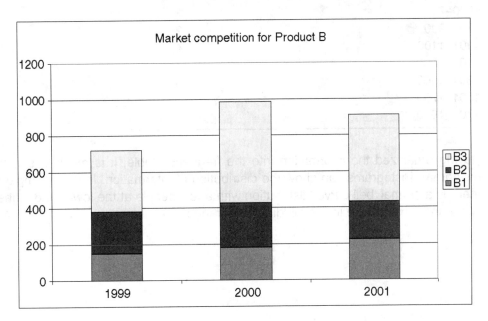

Figure 6.5 A component bar chart

131

Guidelines for producing component column/bar charts

1. The components can be ordered in any way on the column/bar, but must remain consistent if more than one column/bar is demonstrated.
2. The relative values should be kept in order, with either the highest or lowest at the top, and then presented in ascending or descending order.
3. Use shading and/or a key if the components cannot be labelled directly.

Histograms

Histograms should not be confused with bar charts. Bar charts are used for discrete or non-continuous data and so are best drawn using a separate bar for each item that is being represented. Histograms are used to display continuous data such as earnings, mileage, examination marks, heights of people and so on, and as such there is usually no gap between the bars to indicate the continuous nature of the data.

If you were to show the monthly salaries of the marketing staff at Swizzles (listed below), in a histogram, you would first group the information together to produce a frequency table.

Monthly salaries of marketing staff at Swizzles Limited: £1150, £690, £1270, £1450, £1350, £880, £750, £970, £1080, £1290, £1600, £1700, £680, £1090, £950, £1400, £550, £1180, £1250.

From this you can see that the there are three staff whose monthly salaries are in the £500–£700 category.

Frequency table

Monthly earnings (£)	Number of employees
500–700	3
701–900	2
901–1100	4
1101–1300	5
1301–1500	3
1501–1700	1
1701–1900	1

Having organized the information into the frequency table, it is much easier to plot it on a histogram. Histograms can show the distribution of information. In the example in Figure 6.6, there is a normal 'bell curve' distribution with a few people at the lower and higher ends of the scale and most people in the middle salary range.

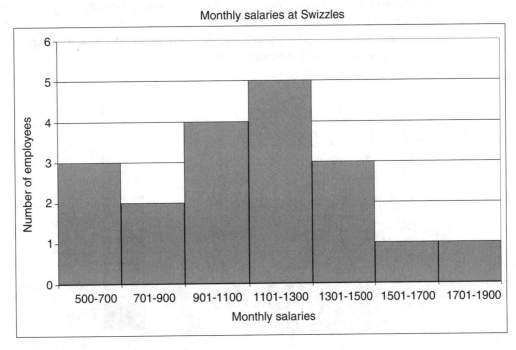

Figure 6.6 Monthly salaries at Swizzles

Pie charts

Pie charts are circular diagrams that are particularly useful for showing the composition of all the data, with the segments demonstrating the relative values of the data. They are used to show the relative size of different items making up a total, and are useful to show proportions of a whole. Ideally there should be no more than eight sections with the largest segment usually shown running clockwise from the top of the pie. Each segment should be labelled, sometimes including a value and a percentage share. The overall total is usually stated.

Guidelines for producing pie charts

1. Pie charts should be drawn accurately with a compass to represent the 360° of a circle and divided up into segments.
2. The component parts must represent 100 per cent.
3. To draw the segment sizes accurately, use a protractor by putting the base line across the middle of the circle and marking off degrees to represent percentages (which must be worked out, based on numerical values). For example, 180° represents 50 per cent, 90° represents 25 per cent and so on.
4. Keep the maximum number of segments to seven, otherwise the chart will look too congested and more difficult to interpret.
5. Place the most important (largest) segment at the 12 o'clock position and the others relative to it in some logical order.

6. Use shading to draw attention to salient features, usually largest and/or smallest segments.
7. Label all the segments and show their relative values either on the segments or beside the chart. A key will be necessary for this.

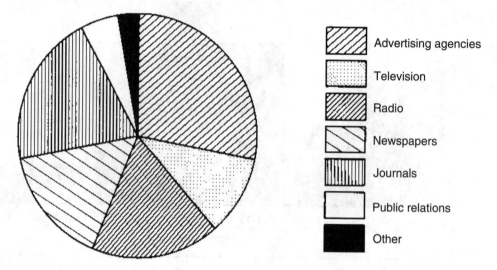

Figure 6.7 A pie chart

Line graphs

Line graphs are a series of points joined together to form a straight or curved line and are usually used to reflect a trend over a period of time or the interaction of two variables. In many cases, several lines will be used to show comparisons between the data.

Guidelines for producing line graphs
1. The horizontal axis should show the time period (years, months, hours, etc.).
2. The vertical axis should show the amount or value being measured.
3. Both scales should begin at 0 and increase in equal amounts, or indicate with a staggered line that the data does not begin at 0.
4. Both negative and positive values can be shown on line graphs.
5. Use different colours for more than one line on the same graph, to distinguish between them.
6. Use solid lines or broken lines to distinguish between different data or to draw attention to significant features of the data.
7. In order to avoid clutter and to make observation of the chart easier, a maximum of three lines on any graph should be used, especially if they are likely to cross over.

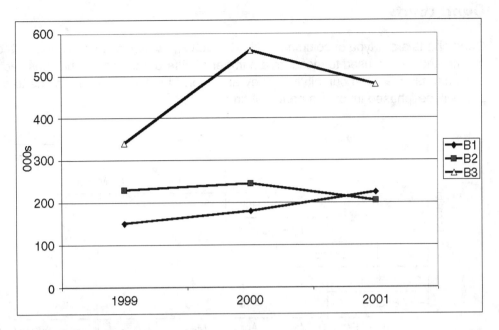

Figure 6.8 A simple line graph

 ## Activity 6.2

The costs of production at two different manufacturing sites during November 2004 were as follows:

	Shawcross site		Marlbrook site	
	£'000	%	£'000	%
Direct materials	70	35	50	20
Direct labour	30	15	125	50
Production overhead	90	45	50	20
Office costs	10	5	25	10
Total	200	100	250	100

The Finance director has asked you to compare the relative costs by site for the next sales and marketing meeting. Which graphical technique would aid the correct interpretation and understanding of the information?

Gantt charts

Gantt charts are a type of column/bar chart which show dimensions of a variable over a period of time and can be used to measure a number of different aspects of business activity in terms of actual, planned and cumulative. They are often found in marketing plans to show how the plan will be 'phased in' over a period of time.

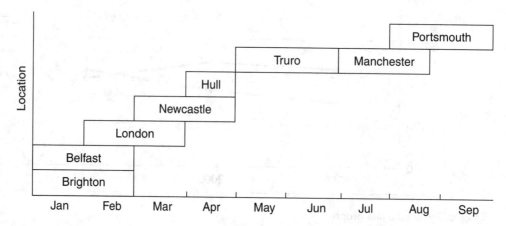

Figure 6.9 Gantt chart. Rolling national launch of Brand Q in different regional cities in the UK from January to September 2006

Pictograms

Pictograms are charts in which the data is represented by a line of symbols or pictures. They are usually used for presenting information in a novel format and are often used in the transmission of simple messages. They can give impact to data as it can be represented by a striking image or picture. For instance, numbers of employees or customers can be represented by matchstick people; aeroplane sales can be shown as drawings of aeroplanes.

An increase in quantity can be shown by more images (where the image is given a value) or the size of the image might increase to represent the quantity change. However, the problems with doing this are that quantities can be misrepresented because the scaling is unclear.

In addition, although pictograms can make a visual impact, certain audiences could perceive them as frivolous or patronizing.

Guidelines for producing pictograms

1. Use a symbol which will be clearly representative of the subject matter, eye-catching and appealing.
2. The number of pictures or symbols must reflect the values they represent.
3. Use a key to indicate the value of one picture or symbol.
4. Keep the size of the pictures and graph consistent with the overall presentation.

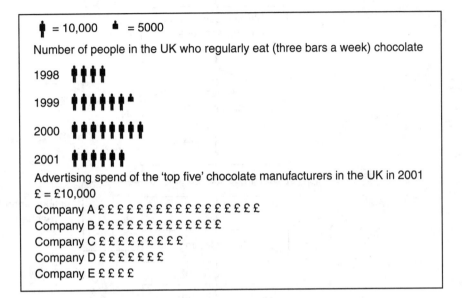

Figure 6.10 Examples of pictograms

Flow charts

Flow charts are useful for demonstrating conceptual relationships, processes, and procedures and business activities, where numerical values are not important. The relationships between various parts of the activity being demonstrated are shown in sequence from beginning to end and geometric shapes are used to distinguish between various aspects.

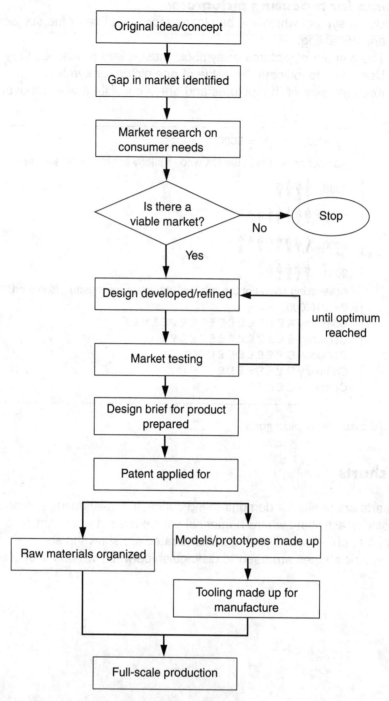

Figure 6.11 A flow chart for the stages involved in the introduction of a new product

Organization charts

Organization charts are frequently used in business organizations to show the hierarchical positions and relationships of employees, which also represent the main formal channels of communication.

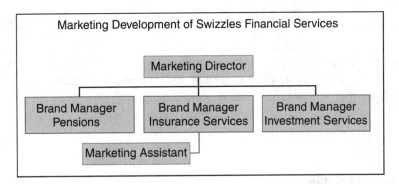

Figure 6.12 An organization chart for the Marketing Department of Swizzles Financial Services

Problems with distorting information

You should avoid using value-loaded expressions to alter how a statistic sounds as this could distort the information. For example, 47 per cent sounds different when described as 'nearly half the population', which sounds different again from 'barely half' or 'not even half those questioned'. Similarly, you should remember that if 'nearly one in ten of the population has a problem with x, y or z', it means that over 90 per cent of people don't have that problem.

Graphs and charts can be very effective communication media, but it is easy to confuse an audience or be confused yourself if the wrong medium is used to communicate data or if it is constructed incorrectly.

Be aware that you can distort the information you are presenting if the axis on graphs and charts does not start from zero. Trends in the top part of a chart will be more exaggerated if you see the whole picture with zero at the bottom left-hand corner.

Similarly, if you use a set of line charts but use a different scale on each of them, you could distort the information. For example, if you expanded or compressed the y axis (vertical axis) you could make a curve showing sales steeper or flatter which could affect the way that sales performance is perceived. Spreading out or compressing the distance between values on the x-axis (horizontal axis) could cause the same effect.

Computer packages offer you the facility of producing graphs and charts that have a three-dimensional appearance. However, sometimes the cosmetic benefits of blocking out areas of graphs and charts can be outweighed by the problems of readability. The problem is that it is difficult to see how the 3-D lines and bars line up against the relevant scale and so data values are difficult to determine.

Summary

In this unit you have studied:

o Why data is relevant to marketing
o How to interpret and summarize data
o Why visual data is an effective communication tool
o How to present a range of visual data, including charts, graphs and diagrams
o How to avoid distorting data.

Further study

If you require further exam practice then attempt Question 1(b) from the June 2005 examination paper and do Question 1(b) from the December 2004 paper in Appendix 4. Go to www.cim.co.uk to access Specimen Answers for these exam questions.

Hints and tips

Candidates studying for the examination should be aware that this unit is particularly relevant to the compulsory Part A question. Ensure that you can interpret written and/or visual data in order to undertake a number of tasks, such as, writing a report (see unit 'The communication process' for information about report writing) and producing graphs and charts. Ensure that you can analyse, interpret, summarize and present information in a concise and accurate manner.

Also extend your communications diary to include graphical information. Analyse what the raw data may have been and why this was decided to be the best format.

unit 7
the promotional mix – below the line

Learning objectives

In this unit you will:

- Extend your knowledge of the communications or promotional mix. See syllabus section 3.4.

- Examine the characteristics and use of below-the-line promotional tools. See syllabus section 3.6.

- Appreciate what influences promotional decisions. See syllabus section 3.1.

- Appreciate the benefits of a corporate identity. See syllabus section 3.9.

By the end of this unit you should be able to:

- Explain the concept of, and need for, an integrated marketing communications approach and the links between communications and marketing planning (3.1).

- Explain the role and importance of promotion in marketing (3.2).

- Describe the tools of promotion (the promotion mix) (3.4).

- Explain the planning process for developing and implementing promotional strategies and individual elements of the promotional mix (3.5).

- Explain how below-the-line activities are used (3.6).

- Describe the role and scope of PR and its contribution to the promotional mix (3.8).

- Explain the role of corporate identity, brand image and logos in corporate communication with customers (3.9).

- Distinguish between the different forms of integrated mail media, such as direct mail leaflets and mail order advertising (3.10).

- Explain the role of Point of Sale (POS) material and how it is developing in response to changing customer needs (3.11).

o   Explain the role of Packaging in the promotions mix (3.12).

o   Describe the role of exhibitors as a communications tool and their role in promotions (3.13).

This unit relates to statements of practice

o   Cb.1   Develop direct or indirect communications

o   Cb.2   Deliver direct or indirect communications

o   Gb.1   Support the management of customer relationships.

Study Guide

This unit along with Unit 8 provides you with a basic understanding of the marketing communications or promotional mix and covers parts of indicative content area 3.1–3.13 of the syllabus. Other elements of this syllabus section are covered in Unit 8.

It links with the Marketing Fundamentals syllabus indicative content area 1.2.9, which is covered in Unit 7 of the Marketing Fundamentals coursebook. With the Marketing Fundamentals syllabus you are looking at the promotional mix as one element of a total marketing mix; with Customer Communications this topic is the key to understanding how organizations communicate with their external customers.

The units have been split arbitrarily to echo how the promotional mix is viewed within the Communications industry.

Interaction of the organization with the communications industry as external suppliers to the organization will also be covered in Unit 8. Unit 7 will cover the more tactical short-term use of the promotional mix. Unit 8 will cover the more strategic use required for long-term brand building.

You not only need to know about the various communication tools but also need to be able to use them and combine them into integrated marketing communications.

In terms of the depth of knowledge you will need to demonstrate in this area of the syllabus, you need to be able to write a press release, suggest the layout for a press advertisement or write the copy for a mail shot. However, you would not be expected to be able to make a television or radio advertisement because these are very specialized activities that would be difficult to assess in a written examination.

Although Unit 9 focuses specifically on ICT, this unit will provide you with a brief insight into its role within the communications mix. You will look at how technology specifically affects your communication with customers, and especially how ICT can help in feeding back the customers response to the message being communicated as detailed in the Schramm model in Unit 3.

For further information on how this material in this unit will be examined, read the Exam Hints section at the end of this unit.

This unit will take you 3 hours to read through and a further 3 hours to work through the activities.

The communications or promotional mix

We have already looked at the various ways individuals inside an organization communicate either with colleagues or others outside their organizations. The concept of *Internal* marketing is mostly served by the methods of communication that we have considered in Units 5 and 6. The *communications or promotional mix* refers to those forms of communication that are used not on behalf of an individual but on behalf of the entire organization to promote either itself or its goods and services to *external stakeholders*. The emphasis here being related directly to the marketing mix and the role of promotion within that, to arrive at a message which *differentiates*, *informs*, *reminds and persuades* the end-user to purchase the product/service, through targeting sections of the promotional toolbox to deliver that message to them.

Refer to Figure 1.3 in Unit 1 for an example of the communications or promotional mix and Figure 1.1 for the target audiences that organizations may want to communicate with.

As stated in Unit 2, it is important to realize that external communications are not just targeted at the *end-user*. All the external messages, which emanate from an organization, carry other hidden messages encoded within them, as was demonstrated with the Persil Non-bio advertisement in Unit 3.

If we are supporting the launch of our new product range with an extensive advertising campaign, using television, press and posters, then we are also communicating how convinced we are that the new launch will be a success. This sends out positive messages not only to our suppliers, who may get to supply us with greater quantities of raw material through increased sales, but also to our distributors who can see how serious we are about building sales and hopefully increasing their profitability as well as our own. Consider the following message BP placed in all newspapers after the fuel crisis of 2000.

Britain's fuel crisis.
BP's promise to its customers.

This weekend, and for as long as it takes, our tanker fleets and delivery terminals will operate at maximum capacity to supply fuel to vital public services and to stock our retail sites

By Monday we aim to make petrol available to 70 per cent of our forecourts.

Our object is to distribute our products fairly and safely. While emergency vehicles will be given priority at all sites, we intend to serve fuels on a first-come, first-served basis, unless otherwise instructed by Government.

We thank our customers for their patience and assure them that our thousands of UK staff will work around the clock on their behalf.

We have not increased the price of our petrol during this crisis. The level of fuel taxes in the UK is a matter for Government and Parliament alone. But if any tax cuts were to be made, we would ensure our customers received the benefits.

That is our firm commitment. And that is what our relationship with you, the fuel-buying public, is about.

For latest information, call 0800-402402 or visit our website at www.bp.com

© 2000 Bp Amoco plc.

 Activity 7.1

Read the text of the newspaper advertisement above. How many stakeholders are being targeted and what is the message being transmitted to each group?

The communications or promotional mix can be categorized as *above-the-line* activity and *below-the-line* activity. These are slightly out-of-date definitions but do still exist and are still used within the communications industry.

Above-the-line methods, also referred to as *advertising*, have traditionally incorporated media such as television, press, radio and cinema and outdoor poster and transport advertising. Use of these methods usually resulted in commission being paid to the *advertising agency* that was responsible for booking the advertising space. The characteristics that these media have in common are that they can be utilized for mass-market communication usually targeted at the end-user or customer. These media are most often utilized (although not totally) to communicate between the *business to consumer market* or *B2C*. These media tend to concentrate on the *differentiate and persuade* messages and tend to rely on the availability of fairly sizable media budgets.

Below-the-line methods are those where commission was not paid, again a rather old-fashioned definition. However, these do tend to meet more specific promotional objectives. These methods can be seen in Figure 7.1 below and will be dealt with in detail in this unit. You will learn that each category splits down into further media tools, which will also be covered. Within B2C markets these can be used alongside above-the-line media within a combined campaign to communicate an integrated message to their target audience. These are often used to convey the *inform* and *remind* messages.

These are also quite widely used in the *Business to Business market* where the promotional message is to a much smaller and easily targeted group.

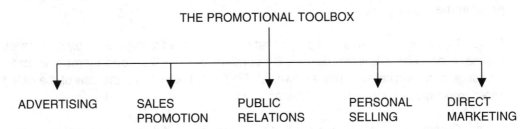

Figure 7.1 The promotional toolbox

As stated above, each of these categories includes specific media tools, the use of which will be examined in detail within the relevant unit, and are jointly referred to as the promotional or communications toolbox. As with any toolbox the promotional 'problem' will require the use of more than one tool or medium. It is necessary to consider the characteristics of each in turn to be able to decide which tools should be used in which combination to best construct the 'Promotional solution'.

Why communicate externally?

In Unit 1 we examined the wider definition of the term customer and the difference between customers and end-users. In Unit 3 we investigated the communication process and theory, which included the *encoding* and *decoding* of messages. In this unit we need to consider how, once the promotional message has been successfully *encoded*, we then send that message to ensure it reaches the right group of people at the right time in relation to the buying decision process.

The customer decision is ever more complicated with numerous different product and service combinations designed to meet their needs. The customer has more power and is determined to exercise that power whenever they can by getting what they want, when they want it and at a price they wish to pay. This will be developed further in Unit 10. It is often the job of the promotional element of the marketing mix to be the differentiating factor between products and services in a crowded or saturated market. In Unit 1 we looked at the DRIP factors and how they can be used to develop the promotional message.

We need to choose a promotional mix that will also:

   o *Differentiate* – by the intelligent use of media to build awareness in a more precisely targeted manner.
   o *Remind* – by prompting customers at the point of purchase and reminding them why.
   o *Inform* – by establishing two-way communication to help remove those lingering barriers to purchase.
   o *Persuade* – through reassurance of the quality aspects that the brand/service conveys.

For example, if our only promotional effort is a hastily produced A5 flyer, pushed through our door at 6.30 a.m. on a Saturday, with a phone number that never seems to be answered or has only an answer-phone, then we can hardly forgive our prospective customers if they don't believe we produce a high quality product/service.

Our use of media reflects on us as an organization, and as customers get more used to travelling globally and receiving ever-more sophisticated messages we have to ensure that what we say and the way we say it is the result of a carefully integrated communications programme.

Fill (2002) informs us that a campaign that is co-ordinated is planned, communicates the same message and has a uniform design. By combining more than one element of promotion, the message communicated is more powerful. Fill (2002) advocates the use of the 4Cs framework when making the media choice. This advises:

   o *Communication* – How effectively can the media deliver a personal message, how able is it in reaching a large audience and in prompting the message receiver into action?
   o *Credibility* – How believable is the medium?
   o *Cost* – In absolute terms how much will it cost to contact each individual? What is the total investment required and how much of the investment could be wasted?
   o *Control* – How much control do we have over the message transmitted? How easy is it to adjust that message if research finds that to be necessary?

Within the Professional certificate syllabus, the start point of the marketing communications process is to determine our promotional objectives.

The promotional objectives

With any intended course of action it is necessary that we first carefully construct the objectives, which will drive the process forward and provide a basis of measurement for evaluation at the end of that process. Before constructing the promotional objectives we need to have an appreciation of where those objectives 'sit' within the overall context of the marketing planning process. To do this we will re-visit some of the concepts that arise within the Marketing Fundamentals module.

Within the marketing plan we will develop our marketing objectives that could be:

- Gain 10 per cent market share in the xyz market through increased sales of existing product in the next 12 months

or

- Introduce three new products to market within the next 12 months to increase company share of market to 40 per cent.

Marketing strategies using tools such as Ansoff's Growth Matrix and the concept of Segmentation targeting and Positioning will help us to develop ways of achieving those objectives by developing appropriate strategies.

We will then need to develop or adjust the marketing mix for each of those products/services in order to facilitate the chosen strategy. As part of the marketing mix, promotion will have its own objectives designed to help the organization achieve its overall marketing objectives.

Taking the above *marketing* objectives as an example, the following *promotional* objectives could be developed to support the achievement of those marketing objectives:

- Change consumer attitudes towards current products in the *xyz* market to generate a greater positive customer perception of the company's existing product portfolio, in the next 12 months.
- Gain awareness of between 40 and 50 per cent in the minds of selected target customer groups to support the launch of three new products to market over the next 12 months.

Therefore, we must remember that promotional objectives are concerned purely with communications and issues not market share or product development.

To arrive at a realistic set of promotional objectives we have to consider the following issues:

- What is the purpose of your communication? Are you building awareness of a new product or reminding of an existing one?
- Who is your primary target audience? How big is that audience? What are their media habits?
- Are there any secondary/tertiary target audiences? How important are they? What are their media habits?
- Can all media convey the message? Does it need to be transmitted visually, audibly or by the written word?
- When do you need to communicate your message? Is it a seasonal purchase? Are there legal restrictions?
- What is the budget? How does this affect your media choice?
- How complex is the product or service choice? What is the level of detailed information required?

When constructing your promotional objectives we must also remember the SMART mnemonic to ensure that the objectives are Specific, Measurable, Achievable, Realistic and Timed.

Here is a selection of beginnings for promotional objectives:

- To create an image
- To create awareness
- To inform about a new feature
- To change attitudes
- To correct misconceptions
- To reassure
- To remind
- To generate interest
- To generate response
- To encourage trial
- To prompt purchase
- To support other promotional activity.

 Activity 7.2

Refer to some of the examples within your communications diary and consider what the likely objectives are. Write out the objectives and then try to build them into a SMART objective. Make sure that all your objectives relate to communications and not other areas of the marketing mix.

Case history

Ford targeting women

As the car market battles to boost sales to the mid-1990s levels, Ford is having to get more creative. And we are not just talking about flashier TV ads. Its whole approach to marketing is shifting as Ford makes a big effort to romance one of the most influential, affluent and growing market sectors – women with spending power – by building promotions revolving around the shopping centre rather than the dealership forecourt.

Like most clichés, there's a great deal of truth in ones about women and car showrooms. 'I've lost count of the number of times I've heard a woman say that she'd rather go the dentist than into a dealership,' says Patricia Hogan, partner at JD Power & Associates that conducts consumer research in the automotive sector. 'They feel intimidated, confused and almost as if they are under attack when they walk in.'

Yet women are the very audience the carmakers cannot afford to alienate. According to JD Power, women make up 40 per cent of all light vehicle principal drivers and have influence in well over 50 per cent of purchases. In fact Ford estimates that women could make up to 80 per cent of car buying decisions.

From November, Ford is looking to locate more of its cars in a female friendly environment – the Bluewater shopping centre in Kent. 'Thirty-something single women do not spend their weekends at dealership forecourts, but they will spend their time at places like Bluewater' says Peter Fleet, Marketing Director at Ford of Britain, who is leading the scheme. 'It's about putting the brand in front of people in a different way.'

Earlier this year, Ford ran a number of pilot projects at busy locations and the shopping centre emerged as the best place to find new customers. According to Fleet, 915 of the people Ford spoke to at shopping centres were new prospects, with the percentage of those who went on to buy a Ford being 14 points higher than the average. Most strikingly the sales conversion rate was 50 per cent higher for women than men. Encouraged by this, the company is now spending £500 000 to run 6 months of promotional events at Bluewater, featuring a range of its cars.

Another project involved joining the Nectar loyalty card scheme. It has also made more efforts to advertise in women's magazines over the past 18 months.

Liz Kershaw, executive group publishing director at National Magazines, says that in the past 10 years, car makers have become better at taking the female market into account, but the volume of female-targeted advertising is still woefully small compared to the spending power women represent. 'They're getting switched on,' says Kershaw. But considering that women make up 50 per cent of the population it's surprising they aren't doing more.

Extract taken from the *Financial Times*, 30th September 2003.

Below-the-line media

When combining the promotional tools together to produce a customized communications package to meet the needs of our own organization it is important to consider how each of the tools we use will complement and support each other. Some methods slot more naturally into the role of primary media, enabling mass communication and building awareness on a large scale. These tend to be *above-the-line* media and will be covered in Unit 8. *Below-the-line* media usually perform a supporting role or fulfil the role of *secondary* media. The promotional toolbox contains the following below-the-line tools:

o Public relations
o Sales promotion
o Direct marketing
o Personal selling.

We will now consider each of the media within these sections of the toolbox in turn. You will need to know some of these and should be able to apply them in context, while some you may be required to actually do so only in an exam situation, for example write a press release. More detail will be given in these specific areas.

Public relations

The Institute of Public Relations has defined public relations as 'the planned and sustained effort to establish and maintain goodwill and mutual understanding between an organization and its publics'.

Public Relations are essentially concerned with developing a corporate personality that communicates the general philosophies of that organization to its publics (as detailed in Figure 1.2). The PR activities therefore fall into three main categories:

1. Development of the corporate image – the face of the company.
2. Communication of that image and all that falls within it.
3. Specific related activities where the image is used.

The spectrum of Public Relations is increasing all the time in an era where there is little discernable difference between products and services. It is often the customer's perception of the *Corporate personality* which PR seeks to create that offers the differentiation point.

In relation to the 4Cs mentioned earlier in this unit, Public Relations can convey greater *credibility* than an advertising message as it is perceived to have originated from a more independent source. The credibility of the newspaper that is reporting on the organization will be considered rather than the organization itself.

Cost is relatively low in comparison to advertising. The cost of a press conference is relatively of good value when you consider the amount of press reporting and TV coverage you can achieve with a good PR message.

Communication to the correct target audience is reliant on the PR agency ensuring all the relevant press attend the conference, or that the vehicle to be sponsored is one that has links to the target audience.

Control can be an issue. Although you can make sure the press have all the information to pass on a positive perception to the stakeholders, if a particular journalist is looking for a more sensational story that day, then he/she can re-position the information to give a negative slant.

Public relations cover the following activities:

o   Corporate image and corporate social responsibility
o   Exhibitions, conferences and special events
o   Press conferences
o   Press releases
o   Sponsorship.

Development of the corporate image

The visual manifestation of the corporate image has many facets, but each must support the other to support the overall 'personality' of the organization. Therefore, the logo, branding strategies used, organizational culture and corporate activities all play their part in creating the corporate image or personality.

Activity 7.3

The airline industry has changed significantly in the last 10 years with many new entrants into the market delivering a 'No Frills' service, decreasing the cost of flying and the increasing amount of flights we buy up.

Consider the different 'Corporate Personalities' of three competitors in this field: British Airways, Virgin Atlantic and easyJet.

Do these different personalities stop at the boardroom or manifest themselves in the type of service offered?

The corporate image becomes the 'synonym for reputation which can be the single most significant point of differentiation between competing companies' (Dolphin, 2000). Our image portrays to our stakeholders who we want to be. Many organizations actually have straplines to convince us of this, for example 'Cadbury. The first name in Chocolate', and every communication which emanates from the organization supports this claim.

Dolphin also made the point that corporate image is concerned with a mental impression. If the public think well of an organization they are more likely to do business with it and a well-regarded organization can build upon success to be stronger and one step ahead of the competition.

The development of the image has to start with the visual identity or *logo*. The development of a logo is essentially the corporate badge and it can be used to create instant recognition for that organization and its products/services. This differentiates those products from others in the same field and conveys a consistent imagery across the products/services it markets. See Figure 7.2 where the CIM logo can be used by accredited colleges to enhance their credibility in the minds of marketing students. The traditional design of the logo lends support to the 'Chartered' status; use of entirely different graphics could have just as easily detracted from it.

Figure 7.2 The CIM logo

Figure 7.3 Adapting a logo for different purposes

151

The *logo* is then used as the basis of the organization's *corporate literature* which, when used to communicate with the stakeholders of that organization, reinforces the corporate image in the minds of those connected with the organization. The *logo* will appear on all literature such as letter heads, business cards, brochures and annual reports to again convey that consistent message about the organization. The colours and symbols used within the logo can then be used in uniforms, buildings, headquarters, vehicles, newsletters and everything that bears the company name to overlay the image.

In developing the logo every small part must be considered in how it can support or change the perception of the corporate image. Size, colour, typeface, graphics and straplines all combine to create the image, which encapsulates and communicates the corporate image.

Insight

Royal Mail

Royal Mail is one of the most trusted brands in the UK. It is a valuable asset that has evolved and grown since its inception in 1635 when the service of accepting and handling of mail by the Royal posts was opened up to the general public by Charles I.

However, the market in which Royal Mail operates has become more competitive. Parcel delivery is a competitive environment especially with the increase of online and mail-order purchasing. Operators such as UPS and DHL have managed to perform well in this market against a rather jaded Royal Mail image and a degree of negative customer perception.

The increasingly likely prospect that soon Royal Mail will need to compete on a letter delivery platform and the increased usage of e-mail were two very significant threats to the organization. In the year 2000, the newly appointed Chief Executive and the incumbent Board decided to rename the Royal Mail, changing it to Consignia, and a multi-million pound advertising campaign was developed to re-brand and re-position the organization in the minds of the consumer.

However, by the Chief executive's own admission, 'Consignia' was a made-up word and it had no meaning. Hence, it was unable to develop a set of brand values to support the corporate image.

After 18 months of declining sales resulting in the organization losing a million pounds per day, it was decided to go back to the 'Royal Mail' brand that still represented the brand values of its 350-year-old existence and to replace the Chief Executive.

New Chairman Allan Leighton (ex Asda) and his team led the development of a relaunch campaign that highlighted the scale of the brand's capability and demonstrated its unrivalled reach of households within the UK.

Royal Mail is predicted to have turned the previous losses into a £500 million profit for the year 2004.

Communicating the corporate image and Corporate Social Responsibility

Once the visual depicting the image has been developed, we must consider how to communicate that image to give greater weight and credibility to the organization's chosen personality. Within the stakeholder groups, corporate communications tend to diversify the communication channel slightly to appeal more to the recipient needs. Therefore:

o   Business-related stakeholders such as suppliers and distributors in the city receive gifts such as calendars, key rings, desk items and umbrellas carrying the logo. Business dinners or sponsored charity events will be ideal opportunities to further develop the caring side of the personality.

o   Community-related stakeholders such as employees, the local government and so on can be targeted similarly by sponsorship of local events and teams. Scholarship and bursaries for employee's families can be awarded.

o   Customer-related stakeholders – the way that the organization deals with customer complaints is another form of communicating the image. The no-quibble guarantee and well-trained front-line staff communicate the message that the organization cares.

o   Corporate Social Responsibility (CSR) is a significant contemporary marketing issue. Alliances with ethical and environmental issues or charities can develop the caring side of the corporate image. For example, The Body Shop support Fair Trade Organizations who source ingredients from around the world, making sure that they are harvested by labourers who get fair wages and good living conditions. There are many relevant articles within the press praising and berating organizations upon their CSR stance and it would be a good idea to include some of these within your Communications diary to use as examples where necessary. CSR activities should be relevant to the business. A company that invests in schemes that have no connection smacks of opportunism and jumping on the CSR bandwagon. Consumers are becoming wise to this and 'see through' the hype. The CSR choice then becomes a negative message rather than a positive one. Relevant opportunities such as toy companies sending unsold stock to child care homes indicates commitment and behaviour in relation to a moral code.

British Petroleum – bp

Take a look at the advertisement on page 156 that was placed by bp in a variety of newspapers around January 2006. Its Corporate Social Responsibility stance is being communicated in a number of ways within this one advertisement.

The actions taken in relation to their corporate values are described; in this case, educating children in relation to energy issues.

The logo utilizes the environmentally friendly colours of green and yellow – evocative of fresh green grass and sunshine.

The added strapline 'Beyond Petroleum' signifies that the values of the organization extend beyond sales at the petrol forecourt.

Also included is the website address where further information can be found on what BP is doing to ensure they behave in an ethical and responsible manner.

When it comes to green matters we develop grey matter.

Our investment in environmental and science education has helped inspire British school children for 37 years. In the past 12 months, teachers in over 2,400 UK schools have chosen to use our resource packs, which help teach children about energy issues.

bp

beyond petroleum®

© 2006 BP p.l.c.

bp.com

Figure 7.4 Use BP – Beyond Petroleum

Insight

Centrica – British Gas 'Here to Help' campaign

The British Gas 'Here to Help' campaign was set up in 2002 in response to the Government's increasingly stringent targets in terms of energy, efficiency, which all energy suppliers must meet. The campaign's objectives are not just concerned with environmental issues but also the issue of 'fuel poverty' in the 4 million homes, within the UK, living below the poverty line. By investing £150 million over 3 years and working in alliance with the public and voluntary sectors, it has already made substantial inroads into improving the living conditions in those deprived areas, by enabling them to keep warm and save money on energy-related areas.

'Help' was targeted to finance a team of well-trained people to visit houses in deprived areas to carrying out assessments to see what energy efficient measures could be implemented. Checking that people were also receiving the benefits to which they were entitled, by finding out if they knew how to claim was an important part of the campaign.

Charitable help was also targeted to those in most need. The results speak for themselves:

- o The programme has covered 330 000 homes and 650 communities.
- o Assessments have been completed in 100 000 homes.
- o Around £5.5 million of previously unclaimed benefit, equivalent to £1400 per person has been uncovered.

The programme is on target to deliver 40 per cent of the government set fuel poverty energy-saving target for the period 2002–2005.

Extract from 'How to help' – Laura Mazur, *The Marketer* – January 2005.

Corporate people

Sometimes, an organization can choose to develop their personality by using certain industry specialists or celebrities as their 'face'. This can take the form of recruiting a personality into a position of power to send out messages to the buying public which are related to that person's past performance in other areas. George Davies was recruited to develop the 'Per Una' range for an ailing Marks & Spencer, based on his previous success as one of the key people who established Next and his success with Asda range of 'George' clothing. It remains to be seen if his recent departure will affect the success that the Per Una range has achieved.

Richard Branson and Stelios Haji-Iaannou are the public face of their organizations, and their personal values, attitudes and beliefs are echoed in the way their organizations operate.

Kate Moss – Role Model or Not?

Last year's press reports linking Kate Moss to alleged cocaine use led to a number of the organizations with which she was linked, ending their association with her as their public 'face'.

These included Burberry, who, in the wake of the photographs and other lurid tales that came to light, announced that they were to cancel a planned advertising campaign featuring Moss. Their press statement said: 'At the current time we had one project scheduled this Autumn with Kate and in the circumstances, both Kate and Burberry have mutually agreed it is inappropriate to go ahead.'

Chanel will not be renewing their contract with Kate Moss when it ends. In a statement a spokeswoman denied that the model was sacked, saying:

'Kate Moss had a contract until the end of October. We don't have any further projects with her.'

Retailer H&M were one of the first organizations to review their contract, issuing a statement saying that Moss's actions were 'inconsistent with the company's anti-drugs policy.'

Several other companies have chosen to remain aligned with Kate, including Rimmel, who target the younger female sector. It remains to be seen how public opinion will swing and who will have been judged to have made the right decision.

Excerpts taken from *The Independent*, 22 September 2006.

 ## Activity 7.4

Asda have used Sharon Osborne as 'the face of Asda'. Asda identified Sharon as being representative of someone its shoppers believe to stand for 'caring, providing and coping.'

The campaign featuring 'Mums in a Million' to show Sharon testing out an Asda store and talking to staff and customers. It features a new strapline 'Pocketing the difference' which replaced 'Always low prices'.

Consider the advantages and disadvantages of using a celebrity as the 'face' of your organization.

PR activities

Once the corporate image is fully developed in terms of the visual and personality we can then start to utilize selected activities to convey our organizational message to targeted groups. The most commonly used are described below.

Exhibitions, conferences and special events

In many business-to-business marketing situations, organizations have a sales force that visits the customer. With exhibitions, road shows, seminars and conferences, customers come to see the supplier. This provides organizations with a valuable opportunity to communicate with their customers and potential customers in a face-to-face situation; hopefully generating sales leads to follow up at a later date.

Exhibitions, trade fairs and mobile road shows are all used to combine an element of personal selling with a chance to display one's wares within an industry arena. Visitors to these are usually in the same industry and will be attending to see the range of products and services on offer that they can then incorporate into their own business to enhance the end-user experience, for example the Spring Fair held in February every year at the National Exhibition Centre (NEC) in Birmingham is visited by many small gift shop owners to stock up for the summer tourist trade. Some exhibitions are also aimed at the general public such as the National homes exhibition. The Food and Drink Exhibition held during November at the National Exhibition Centre in Birmingham is fast gaining a reputation amongst 'conspicuous consumers' as a place to go to discover the new innovations in this area and is generally considered to be a good day out.

Exhibitions and trade fairs are generally held in large exhibition halls where firms book a stand area and either hire a stand or pay for one to be designed. The stand and the corporate literature have to be presented in an eye-catching way to attract visitors to the stand.

Companies also have to cover the cost of staffing stands, pay for staff travel and accommodation costs and hospitality costs incurred, when sales staff network with prospects and customers.

The costs of attending exhibitions rose substantially in the early nineties and organizations began to reconsider if attending even the most prestigious exhibitions, such as the Motor Show, was actually worthwhile. Some found alternative methods of more closely targeting the suppliers and distributors and have not returned to exhibit. Mobile road shows are often used when there is a benefit if the customer can trial a product. Alcohol manufacturers often use this method to target young pub-goers.

Conferences and seminars are a place to be seen, to network with other people within the industry. These provide an opportunity for a 'softer sell' than exhibitions and the emphasis is on information gathering and sharing. Organizations gain certain kudos by sponsoring a conference or having one of their employees booked to speak at an industry conference.

For example, many of the larger accountancy firms provide breakfast budget briefings to discuss the implications of a new budget or taxation laws. Similarly, pharmaceutical firms arrange seminars for doctors to discuss new drugs that are available on the market.

Another additional cost to participating in these events is the need to undertake pre-exhibition publicity to attract people to your part of the exhibition or conference.

Special events or corporate entertaining can also offer PR opportunities. Having a corporate box at a race meeting or a premier league football club are all activities that can aid the wheels of business to run more smoothly in the B2B world.

A recent development in this area is to create clubs of loyal users to develop PR-based messages to sustain and stretch the product/service. Marmite have recently announced the launch of an online fan club. Two separate websites have been developed for both lovers and haters of the brand. By their own admission it's unlikely to change either side's opinion but it does keep them talking about it!

All of these issues allow two-way communication between the supplier and customer. Interaction on a social, as well as business, level can help mutually beneficial relationships to develop. The ability to demonstrate a product can also lead to consumer objections being minimized.

Insight

Renault – open days

Renault dealers have hosted special 'open days' to accompany the re-launches of some of their new models. Existing and lapsed Renault customers were invited to test-drive the restyled Megane Scenic at locations of general family interest, such as Ragley Hall in Worcester.

The environment was perfect for the whole family to test-drive the car within the grounds on a simulated family trip out. Once the test-drive was over, the house and grounds, which featured family-friendly facilities, such as a maze and woodland assault course, were open to the attendees.

Press conferences

In marketing, *press conferences* are usually used only for very high-profile product launches and will involve the organization presenting the business rationale behind the launch and details of the communications package supporting it.

The industry press, national press and marketing press will be invited so that the message will be disseminated to all the relevant stakeholders. *Publicity stunts* often accompany press conferences to make them more newsworthy and hopefully gain national or even international news coverage. When Pepsi decided to change the can (in line with the corporate image) to be mainly blue in colour they arranged for a Concorde to be painted blue and 'fly past'. Such displays are now considered to be somewhat wasteful in these days of ensuring all resources – environmental and financial – should not be used in such a flippant way.

Press conferences or press releases can also be used in terms of *Crisis management*. According to Fill (2002), crises are occurring more often. Fill cites a number of reasons for this: first, the rise of consumer groups such as Greenpeace has increased the publicity of organizations' less favourable activities. Second, the age of instant communications also results in any potential crisis having been aired to the general public before an organization has had a chance to make a planned response. Another reason is that the rate of technological advances, especially in transportation, can lead to disasters both linked not only to the speed and mode of travel but also due to human error. All of these issues need to be handled carefully if long-term damage to the organization's reputation is to be minimized.

Insight

Marmite pulls TV and poster campaign – December 2005

Marmite had planned a post-Christmas TV and Poster campaign featuring a much publicized new creative treatment. The cult 1950s horror film 'The Blob' was the inspiration for the campaign, which featured screaming people running away from a giant glutinous blob of Marmite – supported by the well-known strapline 'You either love it or you hate it'.

The campaign was pulled before its 27th December start date as it was felt to be in poor taste in light of the Tsunami tragedy.

www.brandrepublic.com.

More commonly, *press releases* are used to convey the same information on a smaller scale. You may be required to write a press release within your marketing role or in an exam. We shall examine this promotional tool in greater depth.

 ## Activity 7.5

Before you start reading the section on how to prepare a press release, read the following abstract taken from a press release that was sent to a local newspaper in a farming region in England. Ignore the format but explain why the content is not suitable and suggest how it could be improved.

PRESS RELEASE FROM XYZ FARMING LTD

Dear Editor,

We believe that we can offer your readers an interesting news story and will be happy to provide fuller details if required. A new concept in dairy cow feeding has been pioneered by XYZ Farming Ltd, which is specifically designed to meet the demand of consumers for milk of higher protein content and reduced fat levels. These requirements are reflected in differential prices paid by most dairies to farmers with greater emphasis on protein content rather than butterfat: high butterfats also act as an effective constraint to the full use by the farmer of his quota allocation. In the new Granary range of compound feeds the high levels of rumen bypass starch, derived from rolled wheat, is pelleted in combination with high vegetable proteins.

Preparing a Press Release

Most organizations have a PR policy, which means that press releases go through a rigorous checking and signing-off procedure whether they are produced in-house or by an agency. It is a specialized job, and one that you will not be involved with unless it is specified as part of your job role.

Nevertheless, you should be able to produce a draft release to show that you understand how they should be written and presented, as it could become a task that is part of your job.

You should be aware that while organizations can pay to obtain advertising space, obtaining editorial space through press releases is subject to the editorial team finding the press release interesting and usable. Even if this is the case, the space that can be given to your press release will probably be limited and they will usually change it so that the angle suits their news purposes.

It is wrong to consider that press releases are 'free' advertising, as the time and effort put into writing a good press release has a cost associated with it.

The format of a press release
A press release format should:

- Feature your organization's logo at the top.
- Be entitled 'Press Release'.
- Show the date the release was prepared or indicate when the news can be released (an embargo).
- Have a headline that sums up the story.
- Be typed with double spacing and have wide margins.
- Only use one side of the paper.
- Indicate that more 'copy' or text follows by using the abbreviation m/f at the end of each page.
- Clearly mark the end of the release with the word 'end'.
- Contain contact details for the media to make further enquiries.
- Contain additional notes in the form of 'background notes for the editor'.

The press release content should:

- Answer the questions who, what, when, where and how.
- Encapsulate the nub of the story in the first paragraph.
- Start with the key point at the top and add the 'bones' of the story in each succeeding paragraph.
- Contain interesting quotes that are attributed to a person relevant to the story. Be geared to the media, so you may have one version for the trade press and another for the local press.
- Use factual, not flowery, language.
- Be clear and concise.
- Relate to any accompanying photographs.
- Have a 'pic caption', that is a few sentences that explain the contents or name the people in a photograph.
- Usually be written as if the event has just happened (even if the presentation or the contract was won a few days ago), although some press releases detail what will happen in the future.

Sponsorship

Sponsorship is another communications tool that can be used to put an organization's name across to a variety of the public and promote an image. Organizations can sponsor the arts, sporting events, individual sportsmen and women or even television programmes.

The section that sponsorship occupies in the promotional toolbox is still a subject for discussion. Sponsorship as described above clearly sits alongside PR, but more commercially based programme sponsorship that has audience coverage as its primary objective could be viewed as a form of advertising. We shall therefore be looking at sponsorship in both categories and the way it is utilized within that category.

Organizations are usually interested in the type of sponsorship that either attracts publicity and media coverage or puts their name in front of their target audience in an interesting, and maybe novel, way. For sponsorship to work, it should be in keeping with the organization's, or its brand's, image.

Sponsoring individuals can be risky if they attract bad publicity and are involved in some form of scandal. This could result in the organization's name being tainted by association. However, most organizations would withdraw sponsorship in the case of a scandal.

Kit Kat Crescent Football Stadium

York City's Bootham crescent ground is to be re-named Kit Kat Crescent as part of a £100 000 rescue package from Nestlé Rowntree, whose UK confectionery headquarters are in York.

The sponsorship deal announced yesterday will secure the future of the ground, York's home for the past 73 years, although now to be named after a chocolate-covered wafer biscuit.

The company will provide the £10 000 needed for the Conference club relegated from the league last season, to complete the buy-back of their ground, sold as they almost went out of existence in financial woe 3 years ago.

'Kit Kat Crescent was the obvious choice of name,' York's Managing Director told the city's *Evening Press* newspaper.

'The product is made in York and, like our home kit, is red and white,' he added. The deal gives the company naming rights for 2005 and 2006.

Extract from *The Guardian* – 20th January 2005.

Advantages of PR as a communication tool	Disadvantages of PR as a communication tool
Communicates and builds the corporate personality enabling relationships with key stakeholders to be developed	Difficult to control the message that the target media subsequently publish
Supports the other elements of the promotional mix by building all-round awareness of the organization and its products/services	No guarantee of gaining any coverage so opportunities can be restricted. This is especially true if your PR event happens on a very newsworthy day
Credibility increases dependence on the source of the message	Communication has a short life
Fairly low cost – just the cost of preparing materials and supporting the sponsored cause	Difficult to measure the effectiveness of PR activity other than column inches or TV seconds generated
Can become more newsworthy if linked events or celebrities enjoy other successes	Can become newsworthy for the wrong reasons (e.g. celebrity gets arrested on drugs charge)

Sales promotion

Sales promotion is another communications tool that marketers use. It is often described as 'A short-term tactical marketing tool that gives customers additional reasons or incentives to purchase.'

The incentive will be linked directly to the promotional objective. With an entirely new product the promotional objective will be to build awareness and the sales promotion objective will be to induce trial of the new product to turn *trialists* into *end-users*. With products in the maturity stage of the Product Life Cycle (PLC) the promotional objective will be to remind people of the product benefits, the sales promotion objectives will be to get them to buy more (3 for 2) and render them less able to switch brands.

Sales promotions can be used as a dual-purpose tool by targeting two different customer groups. Consumer promotions to encourage consumers to go and buy, these are referred to as *pull* strategies because the customer by demanding the product is *pulling* it through the distribution chain. Trade promotions targeting the intermediaries in the distribution chain are used to encourage the intermediaries (often wholesalers or retailers) to stock or recommend the product. This is known as a *push* strategy as the organization seeks to *push* the product through the chain towards the end-user. By using a combination of *push* and *pull* it should be possible to have the product in store at the precise moment the customer demands it.

So the objectives of a sales promotion can be expressed in any (or all) of the following ways:

- Encourage trial of product – to overcome any negative perceptions, encourage brand switching.
- Extend existing customer base – by reducing the cost of brand switching.
- Prompt customers to change brand.
- Generate bulk buying – your consumers will not brand switch if they have residual stock of your product.
- Overcome seasonal dips in sales – which may result in peaks and troughs smoothing out in time.
- Encourage trade to stock product – as they know customers are to be incentivized.

Consumer sales promotions usually offer temporary added value to the customer at the point of purchase. There are many different versions of sales promotions that are directed at consumers:

- Price reductions
- Coupons/money-off vouchers
- Entry to competitions/free prize draws
- Free goods
- *x* per cent free
- 3 for the price of 2 (or Buy one get one free – BOGOF)
- Free samples or gifts
- Guarantees or extended warranties
- £*x* goes to y charity if you purchase
- Reward points/tokens against a free gift (e.g. Air Miles)
- Refunds or free gifts on a mail-in basis.

Sales promotions aimed at the trade include:

o   Discount on bulk orders
o   Free supplies
o   Incentives (e.g. shopping vouchers for Marks & Spencer or a free alarm clock)
o   Free prize draw competitions
o   Deferred invoicing
o   Merchandising and display material.

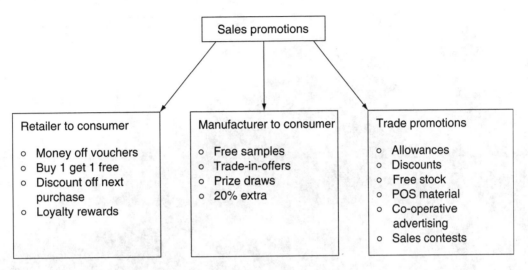

Figure 7.5 Range of sales promotional techniques

When developing a sales promotion it is beneficial to build in a response mechanism where possible. By asking a customer to put their name and address details on a money-off coupon, you can then add them to your customer database and target them with future offers in a more specific way. Often, product guarantees have a section where customers fill in 10–12 questions about their lifestyle and the other types of product/services they are interested in.

By placing a media code on each communication concerning the sales promotion you can then measure which media produces the highest number of responses. Look at many coupons and advertisements in the press to see how these media codes are used.

See the example used by McDonald's below to promote their healthy eating alternatives as they seek to re-position themselves following the bad press as a result of the film 'Supersize Me' where a journalist ate only McDonald's products for three months and then publicized the effects on his health.

Figure 7.6 McDonald's – the healthy options

In terms of the 4Cs *Cost* can be relatively easily controlled. Giving consumers additional products is probably the cheapest form of reward and ties them into the product for longer. Rewards or loyalty schemes often represent a fraction of the cost they are perceived to have. Sales promotion can often utilize the product's packaging or be in the form of a direct marketing method, which is relatively cheap.

Credibility is dependent upon the perceived value of the input in relation to the benefits given. Cadbury were subject to bad press by linking a sales promotion where consumers were encouraged to collect chocolate bar wrappers to receive free sports equipment. Apart from the strange concept of eating more chocolate to obtain free sports equipment, the logistics of the campaign meant that a football worth approximately £5 required an individual to munch through an incredible amount of chocolate bars. The negative PR resulting from this promotion outweighed any benefits.

The links between the visits to National Trust sites and an enjoyable picnic has been evoked by the free gift offer of a free coolbag – seen in the insert below which was distributed in Sunday supplements. The other promotional device – an additional three months membership free if the subscription is paid by Direct Debit – is a small price to pay if you consider how likely the consumer is to forget to cancel the direct debit at the end of 15 months.

THREE MONTHS' MEMBERSHIP FREE – when you pay by Direct Debit

YES I wish to pay for my membership by Direct Debit – please enrol me for twelve months for the price of nine.

THE NATIONAL TRUST

Instruction to your Bank or Building Society to pay by Direct Debit

DIRECT Debit

10109

Please fill in the form and send to: The National Trust Membership Dept, FREEPOST NAT9775, Warrington WA5 7BR

Name and full address of your Bank or Building Society

To: The Manager Bank/Building Society

Address:

Postcode:

Name(s) of Account Holder(s)

Branch Sort Code

Bank/Building Society account number*

Originator's Identification Number

4 1 0 0 4 5

Reference no. (for office use only)

INS001

Instruction to your Bank or Building Society

Please pay the National Trust Direct Debits from the account detailed in this instruction, subject to the safeguards assured by the Direct Debit Guarantee. I understand that this instruction may remain with the National Trust and, if so, details will be passed electronically to my Bank/Building Society.

Signature(s)

Date

*Banks and Building Societies may not accept Direct Debit instructions for some types of account.

The National Trust Membership Department, PO Box 39, Warrington WA5 7WD. Tel: 0870 458 4000 Minicom: 0870 240 3207 Reg. Charity Number 205846

Figure 7.7 National Trust – Building Loyalty

Control is possible but requires careful planning of the likely level of response. Hoover's well-known but ill-fated sales promotion grew well out of control when they underestimated the response to their 'Free flights to USA' promotion in the 1980s. The negative publicity and cost to fulfil all applications resulted in Hoover slipping from the number one slot in that market.

Communication is about linking your promotion with a device that echoes the right kind of values – Tesco's 'Computers for Schools' promotion has run successfully for many years, linking into the minds of their high volume customers – families with young children.

Insight

Sony wrapping paper

The pre-Christmas games market grows year on year. Sales in the run up to Christmas 2003 topped 1.26 billion games. To gain their share of the Christmas 2004 market, Sony sent 300 000 computer gamers playstation-branded wrapping paper which carried the message 'Happy Christmas to me'. The paper was accompanied with gift tags and a card, which offered the chance to win a limited edition console and copies of the games featured in the mailing.

www.brandrepublic.com.

Packaging

Aside from the functional role of packaging, which is to actually provide a container for products, packaging has a role to play in communicating with customers. It communicates the product name and the brand image. Following on from advertising and other promotional activity, this can act as a reminder to consumers at the point of sale to purchase the product in favour of a competing product. Often, some element of the packaging is inherent within the branding and can be used to extend the brand connections into other areas; for example, can you imagine a Toblerone that was not triangular? These links can be used to determine the type of sales promotions developed, for example a triangular puzzle for children.

Recently, the chocolate-coated sweets Smarties switched their packaging from the age-old tube with a removable plastic top to a hexagonal cardboard tube. It will be interesting to see how the consumer reacts to this change.

Stimulus generalization is a concept often used by own label manufacturers when they often emulate a style of packaging of a leading competitor to gain the same response as the original. Cadbury utilized the same type of packaging as Pringles to launch a new range of chocolate nibbles called 'Snaps' prior to Christmas 2004. Originally a seasonal line, these have now been extended to all year round.

Family packaging is when a consistent style of packaging is used across a range of products. Cadbury also do this by using the distinctive purple colour in all their packaging regardless of whether it is an ice cream or a biscuit.

Secondary use packaging is used to lengthen the brand's presence in the home. Lurpak produced a promotional butter dish for users of Lurpak butter, hopefully linking consumers into repeat purchase.

Point of sale display and merchandising

Point of sale display and merchandising refers to the in-store display that can influence consumers to purchase products in shops. It involves the layout and design of the shop and the way the goods or merchandise are presented. Manufacturers can have in-store display material produced to remind customers of their products at the point of purchase. For example, manufacturers of chocolates and confectionery might arrange with shops to display special branded stands, mobiles or life-size cardboard cut-outs of characters used to advertise the chocolate brand.

This has now been extended to actually branding the whole shop facia – a technique used with newsagents by Cadbury and Mars confectionery.

Similarly, cosmetics manufacturers might supply shops with hanging signs or revolving display stands. This is another tool for marketers to communicate brand imagery and act as a reminder at the point of purchase.

Powerful manufacturers who spend vast amounts on advertising tend to have more influence on retailers in terms of where their products are displayed. The most effective display areas are at 'eye level', where products are easy to see and reach for. Powerful retailers will use this tool, often charging manufacturers to move their products to more visible and high traffic sites.

POP displays and beauty products

A point-of-purchase (POP) display is the final chance for a cosmetics company to convince the consumer to choose its brand over the competitors. Almost one-third of the sales of cosmetics can be linked to being noticed and attracted to a display. Many cosmetics are also, in part, impulse buys. Consequently, the design and placement of POP displays represent a key element of the promotional efforts of cosmetics and manufacturers.

Colours are one key ingredient. Colours can create sophistication, fun and various emotions. Colours are often linked with individual companies. The colours of the display should match the packaging of the product and the Integrated Marketing Communications theme that the cosmetics firm presents in other places.

POP displays should lead the consumer to touch or pick up the product. Once a consumer has touched a product, a purchase almost always follows. Teenagers are more likely to pick up items with bold and bright colours and designs. Global Beauty Concepts targets 12 to 15-year-old girls with its brightly designed Petunia range of cosmetics. On the other hand, Fine Fragrances uses simple lines and colours in the attempt to reach key 'high street' retailers and their customers.

Males prefer more neutral colours than females. Products such as razors and colognes are more likely to sell with more minimalistic POPs. Unisex products also sell better with a more subdued approach. Calvin Klein cosmetics has led the way in promoting unisex products in its displays for CK fragrances.

A more recent trend in POP displays is to make them interactive. Clairol Cosmetics pioneered the use of interactive displays. Customers use a keypad or touch screen to select more information about the company's products.

Beyond a sturdy display rack, many factors go into the design of an effective cosmetics POP display. Colour, shape, size, positioning of 'testers' and other elements of design are key ingredients in the sale of these highly profitable items.

Source: Clow and Baack (2001) *Integrated Advertising, Promotion and Marketing Communications.*

Advantages of sales promotion as a communication tool	Disadvantages of sales promotion as a communication tool
Can provide a quick uplift in sales and be used as a quickly arranged competitive tactic	If overused, consumers only purchase if there is a promotion on, especially in low interest products
Can gain better in-store presence on the strength of the promotion	Can be over subscribed and cause fulfilment problems which are very costly and damaging in the long term, for example Hoover flights promotion
Can be creative and forge links with other brands, for example Coffee and Baileys	Promotion-led customers often have low brand loyalty, therefore you are giving away product for no long-term gain
Can generate good quality customer information	

Direct marketing

Direct marketing is a medium that is changing rapidly and could become a more strategic tool in the future. At present most of the uses are tactical in their nature and are methods of generating short-term sales leads.

Direct marketing allows us to send a personalized message to a consumer, generating a one-on-one communication. It is possibly the most targeted method of communication available to us marketers, yet the one that is least welcomed by the recipient.

Technology is enabling many changes within the direct marketing arena. We need to ensure that those changes allow us to use direct marketing techniques more sensitively in order to try to reduce negative perceptions of the medium in the minds of the consumer.

Technological advances mostly generate the changes that are occurring within direct marketing. At present this coursebook still has a unit dedicated to the role of ICT in communicating with the customer (Unit 9), the contents of which will be referred to within this section. With direct marketing the changes have been primarily concerned with the collection, and manipulation of data – namely customer data and databases. We can now collect much more data than ever before from many different sources. Digital technology and the ability to establish more two-way methods of communication mean we can now access and process many more pieces of information into intelligent useable data. We can buy lists of customers of certain demographic profiles and product usage that are of a higher quality in terms of their accuracy than ever before. We now need to use these advances to become more targeted in our approach.

The customers have also evolved and are using their power. More customers are using services to opt out of receiving direct mail by a variety of services that have evolved to rid them of this intrusion into their lives. It is now possible to remove your name from mailing lists, express your wish not to receive direct marketing telephone calls and to bin direct mail communications. Legislation is currently going through parliament to make unsolicited e-mail communication illegal. Further European Legislation is also due to be passed in 2007. The Unfair Commercial practices directive has been four years in the making and will detail a 'Black List' of 31 separate misleading or aggressive practices. These include running a promotion, without awarding the offered prizes and publishing marketing material in the form of an invoice which gives the consumer the impression that they have already ordered the product. The legislation will be applicable across all European member states by December 2007.

Hence, the need for direct marketing techniques to 'grow up' and to be used more sensibly by all organizations.

In terms of the 4Cs *Communication* to the targeted group should be possible resulting in the *cost* per contact becoming of relatively good value. Research into the use of direct marketing techniques found that, on average, one in eleven direct marketing mechanisms resulted in a positive response.

Better targeting made possible by better technology should also make *Control* better, resulting in less wastage and less wrongly targeted messages.

The less unsolicited marketing we receive the more *Credible* the direct marketing message can become. The biggest problem for the industry at present is that while technology is being used to make targeting more specific, it is also being used to make unsolicited advances more cheaply. This can be evidenced by the use of recorded messages that are being used for telemarketing purposes.

Direct marketing objectives

Direct marketing campaign objectives could be to:

- o Generate sales – by generating action, store visit or online order
- o Build up sales leads – for sales people to follow at a later stage
- o Invite recipients to visit a store – to gain information
- o Build the company database – to use for future communication
- o Remind people that an offer closes by a certain date – linking with sales promotion.

Types of direct marketing activity

- o Direct mail (mail shots)
- o Door drops (leaflets/coupons/vouchers posted through the door)
- o Selling via catalogues/brochures/websites (mail order selling)
- o Direct response advertising in the press (off the page selling)
- o Direct response advertising on the television (DRTV)
- o Telemarketing (using the telephone to contact people to sell direct to them).

The most popular form of direct marketing in the UK for both consumer and business-to-business marketing is direct mail. Direct mail usually comprises a sales letter outlining the offer, a response mechanism and sometimes there is a separate piece, which gives details of an incentive offer if you respond by a certain date. Mail shots offer a personalized message. Door drops and leaflets are less targeted and not personalized.

How direct mail can be used?

The principle behind all direct marketing techniques is that organizations build a database of current customers' address details and their previous purchase history. By using this information the organization can target products/services that are tailored to suit the recipient's profile. For example, a bank will have all your financial details and could send you a mail shot promoting a gold status credit card if you fitted the income bracket and financial history for that product.

The same bank could rent a list of people with a gold card customer profile, from another organization, to send them a mail shot in the hope of recruiting additional gold card customers.

Figure 7.8 An example of direct marketing material

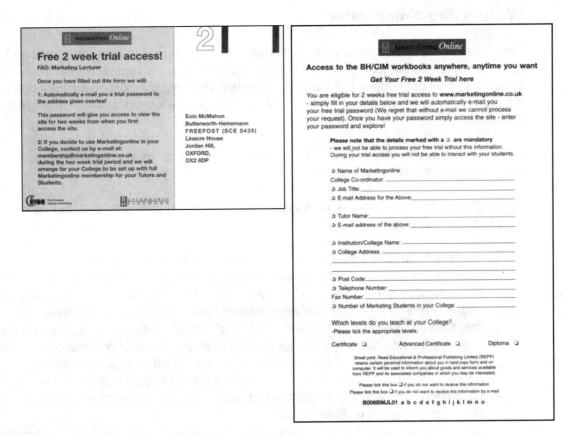

Figure 7.9 An example of a response mechanism

Dear Mrs Wood,

Wouldn't it be nice if someone else paid for the fun things in life? Air Miles do just that.

Take a look at your 'Spring 2001 offers' booklet and you'll find out how. There are 2 great **NEW OFFERS**: earn miles shopping online with Yahoo! UK & Ireland; and earn 100s of miles when you switch to gas and electricity with Scottish Hydro-Electric or Southern Electric. You could also win 10,000 miles at Sainsbury's.

But what are you going to do with all those miles? Well, for only 80 miles you'll get a cheaper holiday than you can find on the high street with 20 leading companies, or a FREE day out; and there are flights worldwide, with three ways to pay.

And remember, the more miles you collect, the more fun you could be having. So take a look at your statement and 'spring 2001 offers' booklet NOW!

Best wishes

Mary Thomas

Marketing Director

Figure 7.10 An example of a direct marketing letter from Air Miles

Writing direct mail letters

Direct mail can be a powerful communication tool but where it is sent indiscriminately it can irritate people and be judged as 'junk mail'. Wastage can be reduced if the mail shots are targeted at the right people. For example, it is very annoying for existing customers to be sent details of a new 'introductory' offer that they cannot take up because they are not a new customer.

If you want customers to respond, you can make it easier for recipients to respond by using a response mechanism (see Figure 7.9).

Although the style of a letter is personal there are some techniques that you can use when writing direct mail letters:

- Say what you mean clearly – be clear what your key message is.
- Sound enthusiastic – if you are writing with an offer, it should sound worth taking up.
- Write personally – where possible use a computer software that enables you to personalize letters with names and even inserting the address or a reference to the customer's current product package in the text of the letter. So, for example, a breakdown recovery service could write to its existing customers and in the text of the letter say, 'Now Mrs Wood, if your car wouldn't start outside 10 Acacia Avenue, wouldn't it be convenient if you had the "home start" service added to your current breakdown cover?'
- Questions can be used to good effect when you are trying to get your recipients to desire or want your product/service.
- You can go into detail in a direct mail letter in a way that you cannot in an advertisement.
- In most circumstances you should use a friendly tone – but it does depend on the situation. So, if you were writing about a critical illness cover your tone would be more serious.
- If you want a response or some form of action from the recipient, make it very clear what it is; perhaps mention it more than once. The P.S. at the end of a direct mail letter can be used to good effect to remind the customer what they need to do and by when. For example, you could say 'P.S. Don't forget that if you want the two free books when you join our book club you need to complete the attached post card and return it before 31 May...'

Other direct response methods

Other methods are not personalized and rely in the message recipient responding to the initial communication. Technology has widened the scope of the messages that can be sent. Mail order used to be totally dependent upon the postal and telephone system, now mail order is changing significantly with the use of websites and online ordering (e-commerce). The inclusion of website addresses on all forms of communicating is encouraging people to contact the organization for either more information or to order the product. For these methods to work, websites must be kept up to date and relevant. Ease of use and navigation is also important online. Security and speed of fulfilment are important when ordering online. More detail on e-commerce issues is available within Unit 9.

Direct Response TV gives the customer two ways of communicating with the organization. Digital viewers can use the 'Red Button' option if advertisers in-build this function into their television advertising. Renault used this with the launch of the re-styled Megane. The red button led the viewer to more detailed information, lists of local dealers and an invitation to test drive. Non-digital viewers are offered a telephone hotline number to gain more information.

Website services are taking over from press direct response as mechanisms to request catalogues or make bookings although it may still be the press advertising that arouses the interest in the first place.

With these two methods it is important that the number or process that the customer uses is evident within the message communicated. Repetition of the telephone number or website address at the end of the advertisement (when using verbal communication methods) will allow people to understand and assimilate the next action required.

It is also essential that the response mechanisms work quickly and effectively. If technology fails or the telephone number rings unanswered then the customer is unlikely to try again.

Newly developed direct response media include the use of e-mail and text or SMS messaging. e-mail can be used in the same way as direct mail with the communication adapted to become screen size and easy to print off. Attachments or hyperlinks to websites can further enhance the message although after many virus scares concerning unsolicited attachments, consumers are choosing to delete 'Spam' in droves without even opening the e-mail. However, the significant cost and time benefits of e-mail over postal methods especially on a global scale will continue to secure its future use.

Text messaging is most widely used by airtime providers to try to get their customers to utilize more paid for services (such as latest football scores). It is probably the most immediate personalized method of direct mail, especially to the ever-evasive youth market. The issue at present is that this form of communication is seen as intrusive, and more creative ways of producing tailor-made messages are required for the consumer to see the benefit.

Telemarketing is becoming a less acceptable way of communicating with customers, as the misuse of this medium by certain product categories (double-glazing) has led to customers feeling intruded upon and response rates are minimal. Legislation has led to this practice being illegal during certain times of the day. The continued misuse can only mean that reputable organizations should avoid this method and use others such as e-mail or mail shots.

Insight

Tesco club card

Tesco club card loyalty device is perhaps the most successful sales promotion of its day. The club card device was instrumental in Tesco overtaking Sainsbury's into the Number 1 Grocery Retailer slot, and going on to build a gap that Sainsbury's have never been able to bridge.

However, the club card continues to reap rewards even now in the arena of direct marketing. By monitoring the volume, frequency and brand choice of shoppers Tesco are able to target direct mail to their customers. This means they can promote not only goods in store, but also other Tesco products such as insurance, credit cards, telephone networks and savings. It is now possible to leave your home, insured by Tesco, drive to the store in your car, insured by Tesco, pay for your shopping with a Tesco Credit card, collecting reward points on your club card for family days out that you can ring people up on your Tesco network to tell people about!

Advantages of direct marketing as a communication tool	Disadvantages of direct marketing as a communication tool
Easy to measure the response and effectiveness of the communication	Customers have negative perceptions of many methods
Precise targeting possible – less costly on wastage	Regarded as intrusive by many
Can send a customized message to different segments of customers	Direct response mechanisms require costly services to cope with customers' responses adequately
Short lead times – to develop the campaign and inform customers	Much of the information generated is only valuable if processed
	Data processing costs can be high

Personal selling

When one visualizes the 'salesperson' many people will call to mind some negative images of either an unhelpful and impolite sales assistant in their local supermarket or a brash and unrelenting hard-sell salesman, usually connected with cars or double-glazing. Both of these scenarios communicate to the customer – in these cases, very badly. The first scenario is categorized under customer care and as such will be dealt with in Unit 10.

The second scenario falls into the below-the-line area of personal selling and as such is a process that can be important at various stages within the customer buying decision-making process. The most important feature of personal selling as a tool of communication is that it involves two-way interactive communications to take place. This can be used in different ways dependent upon who the customer is.

In consumer communications personal selling can provide the confused consumer with additional information at the point of sale. Customer objections can be investigated, discussed and hopefully dispelled. The salesperson can help the customer to evaluate the alternatives and choose the product or service that is best for them. If this is carried out in an unpressured professional manner the customer will feel empowered to decide, and valued as a customer.

In a business-to-business situation, the success of an organization can depend upon the relationships that its sales people have within the industry. This salesperson has more of a differentiating role to play, highlighting the benefits of his products/services across those in the competition. Objections will still need to be overcome, probably with accompanying guarantees as the customer seeks foolproof solutions, which will reflect well upon him in a pressured business environment. More emphasis will be placed on the terms and conditions of the relationship and the level of after-sales service and support on offer.

In terms of the 4Cs, personal selling can be a very positive promotional media to utilize as long as the salesperson is knowledgeable in their field and cognisant of the need to establish the consumers needs before attempting the selling process. *Communication* and *credibility* are therefore dependent upon the knowledge and skills of the salesperson.

The actions, which take place within the remit of personal selling, can vary, as the salesperson is required to take on one of the following roles:

- o *Order taker* – where the salesperson takes a passive role and enables the transaction to take place, but does not play a part in the decision-making process.
- o *Pre-order caller* – where it is the salesperson's role to inform and build up goodwill with the purchaser so that when they are about to make a purchase the products of that organization are in the purchasers mindset, for example Medical representatives.
- o *Order supporter* – here the main skill of the salesperson is skill or technical knowledge, for example B2B software supplier.
- o *Order getter* – where the salesperson has to creatively sell the product/service in a competitive market.

But, in some of these situations, some degree of negotiation is required to take place. If we can examine the objectives and process of negotiation we can look at how this communication method may be used proactively.

Planning the negotiation

It is important to plan the negotiation before it actually takes place. This involves deciding upon the objectives of the organization and the customer. You may think that the objectives of the organization are to make a sale, but actually a more beneficial objective is to start a relationship that will result in more mutually profitable transactions in the future.

The customer's objective might be to buy the cheapest alternative, but a more beneficial objective is to find the product most suitable to their needs and the most competitive price.

In this way all of the communication that has been transmitted to the customer before the point of purchase will be influencing their decision, and so will all the stuff they remember about the competitors' products. Personal selling does not exist in isolation in a marketing-orientated culture; it is supported by all the other promotional messages too.

As well as other promotional methods supporting the salesperson, useful and informative point of sale material (as covered earlier) can benefit the personal selling process.

Negotiation phases
- o Opening the sale – introduction, arranging appointment, asking how to help.
- o Identifying customer needs or problems – getting them to open up and discuss what is important to them.
- o Demonstrating or presenting the product/service – linking into their evaluation of alternatives.
- o Handling objections – again helping with evaluation, by turning negatives into positives.
- o Negotiating – offering other services which may help decision-making (e.g. free delivery).
- o Closing the sale. Both objectives met.

The objective of personal selling is to ensure the customer has a positive experience at the point of purchase and a way to communicate if the post-purchase evaluation stage has its problems. In this way the organization can succeed in retaining valuable existing customers.

Advantages of personal selling as a communication tool	Disadvantages of personal selling as a communication tool
Two-way interactive communication possible	Costly to maintain a sales force
Good information from the marketplace can be fed back to the organization from the sales people	Training needs and updating skills are also costly
Relationship can be developed and be beneficial to both parties – a win–win situation	Lack of control – dependent upon the mood and skills of one person at one point in time
	If negative the customer will retain that perception

Evaluating the effect of using below-the-line methods

In considering which media to use within a communications campaign one of the factors that influences our choice is 'what has worked well in the past', so it is important that we can effectively evaluate what each medium has contributed towards the overall campaign results.

Measuring sales

It is not appropriate to only look at sales when you are measuring the success of an advertisement or a campaign because other factors in the marketing mix or the external environment could affect sales (in either a negative or a positive way). For example, if there was media coverage of a research report suggesting that chocolate improved your IQ and reduced stress at the same time as the 'Chocco' advertising campaign, then this could be the reason for a sales increase and not the effect of the advertising campaign. Or, perhaps weather conditions could affect cocoa production adversely, which could cause price rises and reduce demand for 'Chocco', no matter how effective the advertising campaign.

Message content or media used

Within the promotional message the evaluation has two elements to consider, the content of the message itself and how well that worked at communicating, and the efficiency of the media chosen in transmitting the message.

The message content can be evaluated either by commissioning marketing research or by looking at the accuracy in the feedback we are getting from the consumer. If they are entering retail stores asking for the product or lots of people are walking round singing our jingle, we can assume the message is getting through.

The effectiveness of the media can also be measured by marketing research but although we may be aware that awareness has risen to 80 per cent how can we judge which media helped to achieve that the most.

Many of the below-the-line media covered within this unit have response mechanisms or evaluation measurements built into their use. Some we have mentioned along the way. Some may be worth revisiting.

Measuring the effect of PR

An effective way of evaluating public relations effort is to physically measure the amount of coverage in print and broadcast media. For example, to measure the success of a PR campaign informing consumers about a new type of diet chocolate, you could count how many articles appeared in the national press and specialist press (for example, slimming magazines).

To evaluate the success of a business-to-business exhibition, if the objective was to create leads for sales staff, you could count the number of contact numbers collected by the staff manning the exhibition. You could further refine the evaluation process by measuring how many calls led to sales appointments and from there, how many appointments were converted to sales. A final sales figure could be checked against the cost of the exhibition to see if the activity was cost-effective.

Measuring sales promotion and direct marketing

To measure the response to a sales promotion campaign that used a '20p off' coupon you could set up a system with retailers to count the number of redeemed vouchers. By media coding the coupon you will know which magazine produced the most responses.

Similarly, the response rates from direct marketing campaigns should be evaluated and, if appropriate, a further check made to calculate how much response is actually converted to sales. This way the cost of a campaign can be measured against the monetary gain from sales.

Hints and tips

You do need to have a basic understanding of how organizations communicate with their external customers. You need to have lots of examples of the whole range of promotional activities from your own experience to put into answers where appropriate. So, ensure that you do this type of research well in advance of the examination.

Some questions may relate to how logos and corporate images are used to communicate with customers.

Although it is unlikely that you would be asked a question where you just need to regurgitate facts about various media, you could be given a scenario and asked to suggest relevant promotion activities that could be used in that situation and to justify your choice.

Alternatively, you might be asked to write a letter or a memo in a situation relating to exhibitions, sponsorship and so on; fundamental to the question might be your understanding of the promotional activity that relates to the context of the question.

You need to have a basic understanding of the importance of layout, typefaces and design so that you could either evaluate the effectiveness or produce a draft of an advertisement, leaflet or some other printed material.

You should be able to write an effective direct mail shot, press release or text for a press advertisement or another promotional material and know how to monitor or measure the effectiveness of a promotional activity.

You will not be asked questions on how computers work, the history of the Internet or about jargon connected with technological developments. However, you should be prepared to explain how technological changes are affecting the way that people and organizations do business and communicate.

Be prepared to answer questions that are set in a context of new media and technology but test you on other areas of the syllabus.

Summary

In this unit you have studied:

o How we start to use the communications mix
o The role of various below-the-line promotional activities
o What to look for when evaluating corporate literature
o How to write a press release
o How to write a direct mail letter
o How to measure the effectiveness of various promotional activities.

Further study

If you require further exam practice then attempt Question 3b on the December 2004 examination paper and Questions 5(a) & 1a(ii) on the June 2005 paper. Go to www.cim.co.uk to access Specimen Answers for these exam questions.

Bibliography

Fill, C. (2002) *Marketing Communications – Contexts, Strategies and Applications*, 3rd edition, Prentice Hall.

Forsyth, P. (1999) *Communicating with Customers*, London: Orion Business.

unit 8
the promotional mix – above the line

In this unit you will:

- Extend your knowledge of the communications or promotional mix. See syllabus section 3.4.

- Examine the characteristics and use of above-the-line promotion tools. See syllabus section 3.4.

- Appreciate what influences promotional decisions. See syllabus section 3.2.

- Appreciate the concept of Integrated Marketing communications. See syllabus section 3.1.

By the end of this unit you should be able to:

- Explain the concept of, and need for, an integrated marketing communications approach and the links between communications and marketing planning (3.1).

- Explain the role and importance of promotion in marketing (3.2).

- Describe the tools of the promotional mix (3.4).

- Explain how above-the-line activities are used (3.6).

- Describe current trends and developments in promotions and their impact on organizations (3.15).

Study Guide

This unit provides you with a basic understanding of the communications or promotion mix and covers indicative content area 3.1–3.13 of the syllabus.

It links with the Marketing Fundamentals syllabus indicative content area 1.2.9, which is covered in Unit 7 of the Marketing Fundamentals coursebook. With the Marketing Fundamentals syllabus you are looking at the promotional mix as one element of a total marketing mix; with Customer Communications this topic is the key to understanding how organizations communicate with their external customers.

Unit 8 will now build on Unit 7 in looking at the more strategic promotional tools in the promotional toolbox. These fall into the above-the-line category, whereas the tools investigated in Unit 7 fall into the below-the-line category.

As in Unit 7 you not only need to know about the various communication tools but also how you need to be able to use them alongside those methods covered in Unit 7 to combine them into an integrated marketing communications campaign.

You need to appreciate that although some larger organizations use specialized agencies to work on all aspects of their marketing communication activities, there are many smaller organizations where working in the marketing department will mean you are responsible for drafting press advertisements (or at least knowing what makes an effective one) and being able to write a press release or the text for a mail shot.

Although Unit 9 focuses specifically on ICT, this unit will provide you with a brief insight into its role within the communications mix. You will look at how technology specifically affects your communication with customers.

For further information on how this material in this unit will be examined, read the Exam Hints section at the end of this unit.

This unit will take you 3 hours to read through and a further 3 hours to work through the activities.

Study tip

As in Unit 7 this unit provides an outline of the main advertising media and their main attributes. To provide further examination of this topic you need to spend some time looking at examples of advertising using different media and sourcing examples for your communications diary.

You should collect and analyse the use of one example for each of the elements of the promotional mix. Where you are aware that a campaign is using more than one medium, then try to include examples of all media used. This will help you to evaluate the concept of Integrated Communications.

For each example you should specify the advertising objectives, identify the target audience and consider why that particular medium has been chosen.

You need to extend your knowledge by accessing information outside the coursebook, in the quality press, specialist marketing magazines and specialist technical press.

You should also use the Internet to see how it can be used for advertising. www.brandrepublic. com and www.media,guardian.co.uk have extensive updates on organizational communications and the movements within the Advertising Agency world.

Surf the web for more information about technological developments. One of many websites that you could visit is www.net-profit.co.uk, which is in the form of an online magazine and provides information about technology developments affecting business.

The communications mix or promotions mix

The introduction to this unit is exactly the same as Unit 7 except that we will be examining the use of the last remaining tool of the promotional toolbox – Advertising. If a period of time has elapsed since you read Unit 7 you may wish to re-visit the following sections at the beginning of that unit before you continue with this unit.

- o The promotional toolbox – Figure 7.1
- o Why we communicate externally
- o Promotional objectives.

When combining the promotional tools together to produce a customized communications package which meets the needs of our own organization, it is important to consider how each of the tools we use will complement and support each other in achieving the organization's promotional objectives. Some methods more naturally slot into the role of *primary* media, enabling mass communication and building awareness on a large scale. These tend to be *above-the-line* media. The promotional toolbox contains the following above-the-line media.

- o Television
- o Press
- o Radio
- o Outdoor
- o Cinema
- o Internet
- o Branding.

Much of the inter-media decisions taken will depend not only on the budget available but also the media characteristics that the brand/service requires in order that it be communicated in the best possible way. In looking at each of the following media we must also consider their ability to communicate:

- o At a visual level
- o At an audio level, and
- o At the right level of detail.

Television advertising

This is the most visual medium, and as most people spend at least some time watching television for entertainment, it is a medium capable of delivering audiences in large numbers. This ability to reach numbers means the cost of one spot or commercial break can be very high, but this can very much depend on which television channel is used.

Television is a very creative medium that offers:

1. Sound, movement, interesting visual effects.
2. Entertainment that famous people are happy to appear in – giving source credibility to your product/service.
3. Impact – you can see products in action or being demonstrated, and the lifestyle they fit into.
4. Credibility to the product or service – because of the creative treatment and because the organization uses television – the most expensive medium.

181

However, in order that the television commercial does not look out of place with all the other professionally filmed programmes that appear on either side of the commercial, television advertising requires specialist production, which adds considerably to the cost of using television as a medium.

Television commercials give a relatively short exposure time (most commercials last for no more than 30 seconds), which means that the commercial will need to be repeated many times (often at least 20–30 times) within a campaign in order to ensure the majority of the target audience receives and understands the communication.

This is highly dependent upon the way the creative strategy conveys the message. Consider the case of Honda trying to tell people that they have developed a better diesel engine – not a very interesting message but a very noticeable campaign.

Insight

Honda – Can hate be good?

The Observer reported yesterday that the jingle from the Honda ad 'Can hate be good? Can hate be something we don't hate?' could be released as a single, after generating a huge amount of interest.

Created by Wieden and Kennedy, the animated sequence tells the story of how Honda came to design a better diesel engine. It eschews the 'money shots' typical of the majority of car advertising and is set in a brightly coloured world populated by talking rabbits, flowers and rainbows.

The song was written by Michael Russoff, who created the ad along with Sean Thompson and Richard Russell. *The Observer* reports that W&K is now considering what to do with the jingle, which currently appears on radio and television. It owns the copyright but has an agreement that it will only be used to further the commercial interests of Honda.

If the jingle is released as a single it will be following in a tradition dating back to the early 1970s when Coca-Cola launched the 'I'd like to teach the world to sing' campaign. The song was written as a jingle but people loved it so much that it was rushed out as a full-length single by the New Seekers.

Honda have expanded on the success of the television, radio and poster campaign by launching a new-look website which features an online game. The game (www.honda.co.uk/grrrame) challenges users to steer a rabbit around a garden against the clock. Users can then click for more information of the engine, forward the game or enter their details to win a competition.

The online push will feature ads in the motoring section of autocar.co.uk, channel4.com, whatcar.com and autotrader.co.uk. There will also be banner ads on company car and fleet management sites.

www.brandrepublic.com.

The above example demonstrates that television can, with the benefit of an inspirational creative team, *communicate* in a way that other media cannot. With television being used as the primary media in building awareness for the campaign, it is then possible to use a wealth of other secondary media to extend length and frequency of the campaign.

The absolute *cost* of television airtime is very expensive, but reaches a large number of people. This means that the cost of reaching a thousand of your target audience (cost per thousand, CPT) is comparable with other media, but the high going-in cost means that it tends only to feature in the marketing budgets of the mass-market FMCG (fast-moving consumer goods) brands.

There is a certain amount of *Credibility* within the industry when television advertising is used as it implies big budgets. This credibility is not however perceived by the consumer who often cannot recall what even the most memorable ads are representing.

The *Control* element is high as the ad can be placed where the organization requires it to be – as long as it is willing to pay the price. The absolute cost of television advertising results in it being a popular B2C media but hardly ever used for B2B campaigns.

Television is a very transient medium that can easily be missed. This is more so since people with video and DVD recorders can fast-forward past commercial breaks in programmes they have recorded (zipping) and people with a remote control can quickly change channels (zapping) to avoid television advertising. The increase in Digital TV ownership (see below) will exacerbate these problems. However, satellite channels do synchronize their commercial breaks so that anyone zapping through a series of satellite channels will only encounter more advertisement breaks. Terrestrial channels are trying to institute this between themselves.

Television channels which take advertising are split into *terrestrial* channels which are UK-based and can reach 97 per cent of the UK population, and *satellite* channels, such as those offered by Sky, which are available to those homes within the UK that have a satellite dish or are connected to cable TV operators. The penetration of UK homes is currently well above 50 per cent with a number of channels available, some dedicated to sports and movies.

Advertising is available on both *satellite* and *terrestrial* channels. All satellite channels carry advertising although the audience tends to be smaller and more specific to the programming. The *terrestrial* channels carrying advertising are ITV1, Channel 5, Channel 4 and GMTV.

On ITV 1 it is possible to buy television advertising that appears only in one of the 13 ITV regions, and so target a specific area of Britain. However, it is also possible to buy national advertising airtime covering all the television regions, which makes it ideal for mass-market products or services. Channel 4 can also offer a regional coverage option.

Until recently, it was a difficult tool to use for targeting specific groups, except in a fairly crude way. For example, media planners could make generalizations that mothers mostly watch daytime television, upmarket business people watch the evening news, and teenagers watch late-night television.

With the introduction of more channels via cable and satellite television, there are more opportunities for specialist programmes, for example about specific sports. With this come more opportunities to target specific audiences. For example, MUTV is a channel devoted to the interests of Manchester United fans. With greater audience fragmentation comes greater opportunities for niche advertising.

Digital TV/Interactive TV

Digital Television (13 million UK homes in 2004) allows access to more channels. This can be done by purchase of a set top box, Freeview, which removes the need to subscribe to BSkyB or localized cable operators such as Telewest. Currently the split between households subscribing versus those with a one-off payment, set top box, is that Sky has 7.8 million subscriber homes, whereas Freeview reaches an estimated 5.2 million households. To BSkyB's alarm, Freeview

183

is growing fast and some predict could overtake BSkyB by 2012 when the analogue television signal in the UK will be turned off forcing all consumers to adopt some form of Digital TV.

In response to the threat, BSkyB themselves launched a new general entertainment channel in September 2005 called 'Sky Three' to be shown on the Freeview platform in addition to its own platform. The reasoning behind this move was that Sky gain a presence in new types of homes where it is able to give potential customers a taste of the full Sky service and encourage them to switch to the subscriber-based platform.

The graph below extracted from a report in the Independent (23/09/05) charts the predicted growth of Digital channels over the next 5 years up to and after analogue switch off.

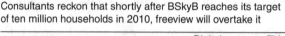

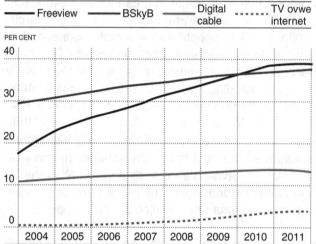

Figure 8.1 Freeview – Predicted growth in digital homes
Source: Spectrum strategy

Digital TV also allows two-way communication (Interactive TV) through the use of the 'Red Button'. Additional information on the products being advertised can be accessed by pressing the 'Red Button' on their remote control if the viewer is interested in the product/service being advertised. This interest can be monitored to establish the interest in the product. They can also interact with some TV programmes such as *Who Wants to be a Millionaire.*

Digital TV also allows viewers to time shift their viewing to suit their lifestyle; they can also filter out advertising whilst viewing in time shift mode. The increased number of channels available means that the audience, which is relatively stable at 21 million homes across the UK, is now fragmented over more channels making it more difficult to reach high audiences with one hit. This makes competition for the high audience slots such as ITV1's *Coronation Street* very high.

All of these issues have resulted in the entry cost to television advertising steadily decreasing and becoming a realistic option for more organizations than before.

Advantages of television as a communication tool	Disadvantages of television as a communication tool
High impact very creative medium	High entry cost – need to produce a commercial and terrestrial channels still expensive
High audience coverage possible. Good for building awareness quickly	Audiences fragmenting with more channels being introduced
Possible to show the product being used	Viewers may not watch commercials but either fast forward or leave the room
Good source credibility	Subject to noise
Certain viewer segments can be targeted	Complex to purchase with long lead times

Sponsorship as an advertising medium

As mentioned in Unit 7, sponsorship can be used as a PR tool but some sponsorship use can be viewed very much as advertising. Sponsorship of television programmes, such as Cadbury's use of Coronation Street, is very similar to using television as an advertising medium and is actually subject to similar restrictions as television advertising, however the advantages are numerous. The product/service is set apart from the usual advertising clutter transmitting at end and start breaks with a tailored message showing the links between the product and the programme. Sponsorship also allows a degree of exclusivity. It is unlikely that Mars will want to advertise in the centre break of *Coronation Street*, even though it is the highest audience break on television, when Cadbury have their own tailored message appearing twice in 3 minutes.

Sponsorship can also be used by linking brand values between the organization and the vehicle it is sponsoring.

It is widely accepted that the best sponsorships occur when there is a link or common bond between the sponsor and the programme. Cadbury claiming to be the first name in chocolate, within the great British institution that *Coronation Street* is, really shows a synergy of two great brands together in a mutually beneficial relationship. Consider how Vodaphone have used this, even adapting the stance when events dictate.

Insight

Vodaphone

Vodaphone also recognized a link between themselves and sportsmen such as David Beckham and Michael Schumacher. At the first level they were both number one in their sport and wore red as their uniform. David Beckham played for Manchester United at the time, also sponsored by Vodaphone. Vodaphone saw links between themselves and the David Beckham brand. Their website stated:

'Beckham's healthy lifestyle allied to his talent suggests an energy and controlled passion for life; an image that Vodaphone would like to project for itself. On a football pitch Beckham is innovative, creative, exciting; characteristics that Vodaphone aspires to. Beckham the family man is seen as caring and empathetic; Vodaphone wants people.'

Vodaphone wants its customers to appreciate that it too understands and cares about what people want and need. Beckham is generally seen as dependable; Vodaphone wants to communicate a similar message. The synergy is clear.

185

But what of recent events that have tarnished the image? It was widely thought that Vodaphone would drop Beckham after the 'alleged' misconduct, but in August 2004 they announced that Beckham would continue to promote the Vodaphone brand and that the company plans to create what it describes as a Beckham 'content suite', including games and screen savers.

David Wheldon, the global director of marketing and brand communications at Vodaphone said, 'We are very happy to have signed a deal with David which builds on the success of our partnership over the last 2 years.'

'The Vodaphone Live! advertising campaigns featuring David were an integral part of the marketing programmes that ran in the UK, Spain and Japan during 2002–2004. We look forward to work successfully together.'

Beckham said, 'I am pleased to be continuing my partnership with Vodaphone. I am looking forward to working on some exciting projects in 2005 and building on the association.'

www.brandrepublic.com.

Marketing communications – Cadbury

Cadbury is one of the best-known brands in the UK and is synonymous with chocolate. In order to communicate and develop its brand with customers and other stakeholders, it uses a variety of communications methods. Some of the main ones are as follows.

Methods of marketing communications used by Cadbury:

- Advertising
- Point of purchase
- Public relations
- Direct marketing
- Website
- Personal selling
- Exhibitions and events
- Packaging
- Sales promotions
- Café Cadbury
- Sponsorship (Coronation Street)
- Trade promotions
- Product placements
- Cadbury World – associated merchandise
- Field marketing
- Vending machines.

One recent addition to this impressive list has been the development of Café Cadbury and its entry into the expanding coffee house market. Positioned as a 'Chocolate Experience', the Cadbury cafés seek to extend the Cadbury brand even though direct sales through these outlets will be small. The objective, as reported by Mason (2000), is to keep the Cadbury brand high in the minds of the public and to maintain the quality and trust that the brand has evoked. Cadbury refers to this brand extension as part of its present marketing programme.

Source: Fill, C. (2002) *Marketing Communications – Contexts and Strategies and Applications*, 3rd edition.

Activity 8.1

The use of celebrities in connection with advertising, either as voice-overs, actors or experts is extensive. Consider how this has developed over time and how sometimes it has worked well but sometimes badly.

Press advertising

Press advertising comprises all printed media. In the UK this covers:

- National newspapers – Quality broadsheets, tabloids; daily and weekend editions.
- Local newspapers – Evening and Weekly. Free and paid for titles.
- General interest magazines, that is female interest, male interest. Television and life-style titles.
- Specialist interest magazines – covering hobbies and activities.
- Specialist trade and technical magazines – one for almost every industry sector and job.
- Children's interest.

Therefore, advertising in print media can be carefully targeted at demographic and geographic segments. A key advantage is that quite complex messages can be conveyed because print media can be retained and seen more than once. One copy of a newspaper will be seen by as many as three different people and magazines tend to hang around the house to be looked at over and over again, giving long life and high coverage to a press advertisement.

Advertisements can also benefit from the credibility of the newspaper or magazine. Often, advertisers portray their products in the same creative style as the magazine and advertise over two or three pages so that the advertisement looks like part of the magazine. This technique is known as an *Advertorial* and is used to infer greater source credibility.

Press is often used as a support medium, as part of an integrated communications package. Consider the advertisement shown below. This reminds potential consumers that Renault not only produce a range of vehicles for everyday use but also play an active and successful role in Formula 1 racing. The values associated with Formula 1 which is the need for constant innovation and reliability therefore become implicit in the normal Renault offering. The press advertisement showing a Formula 1 car parked in a normal street alongside other recognizable Renault cars manages to make these links and communicates a range of messages in one visual.

187

Figure 8.2 Renault – recent press advertisement

However, advertising in the print media has limited impact and the opportunity for the development of highly creative messages is lower than with television advertising. Magazines can be in full colour and quite glossy, newspapers tend to be in black and white with only spot colour. The placing of an advertisement in high-traffic slots, such as the TV page or near articles related to your product/service category can also enhance the readers to 'take' on the advertising message being conveyed.

The plethora of general interest magazines has led to a decline in some of the larger circulation figures (number of copies sold) as people switch to alternative new publications. Many publications are now available globally offering an international advertising opportunity (e.g. Vogue, Hello).

Newspaper circulation is also under threat from 24-hour news channels and Internet access to news sites such as www.bbc.co.uk.

Press advertising can be purchased by the page or fraction of a page. Smaller ads are measured by *single column centimetre*, with the average newspaper having 5 columns on each page and the centimetre measurement referring to the depth of the advert, therefore an ad spanning 3 columns and 20 cm in depth will be 60 s.c.c.

The positioning should also be considered. Apart from the nearby editorial as mentioned above, research tells us that people notice advertisements on the right-hand side of a page more than those on the left, so the price to advertise there is higher. The same theory also raises the price of inside front and back covers.

Advantages of press as a communication tool	Disadvantages of press as a communication tool
Some have high circulation of a mass audience	Newspapers only last a day
Targeting is possible and editorial content gives credibility	No exclusivity – may be next to competitor's advertisement
Flexibility of size, use of colour and creative treatment	Lack of impact in a crowded environment
Possible to convey a complicated message with a short lead time possible	
Long life – ads can be kept and referred to at a later stage	

Tabloid vs Broadsheet

The Daily Press has often categorized itself (and its readers) into a socio-demographic profile through the use of the terms 'Tabloid' and 'Broadsheet'. Although these are technical printing terms concerning the size of the paper the newspaper is printed on, these meanings were also used to imply the quality and integrity of the publication.

However, all is now changed. After research into readers' lifestyles and reading habits it became apparent that the days when father had a pristinely folded broadsheet paper next to his breakfast plate were long gone. Instead, our rushed lifestyle found us more often on the Tube grappling with an ocean of paper.

In a move to retain circulation, most broadsheets are now moving to a tabloid format. This was a move previously witnessed in the women's magazine market where the move by some from the traditional size to an A5 'handbag' size was very successful.

The Times and *Independent* have reported great success and it is thought where the two formats still exist, then sooner, rather than later, the Broadsheet version will be phased out.

At present where two formats exist the copy is the same, thereby retaining the quality aspect. However, once the tabloid only version exists will this still be the case?

Radio advertising

Radio relies only on sound. It does not therefore have the same creative impact as television and cannot show products or how they can be used. The amount of detail that can be conveyed is also limited as overuse of words leads to the listener 'tuning out'.

However, it can tap into the listeners' imaginations with the use of evocative sound effects and voices (including famous voices) to make it a very effective advertising medium.

It can reach large audiences, as in the UK there are several national commercial radio stations specializing in particular types of music (from jazz to classical). In addition, most regions have local radio geared to the needs of people in their catchment area. In this way radio advertising campaigns can be targeted geographically and according to lifestyle/tastes. Listeners tend to be quite loyal to their radio stations with over 50 per cent of homes listening to local radio and around 25 per cent to national commercial radio. They listen for extended periods and do not turn off advertisements in the same way as they do with television.

The size of audience will differ during the day with morning and evening 'drive time' representing the peak of listening. The profile of listeners will also change with a younger audience during drive time than the rest of the day.

Cost varies with the size of audiences reached but production costs are not as high as television and lead times to produce a commercial are very short allowing short-term reactive strategies to be used. However, advertisers usually have to buy a large number of airtime 'spots' because of the transient (and sometimes background listening) nature of the medium.

Radio is usually sold in packages of spots specifically timed to reach certain demographic profiles of listeners.

Advantages of radio as a communication tool	Disadvantages of radio as a communication tool
Both national and regional coverage is possible	Passive medium often used as background noise
Accessible in a number of places, home, work and car	Cluttered environment, advertisements are not distinctive
Companiable medium used by many	Sound only, no visual possible
Source credibility can be gained by use of recognizable voices, often celebrities	
Short production period possible – ability to produce 'reactive' advertising	

Radio can be successful – NSPCC

With radio, practitioners recommend building up pictures in the listener's mind with words. One example of this was an advert by National Society for Prevention of Cruelty to Children (NSPCC) where small vignettes were used to imply how children were being mistreated. Each vignette ended with an intrusive sound such as a hand banging hard on a table to imply the violent act that was unspoken.

This treatment worked well to promote a visual picture in the mind of the listener as radio was used as a support medium to the television campaign, so the visual was already established. The implication of this kind of violence remaining hidden in the family situation was also implied by the use of sound rather than words to represent the violent actions.

The ad was responsible for an upsurge in monthly subscribers that will generate income for a significant time.

Activity 8.2

Start listening to a selection of local and national commercial radio stations to assess how advertisers use it. What do you notice about the profile of advertisers on different stations and across different times of the day or week?

Cinema advertising

Cinema advertising has the same creative characteristics as television and perhaps even more impact because there are fewer distractions and potential interruptions from zipping and zapping. Cinema advertisements are usually longer than those used on TV as the media cost is significantly lower. It is unusual to produce a 'cinema only' advertisement due to the high production cost.

Films that are akin to the lifestyle that the brands and services are targeted at lend source credibility to the advertisement. Categories that are restricted in their TV use (such as alcohol) are able to use cinema more freely in films targeted at over 18s. Cinema is the most effective medium for reaching young adults (16–24s) as they lead a very mobile lifestyle, restricting their consumption of other media.

Orange have recently taken cinema advertising one stage further by sponsoring the 'Turn off your mobile' message at the start of each film. The message is contained in a vignette where a team of film producers interview directors and the film is all about Orange. Sales promotion has also been used as Orange users can now text for free cinema tickets on Wednesdays and receive a text code back to submit to the ticket office on arrival. This links in well to their aim to get 'Pay as you Go' customers onto contract.

In the UK, cinema advertising is sold on a national and regional basis through various cinema chains and two contractors. There is some opportunity for a high degree of geographic segmentation, with a small proportion of advertising aimed at purely local audiences.

Table 8.1 Top Five Spending Brands January–August 2003

Brand	Revenue
Orange – Orange mobile	£7.8 million
Saab – Car range	£2.7 million
3G – Mobile network	£2.2 million
Red Bull – Drink	£1.8 million
Virgin – Mobile Phone network	£1.8 million

(*Source*: MMS)

Advantages of cinema as a communication tool	Disadvantages of cinema as a communication tool
Quite a glamorous environment, which transfers to the advertisements shown. Very easy to target a lifestyle by targeting specific films. Audiences growing	High production cost. High cost of reaching a thousand people within your target audience
Audience captive and receptive to message being shown	Still limited groups being reached. One opportunity only
Can use audio and visual images. Longer commercials can be used to be very creative	No two-way response possible
Coverage possible – national down to just one cinema	

Outdoor advertising

This type of advertising covers a whole range of different types of media that can be found outdoors and indoors. It includes large roadside billboard hoardings, small poster sites on bus shelters and bus stations, underground and ground-level train stations, the inside and outside of various types of transport, such as buses, trains, tubes and taxis, and even peripheral sites, such as parking meters and street furniture.

Many also appear 'inside' shopping centres, leisure centres, football stadiums, health clubs and supermarkets.

This division in the location of sites tends to result in outside sites being targeted at adults in general and is used to raise awareness. Indoor sites, especially those in shopping centres, tend to be more targeted at women and is used to advertise products near the point of sale, for example coffee, chocolate.

Although a poster site can have plenty of impact, it is limited to short messages with bold images. Usually, there is a very short exposure time as people are moving past the advertising. (Exceptions here are people waiting at tube or rail stations.) Most outdoor advertising does not incorporate sound or movement in the message. However, there are some moving poster sites where the image changes every few minutes. Many sites are now illuminated, allowing the media to be used effectively throughout the year; non-illuminated sites tend to lack visibility during the winter months. There are also some well-known three-dimensional sites. For example, an airline has one in the form of an aeroplane at Heathrow and there was a famous one designed to look like a pub that sold Guinness.

Outdoor advertising can be purchased on a national basis by using pre-prepared packages of sites. These are usually packaged using posters of a similar size. It is also possible to buy outdoor advertising on a very regional basis even down to one site outside your own shop.

Outdoor advertising tends to be a B2C medium apart from very specific areas such as exhibition halls and the NEC where a degree of B2B advertising is used. Outdoor advertising tends to support other media, which can give more information due to the spoken word or written word with more time to read. It can be used to *remind* consumers of brands that have instant recognition or a well-known strapline. Marmite tend to give us quite a lot of outdoor advertising because of this.

Advantages of outdoor advertising as a communication tool	Disadvantages of outdoor advertising as a communication tool
Gives the opportunity to reach the target a number of times giving greater frequency to the message	Message can be affected by weather, graffiti and limited daytime hours
Possible to buy sites near point of sale for some products/services	Detailed message not possible
Local/regional use possible for a variety of periods of time	Long lead times. Production requires printing and all need to be posted, which can be a lengthy process
Message gets a long exposure. Creative use possible	

Internet advertising

Within this unit, we will deal specifically with using the Internet as an advertising medium on which to raise awareness of your products/services and of course website.

The use of the organization's website as a communication device and alternative distribution channel will be covered within Unit 9. E-mail as a communication method is covered within Unit 5.

Internet access is available in over 50 per cent of homes in the UK. Although the profile of users is becoming closer to the national profile, it is still heavily utilized by younger more affluent people. Over 50 per cent of e-mail usage emanates from people under 25 years old.

Internet advertising allows varying levels of visual, audio and interactive messages to be developed dependent upon the budget and creativity of the designer. A great deal of information can be transmitted, with the level of interaction being determined by the 'viewer'. Usage will fall into two broad categories: the viewer who requires a specific piece of information to act upon, or those who are 'browsing' – any advertising needs to fulfil the needs of both.

All *off-line* communications must feature the website address to build awareness of the site and its offerings. *Online* advertising is also used to drive traffic through to the website using the following methods:

- o Links with other sites – these can be general sites with a similar profile of users to whom you are targeting, for example Sunday Times, Amazon. Special interest sites, such as the Formula1 website, will provide more targeted opportunities.
- o Advertising on ISP portals (Internet service provider) such as Wanadoo and Yahoo! These can also be targeted as they have the demographic details of their subscribers and have details of their high traffic sites.

193

- E-mail advertising – using information gained from customer details or purchased as lists from many organizations.
- SMS messaging (using mobile phones) is not strictly an Internet medium but is often used in the same way, targeting people by sending text messages. Airtime providers use this a great deal to market their own services but are now providing lists of numbers to other organizations, specifically for targeting hard to reach groups such as young adults.

The type of advertisement used will depend on the target audience, media chosen and the degree of information/creativity needed and possible. The advertisements are created in one of the following ways:

- Banner advertising – The most common form of advertising, banner advertisements appear on linked sites and offer the ability for the viewer to click through into the advertising organization's website. There are also e-banners that allow e-transactions to take place.
- Pop-up ads – Often used not to advertise but to arouse interest via use of a game or clip of a film. Encourages the viewer to leave contact details to allow contact at a later stage.
- Superstitals – These appear whilst pages are being downloaded and provide entertainment whilst that is taking place. British Airways inserted one on the download to the Times newspaper website. However, with the improved penetration of broadband, opportunities may be limited in the future.
- e-mail and SMS as detailed above, where a very specific message can be sent directly to the recipient.

All methods and media allow us to be very targeted or quite general in our target, dependent upon the linked site or portal chosen to carry the advertising. All uses are very measurable in that we are able to monitor the degree of 'click through'. A high level of interaction can also be built in to engage the viewer, and the content is flexible and can be updated regularly – at a cost.

Internet advertising has already made a significant impact in the business-to-business sector. It now ranks sixth among the business-to-business marketing media, just behind direct marketing. The Internet is rapidly becoming the medium of choice for communications with customers and for e-commerce. All estimates indicate that the business-to-business marketing will continue to increase at a very rapid pace.

Advertisements need to become more creative and impactful, and sites used in a more targeted way to ensure that Internet advertising is not viewed as intrusive and 'junk'. Used well, Internet advertising, e-mail and SMS media can add value to advertising campaigns by being able to provide two-way interactive communication being supported by and supporting other media used.

Advantages of the Internet as a communication tool	Disadvantages of the Internet as a communication tool
Can be very creative in producing an interactive message with sight and sound possible	Still quite low coverage – needs to be supported by other media
Very measurable. Can track movement from linked sites and within own site	Speed of access can be a problem with complicated ads. Hopefully resolved via Broadband usage's expansion
Message can be kept as a permanent reminder	Not yet mainstream in its usage – but developing fast

Citroen C3 microsite

Launching the C3 family car, Citroen realized it would have to branch out beyond traditional media channels to target women with young children. It worked with media agency OMD to tie up an ad partnership with AOL Time Warner, which enabled it to use two formidable ad platforms – AOL and IPC media – to target its audience.

AOL launched a branded micro site offering ideas and tips on getting the best day out to support the creative idea, 'Family Days Out'. IPC magazines also ran advertorials and produced its own guides for mums, which supported the micro site.

The campaign was a huge success – 110 000 AOL members visited the Citroen branded micro site with AOL the primary driver of traffic to www.citroenc3.co.uk.

Interactive Advertising Bureau UK – www.iabuk.net.

Insight

Braun raising purchasing intent

Braun wanted to promote the benefits of its Precision Sensor Blood Pressure Monitor by educating people about the risks associated with high blood pressure.

Digital agency i-level determined that the Internet is used as a source for learning about medical conditions, so it decided to associate Braun with sites that the target group used and trusted.

Advertorials were written in the style of each site. Amongst the over-50s primary target group brand awareness increased by 1017 per cent and purchase intent by 119 per cent.

Interactive Advertising Bureau UK – www.iabuk.net.

Brand image

Whereas a corporate image, as covered in Unit 7, refers to the organization as a whole, the organization may be the umbrella for a number of different brands. For example, Virgin is an organization with a corporate image and there are a number of Virgin brands, such as Virgin Vodka, Virgin One (financial services) and Virgin Trains, each with their own brand image.

In a similar way to the corporate image, the brands within that organization can create their own image, which can be communicated by any of the following:

- A name
- A term
- A design
- A trademark
- A symbol
- A logo.

In short a brand is a 'bundle of attributes' that combine together to create a recognizable personality that can help to communicate those attributes to the consumer and help them to link into the attributes that they buy into.

For example, Volvo = Safety = Keeping the children safe on the motorway.

With brands, consumers can be encouraged to associate certain attributes with a product. These attributes can be used to personify the brand and add value to a commodity. For example, it is much easier to promote Andrex toilet paper using the Andrex puppies than if the manufacturers could only talk about the product and show images of toilet rolls. It allows Andrex to distinguish the product from its competitors and allows the manufacturer to charge a premium price.

Branding was the platform for a recent 'Shape the Agenda' debate hosted online by the CIM (www.shapetheagenda.com). The debate raised the issue that trust in brands was not enough for today's media-savvy customer. They are starting to reject the artificial lifestyles and aspirations that brands communicate to them and they know when they are being sold something that does not have meaning in their lives. Apparently, to really connect with consumers, the Brands of today have to be *real*. *Real* people with *real* benefits for *real* consumers. This occurs in three stages:

- *First stage = TRUST* – Brands give the customer confidence that the product or service will deliver on its promise, for example Volvo = Safety, Remington = Closer shave or your money back.
- *Second stage = EMOTIONAL CONNECTION* – Many brands are known as trustworthy but they also have to connect emotionally with the customer, for example Mini, Marmite = MyMate.
- *Third stage = REALITY* – Many brands now engage at an emotional level. Brands have to move on to be relevant to real people and real life events, or they will die. For example Dove firming body wash = As tested on real curves, Bold Non Bio = Part of the fabric of life, Kellogg's Special K = Surely there's an easier way.

Cadbury have a corporate image of a caring yet progressive organization; they also have a large brand portfolio that fits into, and operates within, the corporate image. Each supports and communicates the other.

Corporate identity – online banking

Many financial services organizations have begun to offer online banking. The chance to reduce costs and reach new customer groups has been a major force behind this development. What is interesting, however, is that many have chosen to rebrand their online offering and create a separate identity.

The Halifax uses 'If', the Cooperative Bank 'Smile' and Prudential 'Egg'. Abbey National chose to use the name 'Cahoot' in order to reach a more affluent customer, one who, research shows, would not normally bank with Abbey National. The disguise of the online brand identity therefore enables organizations to use communications directed to particular customer segments without having to overcome the negative values associated with the parent brand.

Source: Fill, C. (2002) *Marketing Communications – Contexts, Strategies and Applications*, 3rd edition.

The media plan

Having considered the benefits and limitations of all elements of the communications mix within this unit and Unit 7, we now have to consider how these should best be combined. In practice this will be carried out by external agencies in response to a brief issued by the marketer (details later in this unit) but in an exam you may well be asked to recommend the best media combination to communicate in a given circumstance.

The starting point is considering who our target audiences are. In Unit 1 we looked at the range of audiences with whom we need to communicate; these will include:

- Distributors – who will need to stock up on our products in preparation for increased demand.
- Employees – who will need to know the details of our message to ensure that they can deal with customers effectively.
- End-users – the person who will actually go out and purchase the product/service being advertised.

To communicate to the trade we will implement a *push strategy* targeting the members within the distribution chain to ensure the product/service is *pushed* through the chain to the end-user. Methods include trade press, personal selling, public relations and trade sales promotions.

To communicate to the employees we will need to develop an *internal marketing plan* communicating via meetings, e-mails, conferences and newsletters.

To communicate to the end-users we will need to develop a *pull strategy* to communicate directly with the end-user to go and demand the product at the point of sale. Most of the above- and below-the-line methods will be considered for this market.

Media choice will be dependent upon the communications objectives and likely communications budget. Building awareness will mean use of more mass coverage media such as TV and press, but these may not be possible within the budget available. All of these requirements need to be considered when putting the media plan together.

Within the plan, different media will perform different functions. *Primary media* will fulfil the main communications objective, for example raise awareness, which means using TV or press. Often, these *primary media* are expensive ways to communicate. In order to provide cheaper frequency and to support the main media in a cheaper way we use *secondary media* such as posters and radio or other tools such as sales promotion to provide support to the main media.

Integrated communications is a further technique that can be built into the external communications plan, to ensure a more powerful message being communicated.

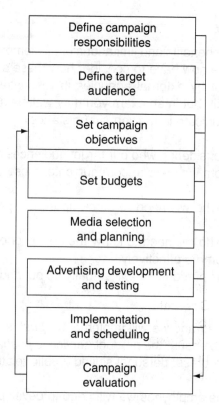

Figure 8.3 Advertising campaign planning
Source: Hughes and Fill (2004) CIM coursebook, *Marketing Communications*, Elsevier Butterworth-Heinemann

Integrated marketing communications

Put very simply, integrated marketing communications is about combining all the elements of the communications mix for the maximum communications impact. If we are to use four different media within a campaign, integrating those media by having a common message, strapline or cross referencing one to another, it will appear to the consumer that the combined campaign is bigger than the sum of the parts which combine to make it complete.

Integrated communications can go further by utilizing the corporate image as an umbrella device, thereby enhancing the brand message by linking one brand/service to the others within the portfolio, for example Kellogg's cornflakes carry the same connotations and message as Kellogg's Frosties. When the Kellogg's company launched 'Winders', a new product, into a new market the familiarity with the Kellogg's name reassured purchasers of the likely brand quality.

Integration is a move away from the traditional use of the promotional mix where marketers have treated the elements individually, almost in isolation of each other. It has been said, however, that:

'The marketer who succeeds in the new environment will be the one who co-ordinates the communications mix so tightly that you can look from [advertising] medium-to-medium, from programme-to-programme event, and instantly see that the brand is speaking with one voice.'

Quoting Spencer Plavoukas, chairman of Lintas (New York), and cited in Laurie Petersen, 'Pursuing Results in the Age'.

Key features of IMC

According to Shimp (2000), 'five key features underpin the philosophy and practice of integrated marketing communications'. These five features are:

1. *Affect behaviour* – According to Shimp, the goal of IMC is to *affect the behaviour* of the communications audience. This means that marketing communications must do more than just influence brand awareness or enhance customer attitudes towards the brand. Instead, IMC's objective is to move people to action. For example, McDonald's would want their customers to be aware of any special promotion they had ongoing with their hamburgers, however, what they really want is the customer to go and *buy* the hamburger.

2. *Start with the customer or prospect* – Shimp indicates that the second key feature of IMC is that the process starts with the customer or prospect and then works back to the brand communicator in determining the most appropriate and effective methods through which persuasive communications should be developed.

3. *Use any and all forms of contact* – According to Shimp, the key feature of this third element of IMC is that it reflects a willingness to use whatever communication outlets (contacts) are best for reaching the target audience, rather than pre-committing to any single medium or subset of media. So, direct-mail advertising, promotions at sporting and entertainment events, advertisements on packages of other brands, slogans on T-shirts, in-store displays and Internet pages are all potentially important contact methods for reaching present and potential customers.

4. *Achieve synergy* – Inherent in the definition of IMC is the need for *synergy*. All of the communication elements (advertising, point-of-purchase, sales promotions, events, etc.) must speak with a *single voice*; co-ordination is absolutely critical to achieving a strong and unified brand image and moving customers to action.

5. *Build relationships* – The fifth characteristic of IMC, according to Shimp, is the belief that successful marketing communications requires *building a relationship between the brand and the customer*. A relationship is an enduring link between a brand and its consumers; it entails repeat purchases and perhaps even loyalty.

Case history

Integration – Haagen-Dazs

Haagen-Dazs demonstrated the effective use of IMC when it entered the UK market. Ice cream was traditionally a seasonal children's food and the market had experienced little growth or innovation. The business strategy adopted was to create a new market segment, one that has become referred to as the super-premium segment.

The positioning intention was to present Haagen-Dazs as a luxury, fashion-oriented food for adults. To achieve the business goals, the entire marketing mix was co-ordinated: the product reflected high quality, the high price induced perceived quality, and the distribution in the launch was through up-market restaurants in prestige locations and five-star hotels where Haagen-Dazs was the only branded ice-cream on the menu.

The promotional campaign used celebrities from many walks of life as opinion leaders to create a word-of-mouth ripple effect. The quality of the media used and messages themselves reflected the same quality theme. The brand has since become firmly established and, although the arrival of Ben & Jerry's and other up-market brands has increased competition and rivalry, the brand remains distinctive and continues to use an integrated approach to its communications.

Source: Fill, C. (2002) *Marketing Communications – Contexts, Strategies and Applications*, 3rd edition, Pearson Education Ltd.

Benefits of Integrated Marketing Communications

What's the use of an excellent advertising campaign, full of creativity, if it's backed up by a second-rate website? The answer is, there is no use. The same principle applies to all the elements of the communications mix.

The key to success is synergy via integration of the individual elements of the communication mix. According to Pickton and Broderick (*Integrated Marketing Communications*, p. 70, 2001): 'Integration is not easy to achieve, but when it is achieved, the 4Es and 4Cs of Integrated Marketing Communications create the synergistic benefits of integration.'

The following are Pickton and Broderick's 4Es of integrated marketing communications:

o *Economical* – Least cost to the use of financial and other resources; not wasteful
o *Efficient* – Doing things right; competent, not wasteful
o *Effective* – Doing the right things, producing the outcome required, not wasteful
o *Enhancing* – Improve; augment; intensify.

The following are Pickton and Broderick's 4Cs of integrated marketing communications:

o *Coherence* – Logically connected; firmly stuck together
o *Consistency* – Not self-contradictory; in agreement, harmony, accord
o *Continuity* – Connected and consistent over time
o *Complementary communications* – Producing a balanced whole; supportive communications.

Case history

Charities and IMC – the National Society for Prevention of Cruelty to Children (NSPCC)

This campaign, which sought to stop cruelty to children, had a number of integrated communication characteristics. The ambitious targets, range of activities and the huge number of people involved needed an integrated marketing communications campaign to make it succeed.

To start with, there was a range of stakeholders involved: police, parents, teachers, businesses, agencies, the media and, of course, children. All needed to be part of the communications.

The strategy was based around two main phases. The first was a strong pull campaign directed at the public, designed to raise awareness of child cruelty, and the second step was action oriented. In parallel, there was a strategy designed to communicate with businesses in order to generate funds, goodwill and support.

The overall profile of the organization (NSPCC) was also to be raised and communications needed to ensure that the integrity of the organization and those associated with it was maintained. In addition, all communications had to be consistent. The promotional mix used to create a dialogue with the public included public relations, TV, posters, field marketing, direct marketing, direct mail, telemarketing and a website.

In the first phase, public relations were used at the initial stages of the campaign, to help create awareness. Public address systems at railway stations and airports were used as a reminder mechanism.

A national TV campaign, supported by posters, broke soon after the public relations in order to raise awareness and provoke within each individual the question, 'what can I do?' The message strategy was very emotional and used strong imagery to create shock and attention.

The heavy TV campaign looked to generate 600 TVRs, 8.5 per cent coverage at 7.1 OTSs. The supporting poster campaign used 48 sheets on 3500 sites designed to deliver 55 per cent coverage with 21 OTSs. Initial enquiries in response to this wave of communications were handled by an automated telemarketing bureau.

In the second phase, the aim was to provide the public with an answer to the question that the advertising had provoked, namely to sign the pledge and/or volunteer as a donor or fund-raiser. An envelope picked up on the TV creative treatment, repeating as a subdued background motif, the image of a nursery wallpaper with a teddy bear covering its eyes with its paws: 'Don't close your eyes to cruelty to children.' This was to be delivered to 23 million postboxes, as a doordrop campaign.

It was thought that the doordrop letter addressed as 'Dear Householder' might offend established donors. To avoid this, 160 000 best donors were sent an early warning letter in advance of the campaign breaking in order to get their support. Another million received personal letters just ahead of the doordrop. It was expected that the bulk of enquiries would come from the doordrop action and these were to be handled through personal telemarketing responses (inbound). The website was also adapted in order that it would be able to accept pledges.

In addition to this, the campaign utilized a call-to-action weekend with volunteers manning 2000 sites around the country, including most city centres, to remind and raise cash donations.

The promotional mix used to communicate with businesses involved sponsorship, the direct mail/ information pack and the Internet. Sponsorship deals were made available enabling businesses to align themselves more closely with the campaign. Microsoft has been closely involved with the NSPCC for a number of years and it acted as a prime mover, encouraging other businesses to pledge their support. The advertising for the campaign was sponsored by Microsoft. Other sponsorship and cause-related marketing packages were detailed in a toolkit distributed to other major organizations. Direct mail was also used to encourage businesses to make donations and electronic communications to promote pledges online.

At this stage, it appears that the co-ordinated promotional plan enabled a simple yet hard-hitting message to be conveyed to a substantial part of the nation. The publicity derived from the above-the-line work and the rigorous nature of the below-the-line activities suggest that many of the objectives have been achieved. However, results declared in December 2000 showed that in its first year, of the £75 million budget, less than half was spent on child-related services, suggesting to some that the Full Stop campaign was more about brand building.

Source: Fill, C. (2002) *Marketing Communications – Contexts, Strategies and Applications*, 3rd edition.

The communications industry

At the beginning of Unit 7 it was stated that the communications industry is an industry in itself with its own specialists and with its own jargon and ways of working. Most of the skills that are required for external communications are not possessed internally by the organization wishing to communicate with its customers (the client). The dynamic nature of the industry requires constant updating of skills, which even the most media-aware client would find difficult to keep pace with on a daily basis. Therefore, most clients employ external suppliers or agencies to provide these services.

Many of these suppliers concentrate on a particular area of the communications industry and the *above-* and *below-the-line* split can be evidenced in the areas of expertise that the suppliers work within. The communications industry is therefore made up of the following groups of companies:

- o Sales promotion agencies
- o Direct marketing agencies
- o Public relations agencies
- o New media such as Internet
- o Design/creative agencies
- o Production companies (of advertising copy and commercials)
- o Advertising agencies.

The last in the list are the largest and most influential members of the communications industry.

Many advertising agencies are global operators, either having their own offices across the major cities of the world or very close working links with other agency groups.

Often, a *Full service* agency will offer a menu of services covering all aspects of below- and above-the-line media to the client. The role of the full service agency will be to provide a complete advertising service incorporating planning, developing and producing creative work, and media planning and buying for above-the-line media.

They may also be able to provide, either directly or through liaison with other specialist providers, a full below-the-line service. It is the client's decision of the breadth and depth of the services they wish to use.

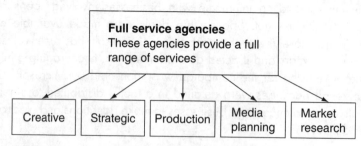

Figure 8.4 Full service agencies

Some clients with large-media spend like to use a different agency to plan and buy their media. These are known as *media independents*. By combining their buying power with one buying agency many clients feel they get better value for their communications spend, as the media buyer is able to gain greater negotiating power with control of larger budgets.

It is the role of the marketing department to ensure a mutually beneficial relationship is developed and maintained with all outside suppliers. The relationship with the advertising agency needs to take priority overall, as these are the specialists who ultimately have control of your external communications with the person most important to your organization – the customer. It is imperative that a close, confidential working relationship is developed between the marketing department and the account-planning department of the agency. Most work on projects start with the marketing department issuing a brief to the advertising agency.

The role of the brief

The brief is commonly used within the communications industry to communicate with external suppliers. As someone working within a marketing environment, you need to be aware of the areas covered by a brief. Below is an example of the headings that could be used in an advertising brief, these would need to be adapted for use with other agencies such as Public Relations or Sales Promotion agencies.

Every piece of communications activity will need to be briefed out to the appropriate agency to ensure they have all the necessary information to complete the planned task/campaign.

An example of advertising brief

Client details
In this section you would include the name of the client and the name of the product.

Background information
In this section you would include whatever relevant information you had about the following:

- The company
- The product
- The market
- The competition
- Previous advertising activity that has been undertaken
- Any relevant research data.

Objectives
In this section you should outline the objectives of the campaign/project. These should be written using the SMART mnemonic and be communications-related.

Target audience
In this section you should identify who the campaign is aimed at. It may be that a campaign could have primary and secondary target audiences.

Message to be conveyed

In this section you should identify what you want to say and how it should be said. This may include the unique selling proposition (the one key benefit that distinguishes the product/ service) and any substantiation for the claims being made. It should also determine the desired tone of voice and brand image that should be communicated.

Media

In this section, you should specify where you want to place the message. This may change once the creative message has been determined.

Timescale

Here you need to specify when the campaign is to run, its length and duration.

Budget

Here you should specify how much money is available for the campaign.

Miscellaneous information

In this section you should specify if there are any mandatory inclusions – for instance, you may have to mention membership of ABTA in an advertisement for a travel agent. You also need to include contact phone numbers or certain logos.

The agency should present their response to the brief within an agreed time limit (as detailed in the brief). This presentation will then form the basis of the campaign and a definitive plan will be developed through discussion between the agency and the client. In this way all internal and external parties should be fully on board and cognizant of all details relating to the campaign being undertaken.

 ## Activity 8.3

You work for a charitable organization that has been established to promote health and safety issues in the workplace. You would like to run a marketing campaign highlighting health and safety hazards in the workplace and the potential financial damages that companies could incur. You also want to send a poster featuring health and safety hazards to a list of companies that are held on your database.

Draft a brief for your Marketing Officer that indicates the objectives of the campaign, target markets and any other details that you consider the Marketing Officer should have.

Evaluating the effect of above-the-line media

In Unit 7, we considered what elements need to be evaluated when using below-the-line media and established that perception, changing attitudes and brand/service awareness are better than simply measuring sales which could have been affected by so many more external and internal influences.

We now move on to evaluate the use of above-the-line media which is often considered more important within an organization due to the higher absolute amounts of money that are spent on these promotional tools.

Accountants and marketers have long argued about the measurability and accountability of spending what is probably the single biggest expenditure that the organization makes.

Television is perhaps the most audited of the above-the-line tools. Day-by-day, minute-by-minute audience figures tell us who is watching at any time during the 24-hour day. Digital television has introduced two-way communication, so for the first time we can actually measure the audience's response by the number of 'red buttons' clicked. The inclusion of website addresses and direct response telephone numbers has also introduced a measurable aspect into television advertising.

But, in real terms, the role of advertising is to develop long-term brand values and the benefit of the expenditure can only be measured by a shift in customer attitudes over time. This is also true of all other above-the-line media in that although they all have a short-term measurable aspect to their use, their real value is as a strategic tool used consistently over time. It is not coincidence that some of the world's icon brands such as Coca-Cola, IBM and Kellogg's are also those that have consistently appeared in the top-ten-advertising spend tables over the last 10 years.

Is it the role of marketing research to measure these shifts over time on both a brand/service level and within the marketplace? It is really the only way we get a complete picture of how customers perceive our offering.

Press research takes place at regular points during the year, establishing the demographic profile and number of readers of particular newspapers and magazines. Coupons and other editorial based offers can be media coded to enable us to evaluate if the *Sun* or *Times* newspapers produce the most response. Again, links to websites and direct telephone numbers can be used to measure consumer response to a promotion.

Radio, cinema and outdoor advertising all have their means of measuring audience but measurement of response to our advertisement is limited to website and direct response mechanisms telling us what people think. Industry research can be linked to product usage in the Target Group Index (TGI) survey but this is used to plan media usage rather than evaluate. Marketing research is the only real tool we have here.

Internet research is in its infancy. We have the benefit of the ultimate measurability in terms of being able to measure click through but that only measures that someone has visited and not what actions they have subsequently taken or what they think. The use of e-mail questionnaires is growing but it remains to be seen how effective these become and how intrusive people think they are. More sites are inviting two-way communication and building in devices to measure where visitors have obtained the website address and other media they have seen. It will be interesting to see how this media which could offer unlimited ability to measure response develops over the next few years.

There will always be significant debate about the validity and effectiveness of the advertising pound. We now have to communicate to compete and we are now in possession of more information than ever before. We now have to learn how that information can be used effectively.

Hints and tips

You do need to have a basic understanding of how organizations communicate with their external customers. You need to have lots of examples of the whole range of promotional activities from your own experience to put into answers where appropriate. This is the reason behind your communications diary. Make sure you have examples of all of the promotional tools. Discuss the use of these with other students, on e-mail if not in class. The use of pertinent current examples in exams demonstrates your ability to apply and analyse the knowledge gained during the module.

As previously stated, it is unlikely that you would be asked a question where you just need to regurgitate facts about various media. It is more likely that you will be given a scenario and asked to suggest relevant promotion activities that could be used in that situation.

Finally, you should be able to draw up a brief that would assist an external supplier, such as a design, PR or Sales Promotion consultancy or advertising agency, to do their job of designing or writing for products or services in a given context.

You will not be asked questions on how computers work, the history of the Internet or about jargon connected with technological developments. However, you should be prepared to explain how technological changes are affecting the way that people and organizations do business and communicate.

Be prepared to answer questions that are set in a context of new media and technology but test you on other areas of the syllabus.

Summary

In this unit you have studied:

- The communications mix
- The role of various above-the-line promotional activities
- How branding works
- How to develop a media plan
- How to measure the effectiveness of various promotional activities
- The role of the brief.

Further study

If you require further exam practice then attempt Questions 5a and 1a(ii) on the June 2005 examination paper and Question (b) on the December 2004 paper. Go to www.cim.co.uk to access the Specimen Answers for these exam questions.

Bibliography

Fill, C. (2002) *Marketing Communications – Contexts, Strategies and Applications*, 3rd edition, Prentice Hall.

Hughes, G. and Fill, C. (2004) CIM Coursebook, *Marketing Communications*, Elsevier Butterworth-Heinemann.

Pickton and Broderick (2001) *Integrated Marketing Communications*, Pearson Education Ltd.

Shimp, T. (2000) *Advertising Promotions Supplemented Aspects of Integrated Marketing Communications*, Harcourt Inc.

unit 9

the role of information communication technology in customer communications

Learning objectives

In this unit you will:

- o Examine technological developments in the field of communication. See syllabus 3.14.

- o Look at the impact of the Internet and e-commerce on customer communication.

By the end of this unit you should be able to:

- o Explain the role of information and communications technology (ICT) in communications, including digital TV and interactive marketing (3.14).

- o Demonstrate an understanding of how ICT is used in customer service, for example, through the use of database (5.6).

This unit relates to the statements of practice:

Cb.1   Develop direct or indirect communications

Gb.1   Deliver effective customer service.

Study Guide

This unit provides an overview of technological developments and trends in communications. This unit covers indicative content areas 3.14 and 5.6 of the syllabus. This links in with 1.5 on the Marketing Fundamentals syllabus, which is covered in Unit 11 of the Marketing Fundamentals coursebook. In Marketing Fundamentals you were looking at how information communication technologies (ICT) affect all the elements in the marketing mix, whereas with customer communications you are looking at how technology specifically affects how you communicate with customers.

For further information for how this material in this unit will be examined, read the Exam Hints section at the end of the unit.

The unit will take you 3 hours to read and a further 3 hours to work through the activities.

Study tip

Because the speed of technological change is so fast, you should use this unit as a starting point to think about how ICT is changing the way you communicate. You need to extend your knowledge by accessing information outside the coursebook, in the quality press, specialist marketing magazines and specialist technical press.

You should also use the Internet to assess how effectively it can be used. Look up some websites that are of particular interest to you and surf the web for more information about technological developments. Look at the elements contained within your communications diary – how are websites being used within advertising and other forms of communication? One of many websites that you could visit is www.net-profit.co.uk, which is in the form of an online magazine and provides information about technology developments affecting business.

In addition, look at how technology plays a part in your day-to-day working environment. How has it changed the way you and your colleagues do your jobs? What are the advantages and disadvantages of technology in the workplace?

If you cannot access the Internet at home or at work, you could find access at your college or local library or even visit an Internet or cyber café, where you can pay for access.

How communication with customers is changing

Technological developments in communications are making massive changes to your personal and working lives. They are changing the way you shop, find out information, communicate with others inside and outside your organization; they are affecting the way organizations promote their products/services and even changing the way organizations do business with suppliers and distributors.

The introduction of computers has transformed the way information is handled and communicated. Data in a digital format means that when a document is typed any mistakes can be quickly corrected before it is printed out and information such as invoices, forms and previous letters can be indexed and retrieved easily.

Electronic point of sale (EPOS) systems allow retailers to record and monitor sales data. Linked to 'smart' card purchases, EPOS data provides organizations with detailed profiles of customer preferences and purchasing habits. Databases can be used to store information about customer purchase history so that mail-merged documents can be sent to customers with offers tailored to their needs. These areas are developed further within Unit 10 which covers customer care.

Even the way you use the telephone has changed. Mobile telephones mean you can be constantly in touch with colleagues and customers even when you are away from the office. People can leave voice mail and fax messages at any time, without having to rely on others to take the information down correctly. Businesses can deal speedily with massive telephone response through voice mail and automated processes.

We are now seeing the general use of videophone technology combined with mobile phones, which will change the way you communicate on the telephone, because your body language and facial expressions can be observed.

Laptop computers mean that you can work away from your desk or while on the move and still access or send information to your colleagues at the office. Wireless technology has removed the need for a docking station or physical connection to access the Internet.

The advent of electronic communication has probably had the most impact, and e-mail in particular has become so popular that for many people it is the main way they communicate with others. However, it is also true to say that new ways of working still have to develop acceptable ways of working and a sense of business etiquette guiding their use.

The ability to use the Internet has had a massive impact on the speed and cost of communicating, especially accessing information on websites or transacting business online.

You can also produce vast quantities of text, sound and picture information and store it on CD-ROM or in Digital Versatile Disk (DVD) format, which is an extremely interactive way for customers to access information. ISDN, and more recently broadband, lines have led to complex downloadable information being transmitted quickly and without the need for the now almost-redundant motorcycle courier.

Business strategy and new technologies – Blockbuster

The development of broadband technology demonstrates the impact that the digital evolution can have in terms of channel structure and the strategic shift that organizations need to make in order to remain competitive.

Films are traditionally marketed first through cinemas, then through video releases and finally through television (as video on demand, then pay-for channels and then terrestrial services). The full financial potential is realized through this channel structure. The development of digital technologies and Internet facilities offer certain advantages to film studios but it is not necessarily to their advantage to cut out these intermediaries. For example, not all films are successful and it is sometimes necessary to go 'straight to video' in which case the video rental store plays a significant part in the marketing channel.

Broadband services enable people to see films online, whenever and wherever they want. For organizations such as Blockbuster video rental stores, this development posed a major threat. With 65 million cardholders and 6300 stores worldwide (Oliver, 2000), the company needed to anticipate the changes in supply and demand. Blockbuster's response was to change the fundamental purpose or mission of the organization to be an overall entertainment provider for the home. The development of e-commerce facilities has been a key part of their strategy.

Central to this strategy was the non-exclusive digital download and video streaming rights agreement with the film studio MGM and independent film operator AtomFilms. This enables Blockbuster to showcase selected films on its website (www.blockbuster.co.uk). (This first step may lead to agreements with other studios and may well prove attractive to other entertainment-based companies that might enter into partnership deals.)

The website also enables people to purchase CDs, DVDs and games as well as the core product, videos. In addition, Blockbuster has used interactive technologies to provide a higher level of customer personalization in the services they offer. For example, its 'Blockbuster Recommends' facility suggests films to customers based upon their previous selections or a list of films rated *I hate it* or *I like it*. Another example of the personalization approach is the facility to suggest films to match the mood of the viewer. For example, if someone is feeling depressed then it may suggest a Gene Wilder film to cheer them up. All of these changes have been supported with a substantial off-line advertising campaign to inform current customers of the changes and to remind them of the Blockbuster proposition and values, to attract and persuade potential new customers to visit the site or a local store, and finally to reposition the brand by differentiating it from its previous position and its main competitors.

Effectively, the company has revised its strategy to accommodate changes in the environment, implemented the necessary changes to its offering, and then rebranded itself to be repositioned in the home entertainment business.

Source: Fill, C. (2002) *Marketing Communications – Contexts, Strategies and Applications*, 3rd edition.

As the introduction to this unit suggests, ICT has affected the way that we do business with our suppliers, distributors and customers. The changes can be categorized in the following four areas:

1. How we communicate with stakeholders to gain awareness of our message.
2. How we gather information from stakeholders to enable decision-making.
3. How we can prompt purchase through the use of ICT.
4. How we obtain measurable feedback from stakeholders in order to evaluate our communications processes.

We shall now progress through the unit looking at each aspect in turn.

Using ICT to communicate our message

Within Units 7 and 8 we looked at how websites and digital technology has been integrated into the above- and below-the-line media. We shall in this unit go into greater depth on those areas that were not covered, but as you read through this unit you may wish to refer back to those units also.

The main ICT platforms that we utilize to communicate with our stakeholders are:

o The Internet via our organizational website
o Electronic mail – e-mail
o Telecommunications
o Digital media
o Electronic Data Interchange – EDI

As we progress down this list, the communication tools become more useful in communicating B2B than B2C as the focus or target audience of the message becomes more specific. However, the combined use of all techniques is necessary in order to achieve the most effective communications.

Internet/Website as a communication tool

The Internet allows people from all over the world to communicate with each other via a global network of computers. The Internet can be used by organizations to do the following:

o Promote and sell products/services.
o Provide information 24 hours a day to people all over the world.
o Enable two-way communication via e-mail.
o Capture contact information when people register details on websites.
o Build ongoing relationships (through e-mail marketing or adding services/benefits to customers who use a firm's website).
o Improve the way businesses do business with each other.

The Internet is the core of the electronic communications methods leading to communication via e-mail and websites and Intra/Extranets. Websites are the electronic face of an organization and could easily be the first encounter between an organization and its potential customer and as such needs to provide that customer with all the information required.

Websites

Internet software is required to access the Internet, and once you have gained access you can visit an address on the World Wide Web. A famous website address is www.bbc.co.uk but you will see thousands of others on business cards, on product packaging and in advertising. Any organization or person can set up their own website. A website might contain information about the organization or about a person's particular interest or hobby. Information can be communicated using a combination of text, image and sound.

The first thing to make sure of is that your website address is:

o Recognizable to your stakeholders as being linked to your organization.
o Easily remembered and usable on other forms of communication.
o Likely to appear as one of the first found when search engines are being used.

Search engines such as Google and Yahoo! search for web addresses that most closely meet the criteria input by the user and then prioritize those in order of complexity. A one-word search will bring up numerous (often hundreds) potential matches. Internet users who are skilled in the use of Boolean operators to link words and make the search effective, can hone these down significantly. However, it is unlikely that our potential customer will possess these skills. It is important to remember that with so many interesting websites to look at we must make the job of finding us as easy as possible. Take for example the BBC website. The actual name of the BBC is British Broadcasting Corporation, but if we had a website address of www.britishbroad-castingcorporation.org then the search results would run into thousands and the required site may be way down the list due to its length. Therefore, by registering as www.bbc.co.uk the search is instantly more fruitful.

In designing a website you should consider what you are trying to achieve with it and consider who your audience are, what they will be interested in and what sort of equipment they are likely to have.

Although attractive design with sound and graphics can bring a site to life, you need to consider if your audience will have the latest equipment and a large screen to enable them to benefit from these facilities. One way to deal with this issue is to have an alternative version of your website so that those not using a conventional desktop computer can still access it without the sound and graphic effects.

It should be easy for visitors to get around or navigate your website. It also helps if it is easy to access and has a fast response. In order to achieve this you need to consider how customers approach purchasing your products. On many websites for clothes retailers they use the same descriptors and sections as in the store such as 'ladies wear', 'home wear' and 'children's clothing'. However, with more complex areas such as audio and visual electronic products a degree of knowledge is sometimes assumed and the categories for choice as to which will hold the product/service you require can be very difficult to assess.

Good web design also creates this directory structure for the information and establishes links between every page throughout the website. Hypertext will allow users to jump to other pieces of related information on the same site or to other sites anywhere in the world. It is also helpful if key words are highlighted and menus of information on the site are listed in bullet points for easy reading.

The contents need to be designed in a non-linear format because unlike a book, where people start at the beginning, a website can be accessed from any page. Books are also generally printed in a portrait format but websites are in a landscape format, where the width of the screen is greater than its height. Consequently, websites should be designed with a landscape format in mind.

The contents of a website can start off quite simply with some company and product information. However, it is important that the content and quality is updated. Whilst looking at websites for relatively large retailers in January it is possible to spot a number who are still highlighting their Christmas offers; this just gives the impression of a lazy organization.

The website could include an organization's corporate video and music to make it more interesting.

Websites are developed all the time, so the published word, the animated graphic, the broadcast picture, digital video clips and voice messages can all be presented and interconnected. It is becoming more popular as home-based computer technology becomes more updated to show your TV commercial and even post some of the outtakes as often happens on DVDs.

Activity 9.1

A good example of a website that meets all these criteria is the Ribena website www.ribena.co.uk.

Under four different sections dealing with Playground, Cinema, Classroom and Supermarket, the interactive website allows interaction by mother and child to a series of games and information-based pages. You can even access the old Ribena ads since 1959. This is an excellent site and provides you with a benchmark to compare other sites.

Websites should also be interactive and allow for an organization to build up a database of customers. One way to get people to register with their details is to restrict access to certain pages until details are registered. Another way is to build in some form of response, such as a 'freebie', if visitors to the site leave their details. For example, one law firm allowed visitors to their website to register their details if they wanted to receive an advent calendar highlighting areas of the law that companies could fall foul of. This allowed them to establish a list of firms interested in receiving legal advice that they could target with information.

It is important that not too many questions are asked at this stage. Because the Internet is a fast medium, users quickly tire of being in one place at a time. Research tells us that the average attention span per page is between 8 and 10 seconds. If they feel you are asking too many probing questions they will dip out of the process. All you really require is their e-mail address and age/family life stage profile to ascertain if a link would be beneficial.

For many companies it is not just about the number of 'hits' on the site but the way a site can generate leads or actually converts people to business when visiting the site. For example, the easyJet site is designed to allow people to make online bookings and the company measures the success of its website by the level of sales. In fact their online booking system is now so popular that 98 per cent of their bookings are transacted this way and instead of giving an online booking discount as they did originally, they now make an additional charge for booking by telephone.

If much of the above relates to website usage/design in relation to B2C communication in terms of the B2B relationship, then the website is more likely to focus on information relating to the performance, strategic direction and competitive positioning of the organization. Most have a section for job opportunities too! Many use websites to publicize their ethical or CSR stance. They are more about providing information for a wider range of stakeholders such as financial institutions, potential employees and perhaps government departments. This brings us to the type of information and purchasing decisions the customer may make via an online media compared to off-line.

Websites are much better at providing rational product- or service-related information to those traditional media methods. Remember in Unit 2 we looked at Cognitive, Affective and Conative attitudes. Web-based promotion is more likely to appeal to cognitive attitudes as it *informs and reminds* consumers of factual benefits. Traditional media are better at conveying more emotional messages to change or alter attitudes by *differentiating and persuading.* This is why neither should exist in a vacuum and clear links should be established. It is also important to remember that online promotion can prompt the customer to buy immediately which traditional media cannot.

We will investigate online fulfilment later on in this unit.

Within this text many websites have been used. These are listed below along with others that you may wish to access to help you with your studies:

o www.brandrepublic.com
o www.media.guardian.co.uk
o www.shapetheagenda.com
o www.thetimes100.co.uk
o www.iabuk.net
o www.FT.com
o www.IPA.co.uk
o www.ebusiness.uk.com
o www.tbcresearch.com
o www.asiasource.org
o www.marketresearch.org.uk
o www.nielson-netratings.com
o www.streamwave.co.uk
o www.broadvision.com

To access some particularly navigable sites try:

o www.markwarner.co.uk (easy to use, innovative, well-designed, clear and informative also won a 'best travel site' award in 2000).
o www.cityorganiser.com (helps busy business travellers find out about hotels, car hire, restaurants, healthcare and leisure options also with bookable services).

Interesting websites that you could access to see how the web can be used on a more global platform are:

o www.Indya.com (one of India's top three Internet portals)
o www.penang.net (about the island of Malaysia).

Website costs

These can vary from a very simple website that would cost around £1000 to set up, to those costing tens of thousands of pounds which can handle online shopping. An average brochure-type, which informs the user but does not allow online purchase, currently costs around £5000 to be designed and set up.

However, many software packages are now available, such as Microsoft FrontPage and Macromedia's Dream weaver, to ease the learning curve necessary to design a website. This is beneficial to small businesses who cannot justify these development costs but arguably may benefit the most by an online presence.

Recently, the interactive advertising bureau (IAB) UK has developed, with the guidance of media owners and advertising agencies, a universal advertising package (UAP) of six key formats, which they hope will start to become a global standard adopted by all for web-based advertising. Already adopted in the US, the IAB hope that widespread use will occur shortly in the UK market. The product is designed to make the production of online ads more cost-effective for all.

Electronic mail

Electronic mail or e-mail is a method of sending text files from one computer to another, which allows you to send messages across the world in seconds. One way to send and receive messages is to set up an e-mail account with an Internet service provider (ISP).

Dependent upon your ISP you can access your e-mails from just your own computer or from any Internet access point across the world. Many people have multiple e-mail addresses to meet all their social and business needs. It is widely accepted to communicate to most business contacts via e-mail – giving the speed and cost benefits of the telephone but the advantages of the written word.

However, it is more than a messaging service because text, graphics, video and sound can be sent and received across the Internet.

The more detailed aspects of what an e-mail needs to contain as a means of communication is covered in Unit 5. We shall be looking here at how we can use e-mail to develop our communications with our stakeholders.

Cost comparison of e-mail with other forms of communication

Table 9.1 shows the approximate cost of sending a 10-page document from the UK to the USA.

Table 9.1

Cost	Communication method	Time taken to receive message
£1.56	First class post	5–7 days
£2.00	Fax	5 minutes
£30.00	Courier	2 working days
15p (cost of local call)	E-mail	Almost instant

But the issue is not solely related to the cost of sending a message. E-mail has replaced more traditional ways of working, which results in further cost savings. Within the B2C context, this helps in a number of ways, for example banks are using the Internet to add value to the service they provide to current customers by allowing them to transfer money from one account to another, pay bills online and find out their bank balance.

Your local doctor may soon be able to improve their service to you by allowing you to order repeated prescriptions via the Internet, which could then be e-mailed to you under password-protected protocol. This will not only save your time but also free up busy receptionists to deal with people waiting in the surgery.

It is already possible to let your utility company know your meter readings – doing away with the poor meter reader who always seemed to call on a wet and windy day.

Table 9.2 UK e-mail penetration by age

Over 54	11%
45–54	17%
36–44	24%
25–34	25%
Under 25	23%

217

Table 9.3 UK e-mail users by socio-economic group

AB	35%
C1	36%
C2	16%
DE	13%

The possibility of change resulting in cost saving is even more relevant in a B2B context. The availability of the Internet combined with the protocols of e-mail has totally reshaped communication between an organization and its suppliers.

Intranet/Extranet

An intranet is an information system that is used to communicate internally within an organization. This allows all employees within an organization, regardless of how many sites they are located at or the geographical location of those sites, to communicate almost instantaneously. This effectively negates the need for memos as we highlighted in Unit 5, but also allows for electronic transfer of any electronically held information such as reports, letters and data to be transmitted as attachments. The organizational address book allows users to select by name without putting in the whole e-mail address.

An extranet extends the intranet capacity to suppliers and distributors. Along with other approaches detailed below, this can replace time-consuming and costly invoice raising and sending out cheques, by fully automating these processes alongside many others. Different media forms can be accommodated with photographs, videos and artwork being transferable.

Insight

Inland revenue – Getting the message across

It is particularly important for a customer service organization to develop good communication channels with its stakeholders, especially its customers and employees. The Inland Revenue operates in a fast changing environment with its culture changing to become more customer-focused. It has assumed responsibility for new areas of work and developed modern internal and external systems to enhance multi-channel Hints and Tips.

It is vital that responsive informed employees identify and meet their customers' needs as quickly as possible. In order to meet this challenge, the Inland Revenue has embraced a range of communications methods that take full advantage of the latest technology.

Core to these communications systems are online communications. Internal e-mails are as part of the internal communications push to ensure all staff are fully briefed on all aspects of their workload.

Online communications also allow consumers to complete their tax return, claim tax credits and transact a variety of business with the Inland Revenue directly online, thereby saving a lot of time. An important advantage to this method is that ongoing 'help' is provided by pop-up help facilities. This is a cheap, quick and efficient method of communication.

www.thetimes100.co.uk.

Electronic data interchange (EDI)

For many organizations the Internet will enable them to source parts, reduce waiting times for stock, cut the storage area they need for stockholding, and will mean cheaper distribution costs.

For example, a network of franchised garages had their purchasing organized centrally using the Internet. This now means that if a franchise operator uses an exhaust from stock, this information is automatically communicated to the exhaust manufacturer, who can then re-stock the garage automatically. Whilst EDI is strictly a communications protocol, which is largely being replaced by tools such as Extensible Markup Language (XML), it is still often applied to other forms of data interchange. Business process and business communication are also transformed so that there are fewer telephone calls and less paperwork, which has a great impact on the efficiency of the organization.

Electronic data interchange is also used to keep track of inventory. For example, FedEx have opened up the 'back room' to business customers so that they can order courier service and track a package. This adds real value to their business relationship with customers. It also means that staff are not tied up with routine queries about the whereabouts of a package but have more time to spend dealing with orders and more complex forms of enquiry.

In organizations with a large number of transactions such as grocery supermarkets the EPOS systems which record the quantity and price of what the customer has purchased on their individual account till receipt can also then feed the same information into the EDI system to keep a check on stock control. If EPOS tells the stock control system that 58 of the 60 tins of beans have been sold, the EDI system can then activate an order for more beans. This results in the large grocery organizations such as Tesco and Sainsbury's having to dedicate less storage space to warehousing freeing up more space to sell customers more products.

The EDI can, therefore, improve a company's ability to work with others in terms of sharing documents and other information, which improves strategic partnerships on a worldwide basis.

ISDN and Broadband

An ISDN or Broadband line allows your computer to connect to other computers much more quickly and enables much faster transfer of large documents than a normal telephone line. This technology has been successfully used in teleworking, where home workers can source information from the office fast and effectively.

An ISDN can also be used for:

- Sending information with graphics
- Videoconferencing
- Broadcasting
- Telemarketing/call centres.

But it is not just Internet-based ICT that has improved our ability to communicate with our stakeholders. Telecommunications in terms of telephone systems and mobile usage has also delivered significant benefits.

Telecommunications

There have been massive developments in the field of telecommunications.

Automated switchboards are now within the reach of even the smallest firms. This enables customers to leave a message for a particular person or department through voicemail. This facility also enables the organization to pre-select the response, so that if the customer requires information they are put through to department 1, for example; and if the customer wants to order goods, they are put through to department 2 and so on.

Voicemail can enable companies to cope with large volumes of calls and should mean that customers are dealt with more efficiently and effectively. However, automated customer-handling systems do not always improve customer communications. Customers become irritated and angry when they have to go through several button-pushing processes and still end up waiting a long time before their call is answered. A customer being put through to someone's out-of-date voicemail does not communicate a very efficient message.

The other issue for customers is that if they have a non-standard problem or query, they often find it extremely difficult to speak to a real person who can help them. There always needs to be a 'speak to a human' facility, and this needs to be highlighted to the caller fairly early on into the call.

Mobile phones and m-commerce

Mobile phones are getting smaller and more powerful. They can be used to access e-mails. The newest Nokia communicator is not much bigger than a mobile phone but opens up into a keyboard mode. It doubles as a mobile office with Internet access, e-mail and telefax, and can receive pictures from digital cameras. The 'Blackberry', which also allows all these functions and serves as a diary too, is currently the businessman's dream. Camera and video technology are now incorporated within mobile phones facilitating face-to-face communication via a telephone connection to a recipient capable of receiving it.

Wireless Application Protocol (WAP) mobile phones can be used to access the Internet. This technology has encouraged m-commerce, which means that people can shop online on their mobile telephones or access their bank accounts. In a B2B environment, mobile engineers can be redirected and can access information almost instantaneously.

The recent introduction of 3G mobile telephone technology meant that the equipment is even more powerful and will be able to download pictures. These mobile telephones have bigger screens and can be used for videophone calls, to send e-mails with photographs attached, play online games with much better picture quality, and conduct shopping and banking transactions more easily.

The use of text messaging (SMS) and mobile technology as part of an integrated communications campaign can be investigated further in Unit 7 of this coursebook.

Mobile marketing is predicted to be huge but up until now, marketers have had to learn how to create concise mobile advertising campaigns with only 160 characters to play with. However, the new generation of mobile phones mean promotional videos/photos/links with websites can be used to target the key segments. The main issue for marketers appears to be not to inundate people with messages but to get them to give their permission and provide interesting and relevant advertising that requires a response such as ringing a telephone line or looking at a website. Therefore, this technology is more appropriate to retention than acquisition marketing.

In summary, the main benefits of e-communication can thus be encapsulated:

- Cost saving
- Quick two-way communication enabled
- Global barriers reduced
- Better logistics management
- Linkage to off-line media – greater integration possible.

 Activity 9.2

Explain how developments in ICT have changed the way that people communicate with internal and external customers. Provide examples of how the Internet is being used to add value, improve customer service or change the way business is being carried out.

Insight

Millward Brown – marketing research online

Millward Brown have launched a new online research tool called ActiveSelector that allows companies to interview hundreds of respondents in their target market to produce instant marketing solutions.

ActiveSelector combines Millward Brown's brand communication expertise with insight agency Invoke Solutions Dynamic Survey to complete online research in a day.

Already launched in the US, ActiveSelector is used for screening concepts in the early stages of development, such as advertisements, packaging, direct mail, web pages and anything that can be shown on still images or video.

Gordon Pinkcott, head of Client Services at Millward Brown, said, 'By offering the robustness of quantitative research with flexibility, interactivity and direct client involvement, ActiveSelector exemplifies Millward Brown's unique offering of bespoke solutions to clients exact requirements, utilising the most cutting edge technology.'

Dynamic survey was introduced by Invoke to harness the power of the Internet to generate immediate insight into new products and concept ideas.

www.brandrepublic.com – 31st January 2005.

Using ICT to aid decision-making

Having evaluated how ICT can help to communicate with our customer and make that communication more effective, the next stage is to consider how we can utilize the information that we collect via the Internet/extranet and website sources.

Database marketing involves using computers to capture and store data relating to customers' past-purchase history. For instance, if a mail-order company sells clothing, each customer file is computerized so that contact (name, address, postcode) and purchase details (type of item, size, colour preference, price, etc.) are stored. All the departments in the firm can access this information quickly and cheaply. For example, the accounts department may need to access it to chase payment and the marketing department could use it to target offers to customers. So, customers who buy clothes for people under a certain height would only be sent information relating to the 'petite' range of clothing based on their past-purchase behaviour.

Loyalty schemes work on a similar principle: the large supermarkets can use their EPOS not only for stock control purposes but also to target offers that are relevant to customers. For example, a customer who regularly buys dog food would not be sent money-off vouchers for cat food to keep the customer 'loyal'.

Customer relationship management systems can work on a similar principle. The key idea is that each customer is treated as an individual and, in particular, organizations can use computer software to segment their markets, identify the most profitable customers and segments and 'cherry pick' them because of their customer lifetime value (CLV). For example, basic current account holders are not particularly profitable customers for banks as compared to those who have (or potentially want) loans, mortgages, insurance business and pensions. The idea behind CLV is to spend marketing time and effort on those customers who are the most valuable. The interrogation and use of this raw data allow the more sophisticated CRM mechanisms to be put into place (covered in greater depth in Unit 10) and the organization to concentrate their marketing efforts by rewarding the most profitable customer segments with rewards that actually meet their needs.

Data warehousing techniques can also be used through the use of bought databases. These used to have a negative perception as they often contained out-of-date details and incorrect addresses. However, improved technology has resulted in the 'cleaning' of databases becoming a much easier process. There are also some large databases out there that are activated regularly due to customer usage. Consider how useful the database of mobile phone users or credit card holders could be to any organization.

Computer software can also be used in call centres where staffs are handling high volumes of calls. For example, when credit card customers ring a call centre and quote their postcode or account numbers, customers' file details quickly appear on the call handlers' computer screens, enabling them to deal with a query or make a transaction.

Database systems can also be used to improve internal communication as a way of creating a 'knowledge management' system. For example, a firm of accountants can have all their customer files in a centralized database so that staff have access to the 'company's shared experience' of how deals and projects have been managed by others within the firm. It also works when the firm wants to cross-sell their services to a client. It is much easier if details from the client's dealings with the taxation department are easily accessible by another accountant who might be advising the client on business acquisition, for example.

Data 'mining' is when sophisticated systems are used to track customer/client files in order to identify products/services that could be targeted in the future. It is reasonable to assume that an online order for maternity wear will also mean the customer is shortly to be interested in baby clothes and nursery equipment. By packaging needs and directing sales promotions at specific times during the family life-cycle stages, we can raise the CLV and keep customers loyal.

However, we must also consider the other more negative effects of effectively removing verbal communication opportunities with our customer base. Not all of our customers are adept at pushing buttons and using voice-activated systems. Some customer queries do not fall into the categories the voice-activated system gives as options. It is important that we do not totally replace verbal communication but enhance the customer experience via the use of combined communication methods, using the best that technology can offer alongside our well-developed business processes that have proved successful in the past.

Customer Communications can be linked to the data to communicate a very specific message to a very specifically targeted market – we shall move on to see how.

How we can prompt purchase through the use of ICT

The purchasing of goods and services online is known as e-commerce. This is different to e-business which covers the area of business transactions as detailed earlier in this unit when the use of intranets and extranets was covered.

E-commerce then covers the online promotion and purchasing of goods and services. In terms of promotional use, websites as promotional tools were covered in Unit 8. However, more tactical use of the below-the-line media can be further investigated.

Online sales promotion is often used to prompt purchase as soon as the customer has completed the search for the item. Registration to many sites automatically generates a voucher to be used against the first purchase. Amazon regularly give free post and packing to orders over £15 or £20. Promotions can be linked to other products – registration on the Guardian website produces a £15 voucher for use with Virgin wines!

Direct marketing is possible via both e-mail and text/SMS messaging. Whilst direct marketing by e-mail is suffering from legislation restricting the use of spam and virus software making the rejection of unsolicited e-mail possible, SMS messaging is growing significantly. By accessing databases that sell ringtones and games, organizations in certain categories have a ready-made receptive market. Ethical considerations need to be considered; many SMS purchases unwittingly tie people into a regular purchase from which they have to unsubscribe.

Case study

Royal Mail

Royal Mail is working closely with a number of online businesses, most notably Amazon.co.uk, for whom it is the contracted delivery arm.

Online retailers face the challenge of creating a real brand in an e-world and this is where Royal Mail can add value to the experience of many brands by becoming the trusted carrier for online orders.

The revolutionary software application 'Decide and Deliver' was launched to make home shopping easier. The service acts as a web-based electronic postman. It saves consumers time when shopping online and provides them with a range of extra delivery options. In addition, the Local Collect service allows consumers to choose delivery to a post office when ordering from participating retailers.

CIM – Knowledge Hub – www.cim.co.uk.

E-commerce

E-commerce is purchasing online using either the Internet or a mobile phone to access websites, where online purchasing is possible. As highlighted earlier, transactional websites are expensive to maintain and therefore only utilized by larger organizations. Shopping online using your phone offers organizations a cheaper alternative as does Interactive TV which we will cover later; these two methods are not so dependent upon costly website updates and can even be linked to non-transactional sites for information gathering.

Virgin offer mobile shopping from your mobile phone across a range of products from electrical goods, wine, music, DVDs and games. Online auction sites such as eBay continue to grow and increase the range of goods and services that they sell online, with the details of the goods and services effectively posted by the seller.

Online shopping has grown mostly in areas where the product is fairly standard in its approach. For example, if a customer sees a book they like in a bookstore at full price then they are likely to go home and look at Amazon to see if they can get it cheaper. Music, DVDs and video games and toys are also often purchased online, as the purchaser is usually aware of precisely what they need.

Food shopping is also possible online. Tesco, Sainsbury's and Waitrose (www.waitrose.com) all offer online grocery purchasing and delivery for around £5. Although it can be a lengthy process to begin with, once the customer has built up a 'regular' list of products the customer can then update by including and excluding items on a weekly basis.

Service-based products have also sold successfully online. Car, home and travel insurance are commonly purchased if, not online, then by telephone.

The Internet has also prompted price and product transparency. Comet's website prompts the user to input a product type and price range and then compares the product benefits of those that meet the criteria. www.kelkoo.com also allows the user to search for the cheapest price to buy a specific electrical product as long as you know the make and model number. The site can even provide hyperlinks to the cheapest supplier to prompt the purchase.

Other product categories, where size or design forms part of the decision-making process, are not so popular as people cannot try out the product. There was a promise of body scanning software where we could ascertain which size was best and try it on, on-screen, but this has not progressed much further.

The last part of the process is the transaction itself. If the purchaser has not already input details to register, then this is the area where customer details such as name, address and so on will be collected. The key aspect of communication here is the display of the 'secure transaction' symbol, which is only given to organizations that meet stringent online financial criteria. Credit cards now have an additional three-digit code on the reverse signature strip, and this should be used as an additional security measure.

Fulfilment after ordering needs to be documented and the order confirmed. This is usually by return of e-mail and acts as the customer's security blanket in case anything may go wrong. This e-mail should confirm the items and prices of the goods/services ordered and the promised delivery date. Details of how they should communicate if the order is not fulfilled on the promised date should also be given, preferably with an alternative form to online communication given (e.g. a telephone number).

Where possible, it is better to allow the customer to track their own order. This can be done by choosing a carrier such as FedEx or Royal Mail special delivery where a docket number can be entered on the websites of those organizations to track the progress of the order. Where this cannot be achieved, the organization should update the purchaser by e-mail if any changes to their order arise. The best rule to apply here is tell them the bad news before they find it out for themselves.

If the order is not fulfilled, then the situation should be handled for what it is – a customer complaint, and the organization then needs to have detailed systems in place to deal with and rectify that situation (see Unit 10).

The payment of delivery charges or postage and packing is also a hot debate at present. Customers are growing wary of the standard cost-levied approach and of online ads, which do not include the cost of postage and packing. Customers will not purchase online if the delivery charge is a high percentage of the item price. Some organizations such as Amazon allow free delivery on large orders but this can benefit the occasional rather than regular user. Loyalty points can be earned with some retailers to soften the effect of delivery charges. It will be interesting to see if organizations start to drop these charges.

The last form of purchasing online is via Interactive TV.

Interactive Digital TV

Interactive TV requires a telephone link into either a cable TV provider or Digital television service such as BSkyB.

Interaction with programmes such as *Who wants to be a Millionaire* and the Renault Megane advertisement have been discussed in previous units. Purchasing online is achieved in one of the two ways.

First, there are the TV channels such as QVC, which effectively televise the personal selling process. Purchases can be made by 'pushing the red button' and registering your purchase. The address and payment details are already known via the Satellite or Cable subscription. If alternative details are required these can be input with a wireless keyboard that can be purchased separately (approximately £20), or alternatively the whole transaction can take place by phone. Fulfilment follows the same rules as online purchasing.

This method is not really used by reputable companies. The selling environment can be perceived as inferior and there are concerns about the level of consumer spending on credit cards, which this method of communicating encourages people to do, hence the ethical concerns.

The second method is to access the interactive section of the digital provider. Here, there are many games and online shopping opportunities, again how this is perceived by the consumer on an ethical stance is not clear. Some games carry a charge to use, which the parent may be pressured into paying, or even find themselves out of pocket due to a technology-savvy child.

Interactive or DRTV needs to be used with caution and a degree of CSR. The example below of Cancer Research UK shows how this can be achieved.

Cancer Research UK in DRTV fund-raising push

Cancer Research UK, the largest independent cancer research body in the world, is unveiling its first direct marketing campaign since it formed in December 2001.

The campaign, through WWAV Rapp Collins, uses direct response TV supported by a 1 million-strong mailing. The advertisement urges viewers to call the freephone number and pledge £2 a month.

It marks the first wave of fund-raising activity for the charity, which was formed following the merger of Imperial Cancer Research Fund and The Cancer Research Company.

The advertisement features people who have lost family members and close friends to cancer. As they look into a mirror, an image of a loved one suffering from cancer appears. In one advertisement, a mother sees a reflection of her sick daughter in the mirror but the advertisement closes on a positive note, with the child, who has successfully fought the disease, appearing fit and healthy.

The approach is in line with the current above-the-line advertising through Abbott Mead Vickers BBCO which uses family photographs and home video footage.

The DRTV advertisements air on Channel 4, Channel 5, satellite and cable stations in 90- and 60-second versions.

Source: Marketing, 21 February 2002, p. 12.

Measurability

The true benefits of all ICT-based communications methods are the immediate measurability of the customer response. Including a website address on an off-line promotional message can then generate online traffic which can be measured in terms of hits (people logging onto the website) and click-throughs (where they click into other areas of the website thereby demonstrating greater interest). The differing response to each message can also be recorded. If a sales promotional message gets more hits than the normal brand building one, then you know your market is becoming price-sensitive. Getting the consumer to register details can help to assess which segments are more price sensitive than others.

Direct marketing via e-mail is also easily measurable by differing message. If you send out 10 000 e-mails and get a response from 1000 then it is pretty easy to work out that you have a response rate of 10 per cent. This can be benchmarked against other messages and off-line media.

We can even measure where people lose interest. If they progress through the purchase up to the final payment and then stop, it may be reasonable to assume that they are either unsure of the security aspects of finalizing that purchase or there is something about that page which is confusing them. Either way, it is easy enough to redesign the page and measure its suitability in the same way.

Measurability of communications benefits the marketing communications process enormously and helps us to more closely target the most effective message.

Summary

In this unit you have studied:

o The role of Information and Communications Technology in communications.
o How communication with customers is changing.
o How e-business is evolving.
o How ICT can be used to improve customer communications.
o What makes a successful website.
o The role of e-commerce, e-business and e-marketing.

Hints and tips

Within an exam scenario you will not be required to have full detailed knowledge about Internet processes and computer jargon. You are expected to understand how the Internet can change the buying decision-making process and how communication can be adapted to take account of those differences. It will help you to have a degree of experience of different websites and the different ways in which they can be used to either supply information, engage the viewer or to sell goods and services online.

If you have never undertaken any form of online purchasing and do not feel confident in doing so then talk to people who have and find out about the positive and negative aspects of their experiences. If someone has encountered a negative experience then consider how communications can put that right in the minds of the consumer.

Questions will often incorporate new media in the context of solving communications problems.

Further study

If you require further exam practice then attempt Question 6(b) on the June 2005 examination paper. Go to www.cim.co.uk to access the Specimen Answers for this exam question.

Bibliography

Fill, C. (2002) *Marketing Communications – Contexts, Strategies and Applications*, 3rd edition, Prentice Hall.

Hughes, G. and Fill, C. (2004) CIM Coursebook, *Marketing Communications*, Elsevier Butterworth-Heinemann.

unit 10
customer service and customer care

In this unit you will:

o Examine the changing context of customer needs. See syllabus section 5.3.

o Appreciate the role of communications in implementing customer care. See syllabus section 5.4.

o See how customer communications help build customer relationships. See syllabus section 5.4.

o Learn how to plan and establish a customer care programme. See syllabus section 5.5.

o Look at why customer care systems sometimes fail. See syllabus section 5.5.

By the end of this unit you should be able to:

o Explain the concept of customer care and its importance in consumer, business, not-for-profit and public sector organizations (5.1).

o Explain the importance of quality and customer care and methods of achieving quality (5.2).

o Explain the relationship between customer care, customer focus and relationship marketing (5.3).

o Explain the importance of obtaining customer feedback and devising contingencies for dealing with customer complaints (5.4).

o Describe how to plan and establish a customer care programme (5.5).

Study Guide

This unit develops the customer theme from Unit 1 and focuses on how customer communications are a vital part of good customer care and customer service.

The unit covers indicative content areas 5.1–5.5 of the syllabus. This unit also links to the Marketing Fundamentals syllabus, in particular, with indicative content 1.1.1. and 1.4.2.

Both syllabuses deal with the issues regarding adding quality to product/service delivery in order to close the gap between customer expectations and their experience, and the importance of creating a dialogue with customers to promote a long-term relationship. However, the emphasis in the Customer Communications syllabus is on the practical aspects of improving interaction with customers. Consequently, this unit deals with how customer service can be improved to meet customer expectations by improving customer interaction and communication with customers.

There is further reading on the areas covered in this unit in Unit 1 and Unit 9 of the Marketing Fundamentals coursebook.

You should take 2 hours to read the unit and a further 2 hours to complete the activities. At the end of this unit you are also directed to relevant examination questions at the end of the book.

Study tip

At the end of this unit you could check what procedures are in place within your own organization for dealing with customer care issues. Consider how these are implemented and identify any possible improvements.

Your own experiences will also guide you. As well as being a student you are a consumer and it is inevitable that you will have experienced less than perfect customer service. Where did the gaps between your expectations and experience occur? How did the organization deal with the issues?

Consider also which organizations you have relationships with. How does that relationship operate and how frequently is contact made? Are the benefits of the relationship measurable or do you find the relationship intrusive?

Changing customer needs

It is fitting that in the final unit of this coursebook we return to the issues raised within Unit 1. In order to care about customers and build relationships with them, we need to have established a true customer focus within the organization. Only by an organization being customer-focused can the organization be sure that the customer care programme and service levels delivered are in line with customer wants and needs.

However, recognizing customer needs and building them into the product/service offering is an ever moving feast. We have also established within this coursebook that consumers' needs are constantly changing and an organization always needs to anticipate how they will need to react to those changes, in order to develop a system for measuring customer experience versus expectations. We are told that we should be aiming for customer 'delight' rather than 'satisfaction' but need to establish what that means in the consumers' minds and what systems we can put in place to ensure we deliver.

Customers are far more likely to complain nowadays. This is simply due to the fact that, in general terms, consumers travel more widely and are more educated than ever before. Many consumers have developed sophisticated tastes and have higher expectations, having experienced superior service during their travels.

Previous research by the Henley centre established that more than half of consumers have complained in the past and expect to complain at some point in the future. The research defined the areas where complaints arise; 56 per cent of people said they complained in person about poor services or faulty goods over the past year, 35 per cent going on to tell a family member or friend about their experience, just under 50 per cent complained by phone. Ethical considerations and unhealthy products were also cause for concern with, between 15 and 20 per cent of customers had concerns about it.

However, things are changing slowly and organizations have begun to realize that they operate in a more competitive and litigious environment, where they must respond to consumer demands. Most organizations also realize that it is far easier and cheaper to retain current customers than it is to cultivate new ones. Moreover, research shows that dissatisfied customers tend to spread the news of their bad experiences very quickly – something that affects not only an organization's image but also the bottom line in the long run.

So generally customers are becoming more powerful, less easy to please and more likely to complain to a range of people. Some organizations have decided to tackle this problem head-on by focusing on meeting the growing demands of customers and developing more innovative customer-focused solutions to their needs. However, by developing product/service solutions the organization merely succeeds in showing the rest of their industry the direction they should be taking and any new innovation is quickly joined by a host of 'me too's'. The real sustainable competitive advantage (SCA) or differentiating factor is how we communicate with our customer in order to build a relationship that results in retention and loyalty. Units 7 and 8 detail how we can use the promotional mix to ensure the product/service message is communicated to our existing and potential customers. This unit will deal with how we treat those customers once they have bought into our product/service concept and how that relationship can be built into a mutually beneficial one that will stand the test of time.

This can be achieved in many ways. The term 'Customer Delight' is now used to demonstrate that organizations seek to add value to the transaction to more closely meet the customer needs. For example, an electrical retailer who previously used his own drivers to deliver goods such as washing machines and dishwashers now puts the work out to contractors, who ensure that they arrange delivery to suit the customer. They now give time slots within which the delivery will take place, so customers do not have to take a whole day off work to wait for a delivery – how long has the patient consumer been waiting for that one!

Customer focus is designed not only to recognize the changing needs of existing customers but also to attract new ones.

With existing customers, retention will increase the Customer Lifetime Value (C.L.V.). They will become positive advocates for the brand, hopefully increasing the frequency and the volume of their purchases. Any new areas we move into are likely to be adopted by contented existing customers leading to further growth. Tesco is a supreme example of this where growth from non-food areas, such as insurance, have given them the resources to compete in the lower margin grocery area.

The other area for growth is new customers, gained either in existing markets or by moving into new market segments or geographical areas. Customers will soon recognize that a truly customer-focused organization can meet their needs in different ways, encouraging adoption and brand switching. Virgin operate in this way, taking the brand values they have established in markets they operate within into new markets. When they moved into the Health and Fitness market with Virgin Active Gyms, they managed to get existing gym users to swap due to the different product offering. The main difference in this case was they welcomed children – hence aligning themselves to the high volume family market.

In switching into entirely new markets and establishing a global position, it is important not to assume that customer needs will be the same. Market research will be required to assess the degree to which the product or service will need to be adapted to meet the new markets needs. For example, Virgin may need to focus on different peak times such as siesta periods when workers may wish to spend that free time having a swim.

Customer retention equals growth, because happy existing customers influence potential customers. In order to achieve that state, we need to have systems and procedures in place to create the environment the customer is seeking. We shall approach these concepts in the following order:

- *Customer service provision* – level and benefits sought.
- *Customer care programmes* – to ensure standards are maintained and problems resolved.
- *Relationship management* – to keep the information flowing to remain current.

Customer service – how do we get it right?

The level of customer service that a customer expects will depend upon their past experiences and the type of organization which they are dealing with. Within a B2B environment the organizations within the supply chain expect all parties to be focused on the needs of the consumer at the end of the chain. They will expect empathy between parties with a recognition that by pulling together the consumer will benefit. There may not be so many documented processes to enable this as in a B2C environment but the end aim is the same.

In the public sector it has been difficult to implement customer service type culture into organizations that are typically very process orientated and are usually in a non-competitive situation. We all have a mind's eye picture of 'the man from the council' and probably go into a problem situation not expecting too much sympathy. It is also important that the service is maintained and that the customer service ethos is not just a thin veneer. With the growth of the MRSA bug in hospitals, more patients are concerned with the level of hygiene than whether the nurse says hello in the morning.

The not-for-profit sector also need to keep in mind customers' perception of their role and how customer service staff communicate. It is unlikely that you will ask for a refund in a charity shop, but will feel more aggrieved if the assistant is rude to you. Customer service in these sectors is about building long-term relationships, which we will cover later on in this unit.

However, in each of these different examples from across different market sectors, the same basic criteria are responsible for delivering good customer service. They are:

- Friendly and Knowledgeable Staff
- Appropriate procedures and processes
- Product/Service reliability.

We shall move on to cover each of these in turn.

Staff – willing and able!

Research tells us that a story about a negative experience travels fast. Although 56 per cent of people said they did complain, we know nothing of the feelings of the remaining 44 per cent. Good communication is essential and the point of communication, whether it is face to face, on the phone or a response in writing, is between the customer and the employee, whose job it is to interact with the customer.

Customers want to feel valued by the employees they encounter. They want their questions answered in a confident and courteous way, not using jargon, and not assuming they have a high level of subject knowledge. How many times have you gone into your local electrical retailer to make a relatively simple purchase to be blinded by jargon and science when you get in there, leaving fairly hastily because you are frightened to reveal your ignorance? Really, what you wanted was someone to listen to your needs and then advise you on which one of the plethora of products available will meet those needs.

Staff need to be easily recognizable, so uniforms are necessary, as well as a level of personal grooming and hygiene. You don't really want to be analysing the last time someone washed whilst asking for their advice on the differences between a washing machine costing £200 and one at £400.

Staff need to be proactive in helping the customer and sorting out his problems. It is far better to be told that although the store has no stock at present, there is a delivery on Tuesday. Can I put one aside and ring you? The alternative is usually 'we might have some next week if you want to come in then'. It is more likely that you will complain about a member of staff who has tried their utmost to help and failed, regardless, than about someone who simply was not bothered.

There also needs to be evident systems in place that staff can refer to. These can be ICT systems that tell them when a next delivery is due or which other stores have stock, but also team management systems where someone can refer to a team member for help or to a manager with a particular sticky problem. It is better for a staff member to tell the customer that they will need to refer to their manager, rather than the customer coming to their own conclusion that the staff member is not competent to deal with the situation.

The ultimate responsibility of how the staff react and perform in relation to customer service lies with the organization itself. Not only is it imperative that, having established the level of customer service that should be operated, staff receive adequate training and regular updates to ensure they have the product/service knowledge to provide that level of service; but also staff should be empowered by their training and have sufficient knowledge to represent the organization that they work for.

The organizational culture will also affect the level of service determined to be appropriate and how the staff carry out that service. Tesco's can-do attitude is evidenced in the store when you ask a staff member where a certain product is in the store. The Tesco worker will ask you to follow them, take you to where it is, and ask if you need any further help. In contrast, some other stores have a more detached attitude and will respond to the same question by pointing (often impatiently), if you inform them that you cannot find the item then the response will probably be 'If it's not on the rails it's not in stock. You can order it downstairs.' It helps to clarify why Tesco are so successful and others have so many problems. Walking the floor is also a practice undertaken by the Tesco Chairman Terry Leary in a concerted attempt to keep a finger on what is happening on the shop floor and to seek out employee opinion.

Some organizations are investing in knowledge management systems to make the most of the skills and knowledge within the organization so that if staff are not sure, they know where they can access help. Internal communication is important to ensure that staff remain as current as possible. Sometimes it is the recruitment policy of the organization itself that needs to be reviewed. It is a sad fact that many organizations pay the basic minimum wage to their most important, customer facing, staff members. This often means that inexperienced teenagers are the only ones willing to take the job, not so bad in HMV but not so helpful in Comet. B&Q have introduced a policy whereby they employ over-55s, some who have previously taken early retirement and have a wealth of experience in DIY products.

It has to be said that organizations must review the procedures behind recruiting and remunerating front facing staff, to ensure the right people are doing the right job in the right way.

Processes and procedures

Ultimately, all systems will impact on the customer and so should be evaluated in order to establish how these can add to the customer experience rather than become a source of complaints. The five key areas where systems exist are:

1. *Sales and ordering* – consider the speed of processing orders. Is the customer updated regularly?
2. *Accounts and invoicing* – accuracy and a variety of payment methods is key here. Is affordable credit required?
3. *Delivery systems* – is delivery time specific, when the customer wants? Are the goods delivered intact?
4. *After sales* – dealing with customer questions. How easy is it for customers to contact you?
5. *Complaints* – how easy is it to complain? Do complaints get resolved?

Marks & Spencer – Christmas Cheer

For many years Marks & Spencer held a unique position within the Christmas gift buying season. It was well recognized that as the M&S 'offering' was the same countrywide, it was possible to buy gifts from the store confident in the knowledge that if it didn't fit the recipient or were a duplication they could pop along to a local M&S and change the present for something more suitable.

However, in more recent times, with sales starting on December 26th, customers were taking gifts back to be replaced, often finding sizes now out of stock and only being allowed the 'sale price' as a refund or as part payment to another item.

Customers felt cheated that goods that had been charged out at full price were now seemingly worth a fraction of the cost through no fault of their own or the gift purchaser.

This belligerence on behalf of M&S lead to a decline in sales, alongside a lot of other contributing factors. The response was actually an idea of other retailers in the sector who provided the purchaser with a special 'Gift Receipt', which although bore no price enabled the price paid to be tracked back to the day of purchase. Therefore, full refunds were able to be issued.

Unfortunately, by this stage M&S had upset a great deal of customers with their inflexibility in this area, and no longer has the same position in the minds of the gift buying consumer.

Technology can help significantly with all of these issues with e-mail, intranets and extranets (Unit 5) allowing quick easy electronic transactions and questioning. However, we must always consider the need for human intervention when a customer requires the personal touch.

Desktop systems now make small-scale videoconferencing affordable and easy to use. A single card, installed in a personal computer, can enable people to hear and see colleagues face to face wherever they are in the world and exchange and amend documents on screen.

Communication tools such as mobile telephones, pagers, voice mail and call routing are used so that personnel can be reached wherever they are working. Similarly, more staff are allowed to work at home or on the move by using remote data access through laptops or computers at home.

Activity 10.1

It is easy to see how these systems can impact on the customer service delivered in a B2B context. In Unit 9 we looked at Extranets and Intranets and how they can speed up transactions such as ordering and payment. But these issues also have application to the B2C market.

Why do supermarkets have express checkouts?

Why did Argos move their tills to the side of the store, from in front of the collection point where they used to be?

Why is there always a queue to pay in IKEA?

Some of these customer experiences are more pleasurable than others because of the process by which the customer selects goods and services and then proceeds to pay.

As demanding customers we are starting to reconsider why things that have been just so for years cannot now change. Different processes and systems are needed to meet those demands.

A Sainsbury shopper can get their groceries by shopping in store either paying at the checkout or via a hand held scanner, they can order online and pay online, and if they just want to buy a paper there is a separate area and checkout to enable this.

Product/Service reliability

It is obvious that when we purchase a product or service we want it to be fault free, which cannot happen all of the time in this imperfect world we live in. However, it is the way in which problems and faults are dealt with that customer service systems need to be concerned with.

The customer needs to be able to complain. Those 44 per cent of people who did not complain, but wanted to, are still remembering and repeating their negative experience, but without giving us the chance to put it right. Therefore, we need to ensure the process of complaining is not a painful one.

This can be achieved in several ways

o   Ensure staff are trained and have empathy with the cause of complaint.
o   Ensure there are systems and procedures in place to record reoccurring faults/bad service to ensure rectifying action can be taken.
o   Ensure the complaints procedure is fully documented and the essence communicated to the customer, for example refunds on faulty goods are only given on production of a receipt.
o   Ensure that the customer knows what action is to be taken and the timescales that are appropriate to the situation, for example 'We will write to you with a response in the next 7 days.'
o   Make it easy – a customer service desk, a contact us section on the website, a helpline number.

It is important to remember that complaints are emotive issues that have many causes, some of which the staff member may be at a loss to see why a certain aspect is such a problem. But there are always opportunities – to rectify faults for the future and to demonstrate how well we as an organization deal with them because we care.

Satisfied customers take up less time, cause less stress and deliver job satisfaction. Word of mouth is the most effective promotional tool. Customer service is essential for survival and growth.

Steps involved in improving customer service
o   Measure standards by finding out levels of customer satisfaction.
o   Analyse the feedback.
o   Act upon the information and develop what people want, for example customer-friendly systems or getting the detail right.
o   Train staff to ensure competence.
o   Review processes and procedures to ensure they are customer-focused.
o   Consider how much further you could go in terms of exceeding customer expectation.

Marketing research and monitoring customer complaints will enable us to complete the first two steps of the process. It may seem strange that the organization should want to encourage customers to complain, but it is essential to find out what aspects of our services to customers need to be improved.

Measurability
Measurability can be achieved with a properly documented system in place as we should be able to monitor the amount of complaints that are received, how they were received and how quickly an acceptable solution was found. Obviously, the aim is to establish a downward trend.

Market research will be necessary to establish both the level of expectation and experience, if service met that expectation. This can be quickly achieved online or by asking the customer to fill in a questionnaire at the point of contact. This is a method used by the AA and RAC who issue every 'callout' with a pre-paid research card to enable the customer to give their feedback.

Activity 10.2

You work in the marketing department of a DIY chain of stores and you have been asked to produce a leaflet for distribution to all in-store staff on how to handle complaints. The leaflet should show how to deal with complaints and also suggest some helpful approaches. Write some draft notes to plan the content of the leaflet.

Establishing a customer care programme

Having established the level of service that customers expect and having put procedures in place to deliver and collect customer feedback on those criteria, it is now possible to move forward and establish. After establishing the appropriate level of customer service for our organization and the industry sector it operates in, we need to establish procedures and practices which will continue to deliver the service out to customers and hopefully continue to delight. The process is as follows

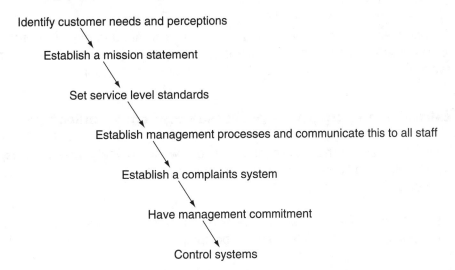

Figure 10.1 Establishing customer care systems

Identify customer needs and perceptions

The work carried out in establishing the level of customer service required will feed into this start point. The aim of the customer care programme will be to continue the provision of what we have established as a base level standard. This area will, as shown earlier focus not just on the product/services provided but also the systems used and staff skills available. Research will be needed to ensure this base standard is current and this could include an element of 'benchmarking' against not just competitive products but also other industries that are considered best in their provision of customer service. UPS parcel systems and Singapore Airlines have excellent service standards, which are recognized across the world. Some of the elements of the service could be transferred into other industry sectors.

Establish a mission statement

Obviously, the organization's approach to customer service must be echoed within this mission statement, as essentially it is the means of communication to both the customer and the employees of the organization. The mission statement gives direction and purpose, also expressing the cultural glue that determines how the organization will interact with their customers. The provision of a mission statement also implies top-level commitment within the organization, which is essential to the success and ease of implementation of the programme.

Set service standard levels

Standards covering all aspects of the service in terms of staff behaviour, appearance and courtesy and responsiveness are required. These should be prescriptive where necessary, that is answer the phone within 4 rings, but also be sufficiently flexible for the staff member to feel empowered to deal with the situation. Situations which should be referred to a senior person should clearly be highlighted.

The complaints procedure should be clearly documented with time scales and supporting paperwork necessary for the smooth running of the system. There should also be a customer-friendly version for communicating in store, on website, or within a telephone conversation. Follow-up procedures also need to be put in place to follow up complaints and to ensure they are all resolved.

Service standards for systems and processes also need to be considered and deadlines set. 'Delivery within 24 hours' or 'You won't find it cheaper anywhere else' are statements that systems need to monitor and highlight where corrective action may be required.

Establish management processes and communication to staff

This is the area which should define who does what, by what and when! Responsibility needs to be allocated and timescales set. Information flow needs to be enabling rather than disabling for the system to work well.

Internal communication in terms of training and team objective setting should take place to ensure everyone is aware of how they should be completing tasks and how they will be measured.

Feedback from staff should be encouraged to ensure procedures that are unworkable are not imposed on the very people who have most experience.

Communication systems may need to be implemented, these could include team meetings, intranet systems and training away days.

Establish a complaints system

Clear systems for encouraging, recording and following up are required. Skills for listening to and empathizing with the complainant will need to be built into staff training. Verbal skills such as clarifying and summarizing will be needed to really ensure that the crux of the problem is identified. It may be necessary to deal with group situations where a number of complainants are encountered at once.

The follow-up system is just as important as the information gathering. It is a much worse sin to not respond to a complaint than the sin of the problem itself.

Have management commitment

This is necessary to gain access to the resources in terms of recruitment, skills and systems that may need to be put in place for the system to work. It is also necessary to echo the cultural push towards delighting the consumer. Consumers quickly pick up on insincere messages and empty promises.

Control systems

The programme must be developed in such a way that measurable objectives can be developed and performance measured against those objectives. Systems need to have defaults that highlight reoccurring problem areas and upcoming deadlines. Performance towards objectives should be communicated and hopefully celebrated. A system of continuous improvement needs to be maintained in order that the service received by the customer continues to evolve and change to meet their needs.

Insight

Online Christmas

Many newspapers reported that Christmas 2004 was set to be the 'online Christmas' with the number of products purchased online to break all previous records. This was thought to be behind many stores recording lower levels of sales year on year for the period.

However, as Christmas approached there were concerns appearing in the daily press that orders were not arriving on the day or including all the items. Many shoppers found themselves having to go and source products in the more usual way. Customers having to check if their orders were to be fulfilled, rather than being notified of the problem by the supplier, compounded the situation.

This was also against a backdrop of no clear winner in the 'Toy of the Year' battle, which usually results in unplanned demand for one particular item.

Even Amazon who had previously been blameless was reported to have incurred problems.

Initial feedback on Christmas 2005 suggests that this problem has mainly been resolved with online purchases increasing significantly year on year – to the concern of the more traditional retail outlets which are reported to be 3.9 per cent down year on year.

Amazon reported that its British business had delivered 480 000 items each day in the run up to Christmas 2005, this was in comparison to a peak of 400 000 in 2004. Amazon added that 99 per cent of orders had been despatched on time.

Figures for the Top Net Shops – November 2005 reported by Neilsen/Net Ratings are:

1. eBay (12.5m visitors)
2. Amazon.co.uk (9m)
3. Yahoo! shopping (5.1m)
4. Tesco (4.4m)
5. Shopping.com (3.5m)

Excerpts taken from *The Times* – 29th December 2005

Potential problems with customer care systems

There are several factors that can result in a customer care programme not achieving its objective to improve the customer experience.

The responsibility of customer care and service resting within a specific department can sometimes result in the rest of the organization not really buying into the concept and not all staff becoming empowered to respond to the standards and systems developed. Although someone has to have overall responsibility, it should be a cross departmental function that involves and communicates to all. Front-line employees have to be involved in the development of the process or they are unlikely to buy into in a committed manner.

The recent move by several large financial institutions to outsource their call centre operations that provide services and monitor feedback has received mostly negative reactions from consumers. There is a feeling that this is customer service being done on the cheap, and the service offered does not fit with the 'organizational culture' evidenced elsewhere in the organization. Consumers feel devalued by the institutions implementing these changes. When the outsourced organization is situated in another time zone, the time-delay in speaking over the international phone lines allows the customer to 'reject' the call before the customer service operative has chance to say why they are calling, and makes complaint calls more fraught because it leads to people speaking at the same time due to being unsure if the other person is still there.

The customer service function must be implemented by valued staff members as discussed earlier, as there are sure to be problems if the lowest paid worker is destined to be the face of the organization. Resources for paying, training and rewarding good performance must be implemented through top-level commitment. People are necessary for this programme to succeed – technology on its own is too impersonal and has the reverse effect than was planned.

Relationship marketing

Having established what we need to do to deliver customer service which delights, and implementing a customer care system to ensure the continued provision, we now look to the benefits of building relationships with customers.

The main idea behind relationship marketing is to build strong relationships in order to retain them instead of concentrating efforts on recruiting new ones.

However, we must remember that relationships with all stakeholders are important.

Figure 10.2 shows the relationships that will need to be considered. Some of these will be maintained through internal communication. Others will take the form of developing more personal one-to-one relationships often achieved via personal selling. Often, in a B2B environment individual staff are given responsibility for 'key accounts' to enable this relationship to develop.

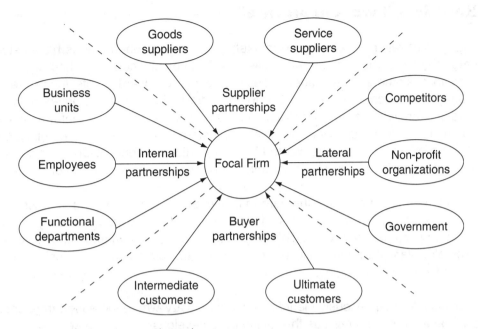

Figure 10.2 The scope of marketing relationships
Source: Hughes and Fill (2004) CIM Coursebook, *Marketing Communications*, Elsevier Butterworth-Heinemann

It has been known for competitors to develop relationships for the good of the industry in total, for example The Tea Council, which promotes drinking tea regardless of which brand, through a jointly funded campaign. Many food manufacturers are funding areas of research into healthy eating options to help their own marketability in the future.

From a customer communications perspective, the most important factor in relationship marketing is the creation of a dialogue between the organization and the consumer. This results in the consumers getting what they want and at the same time becoming a loyal customer who recommends others to the firm. However, it is important to establish the level at which the customer wants to have a relationship. The frequency and intrusive nature of the relationship needs to be linked to the level of involvement in the particular product category. We are less likely to want to develop a relationship with the manufacturer of our shampoo than the manufacturer of our car.

Key elements of relationship marketing

The relationship can only develop if both parties receive something of value – the organization's continued support and the customer benefits from being a valued customer.

The customer must wish the relationship to continue – Pampers nappies are important to mums for the first 2 years of their child life but not necessarily after that. Pampers have extended the range to extend the life of the relationship (e.g. Nite times) but there does need to be a recognized cut off point.

The relationship needs to evolve with the customer's future needs being considered alongside current ones – for example car finance companies giving discounts off-road recovery services such as RAC and AA.

The quality gap between what the customer expects and what they experience must always be filled. Once a customer becomes dissatisfied it is easy for brand switching to occur and revenue to be lost.

How does it work in practice?

A good illustration of relationship marketing is the way supermarkets have established loyalty cards to encourage customers to collect reward points when they shop at stores. The advantage to customers is that after collecting so many reward points these are converted into money-off coupons. The advantage to the store is that when customers register for a loyalty card they provide the store with valuable customer information. This information is used to build up profiles of customers who use a particular store in a particular area. This can help individual stores to stock the products wanted by their particular clientele. So, for example, a store in a location with a large Jewish community would know to stock a range of kosher products.

Each time a customer uses the card to collect points from shopping, the customer's purchase history is added. The value of this information is that past purchase history is the best indicator of future purchase behaviour. This helps stores with many marketing decisions, including, for example, planning appropriate targeted customer communications such as direct marketing and advertising campaigns.

This fits into the previously identified concept of CLV where increased frequency and value of purchase are engendered as the relationship develops.

The Shift to Relationship Marketing

Transactional focus	Relationship focus
Orientation to single sales	Orientation to customer
Discontinuous customer contact	Continuous customer contact
Focus on product features	Focus on customer value
Short timescale	Long timescale
Limited emphasis on customer service	High customer service emphasis
Limited commitment to meeting customer expectations	High commitment to meeting customer expectations
Quality is the concern of production staff	Quality is the concern of all staff

Figure 10.3 The shift to relationship marketing
Source: Payne, Christopher, Clarke and Peck (1998)

Amazon also utilize these techniques. When you first use Amazon you are invited to register using your name and e-mail address. These details will allow an account to be set up in your name and allow your purchases to be tracked – see later on in this unit. As you browse through the various sections, there are on screen hints and tips such as 'people who have liked this book in the past have also liked this DVD' thereby using past customer information to guide you to places of interest and get the order value up. When you have made your selections and proceeded to checkout there may be an introductory discount and also free post and packing if you increase your order value to over £20. If you do this, the action will be logged in your account details as being a responsive device for future use. Once your order is processed you will receive a confirmation e-mail detailing the order, price and intended delivery. The way to check the progress of your order is also given. On receipt of the order you may receive an online questionnaire to give feedback on the service received.

Next time you log in you will be greeted by name and treated as a longstanding friend, again products and services similar to those you have ordered before will be brought to your attention and the attempts to up the order value will begin. However, it could be considered surprising that customer service and relationship marketing as a concept has not developed further. Consider when the case history below was first published. The ideas it espouses are still used today and heralded as good practice – which it is – but we really should be expecting more 9 years on!

Case history

Relationship marketing in the hospitality trade

Every few months the Isle of Eriska Hotel, near Oban, Scotland, sends out a newsletter to former guests updating them on what has been happening in the hotel, any special offers available to them and news of the owners' pets. Although details are obviously derived from a database the former guests are still made to feel special. The personal letter of the proprietor essentially thanks them for staying at the hotel and invites them to visit again.

Thus, the basic components of relationship marketing are implemented: knowing the customer, listening to the customer, competing for the customer and finally, thanking the customer.

This simple example was given by Gordon, R. (1994), The personal touch, *Caterer and Hotelkeeper*, 9 June, p. 26. It is typical of the personalized service that an individually owned hotel owner can offer his guests. But what of the larger organization with hotels distributed throughout the world?

Dev, C.S. and Ellis, B.D. (1991), 'Guest histories: An untapped service resource', *Cornell HRA Quarterly*, August, pp. 29–37, use the example of a business traveller arriving at the airport, being met by the hotel courtesy vehicle and supplied with his favourite soft drink.

On arriving at the hotel he is greeted by name at the front desk, has been pre-registered and all details completed including method of payment. His room has been customized, from his preferred daily newspaper to a selection of the brands of drinks and snacks he consumed on his last stay. Tickets are booked for a theatre production he wanted to see that night. Excellent customer service or invasion of privacy?

This example was only hypothetical but served to illustrate the power of the guest history system if used to its full potential.

Source of both examples: Buttle, F. (1996) *Relationship Marketing Theory and Practice*, Paul Chapman Publishing Ltd.

Key benefits

The increased CLV and feedback of quality information from existing customers has been discussed earlier. However, the valued customer becomes a source of communication in their own right becoming an advocate for the brand and passing on that knowledge to family friends and colleagues. The loss of a bottle of shampoo off your sales is not significant but if that person affects 10 others who in turn affect 10 others each the effect can multiply. In B2B markets where organizations tends to have fewer more valuable clients, the loss of one will inevitably lead to the loss of another which could lead to significant financial difficulty. Conversely, two contented clients recommending your services to two others each can have a very beneficial effect on your business.

At some point an organization will need to assess the customer segments that it wishes to build relationships with, that is who are their key clients. Pareto introduced the 80 : 20 rule which stated 80 per cent of your business comes from 20 per cent of your customers. This is a very arbitrary rule of thumb and each customer or group of customers need to be considered on their merits before action is taken to discontinue a relationship. A supplier to the Queen may not make much money out of doing so but it is unlikely they would disregard the account on that basis.

Activity 10.3

Consider a loyalty scheme that you are familiar with and describe how it works to the advantage of the customer and the organization.

Using information and communication technology in relationship marketing

Relationship marketing requires the storage and manipulation and analysis of huge amounts of customer information in order that the relationship can deliver added value to the customer. The use of customer databases to store and manipulate this data has led to the term 'Database Marketing'.

Database marketing involves using computers to capture and store data relating to customers' past purchase history. For instance, if a mail order company sells clothing in its catalogue, each customer file is computerized so that contact (name, address, postcode) and purchase details (type of item, size, colour preference, price, etc.) are stored. All the departments in the firm can access this information quickly and cheaply. For example, the accounts department may need to access it to chase payment and the marketing department could use it to target offers to customers. So customers who buy clothes for people under a certain height would only be sent information relating to the 'petite' range of clothing based on their past purchase behaviour.

Loyalty schemes work on a similar principle: the large supermarkets can use their EPOS not only for stock control purposes but also to target offers that are relevant to customers. For example, a customer who regularly buys dog food would not be sent money off vouchers to keep the customer 'loyal' for cat food.

Customer relationship management systems work on a similar principle. The key idea is that each customer is treated as an individual, and in particular, organizations can use computer software to identify the customers with the highest CLV. For example, basic current account holders are not particularly profitable customers for banks as those with (or potentially wanting) loans, mortgages, insurance business and pensions are much more profitable. The idea behind CLV is to spend marketing time and effort on those customers who are likely to be the most valuable over their lifetime.

The length of 'lifetime' will vary by industry. Manufacturers of baby products will know that families will probably be in that market sector for about 8 years – the average time between the oldest child and the youngest child moving into the 5 years + bracket. However, these organizations will also have products in other sectors such as household cleaning materials and hair care, where the positive experiences gained from the babycare products will result in the customer entering a relationship for a longer lifetime with different products. Hence, it is possible to have a relationship and retain loyalty for a 'lifetime'.

Data 'mining' is when sophisticated systems are used to track customer/client files in order to identify products/services that could be targeted in the future. The high street retailer Next uses this technique with their mail order catalogue noting when customers make key lifecycle purchases. A sudden change in purchasing, for example homewares, will mean the customer may have just purchased their first home, so Next will send more information concerning their range of furniture or someone ordering maternity wear will shortly be interested in baby wear. Being first to communicate with the customer is a widely accepted mission statement for the approach to customer care itself.

Relationship marketing – the future

The ability to close the communication and receive feedback from customers is the unique selling point for relationship marketing. As more companies perceive the benefits of encouraging a positive relationship with their customers, distributors and suppliers, the growth of two-way communications can grow exponentially alongside the innovation of technology that enables it.

The generation of information that the relationship brings and gives access to, is enormous. It will not be possible to utilize all the information collected. Organizations will need to be selective not only in how they develop relationships but also how they utilize the information they can access.

Trust will continue to be the key factor between a customer and the supplier whether in a B2C or B2B context. This requires an element of mutual benefit and shared values, which the information can enable as long as both parties are willing.

Summary

In this unit you have studied:

o How customer expectations have increased.
o The importance of having a customer focus.
o What is meant by 'customer care' and 'customer delight'.
o How relationship marketing improves communications with customers.
o How customer interaction can be improved.
o How to handle complaints.

Hints and tips

The area of customer service, customer care and relationship marketing is the one that is currently most dynamic in terms of change. The concepts need to mature and, in some cases, re-embed themselves in the culture of the organization. It will be interesting to see how those very large organizations that have moved call centres to Asia will react to the widespread negative perception of the move.

From your own point of view consider which relationships are most beneficial to you. Why is that the case and what are the benefits received by both parties. Consider a family member or colleague of a different age. How does it work for them? How different are the relationships which they value to your own?

You need to be able to describe and evaluate a range of customer care and relationship techniques. Building up a case study bank will be invaluable within the exam situation.

Your communications diary should now be extensive, providing you with examples for use in the exam. Keep adding to it, to remain aware of changing techniques and changing messages. Examine why an organization may have changed its strapline and keep an eye on how it develops.

Hopefully, at the end of this coursebook you are a great deal more attuned to the communications world than at the start. Keep tuned in and you will be able to explore and analyse more complex relationships and messages. This is a skill which will help in all your exams.

Good luck!

Further study

If you require further exam practice then attempt Question 5b from the June 2005 examination paper and Question 5 from the December 2004 paper. To access Specimen Answers for these exam questions, go to www.cim.co.uk.

Bibliography

Fill, C. (2002) *Marketing Communications – Contexts, Strategies and Applications*, 3rd edition, Prentice Hall.

Forsyth, P. (1999) *Communicating with Customers*, London: Orion Business.

Hughes, G. and Fill, C. (2004) CIM Coursebook, *Marketing Communications*, Elsevier Butterworth-Heinemann.

Payne, Christopher, Clarke and Peck (1998) *Relationship Marketing*, Oxford: Butterworth-Heinemann.

appendix 1
guidance on examination preparation

Preparing for your examination

You are now nearing the final phase of your studies and it is time to start the hard work of exam preparation.

During your period of study you will have become used to absorbing large amounts of information. You will have tried to understand and apply aspects of knowledge that may have been very new to you, while some of the information provided may have been more familiar. You may even have undertaken many of the activities that are positioned frequently throughout your Coursebook, which will have enabled you to apply your learning in practical situations. But, whatever the state of your knowledge and understanding, do not allow yourself to fall into the trap of thinking that you know enough, you understand enough, or even worse, that you can just take it as it comes on the day.

Never underestimate the pressure of the CIM examination.

The whole point of preparing this text for you is to ensure that you never take the examination for granted, and that you do not go into the exam unprepared for what might come your way for three hours at a time.

One thing is for sure: there is no quick fix, no easy route, no waving a magic wand and finding you know it all.

Whether you have studied alone, in a CIM study centre, or through distance learning, you now need to ensure that this final phase of your learning process is tightly managed, highly structured and objective.

As a candidate in the examination, your role will be to convince the Senior Examiner for this subject that you have credibility. You need to demonstrate to the examiner that you can be trusted to undertake a range of challenges in the context of marketing, that you are able to capitalize on opportunities and manage your way through threats.

You should prove to the Senior Examiner that you are able to apply knowledge, make decisions, respond to situations and solve problems.

Very shortly we are going to look at a range of revision and exam preparation techniques, and at time management issues, and encourage you towards developing and implementing your own revision plan, but before that, let's look at the role of the Senior Examiner.

247

A bit about the Senior Examiners!

You might be quite shocked to read this, but while it might appear that the examiners are 'relentless question masters' they actually want you to be able to answer the questions and pass the exams! In fact, they would derive no satisfaction or benefits from failing candidates; quite the contrary, they develop the syllabus and exam papers in order that you can learn and then apply that learning effectively so as to pass your examinations. Many of the examiners have said in the past that it is indeed psychologically more difficult to fail students than pass them.

Many of the hints and tips you find within this Appendix have been suggested by the Senior Examiners and authors of the Coursebook series. Therefore, you should consider them carefully and resolve to undertake as many of the elements suggested as possible.

The Chartered Institute of Marketing has a range of processes and systems in place within the Examinations Division to ensure that fairness and consistency prevail across the team of examiners, and that the academic and vocational standards that are set and defined are indeed maintained. In doing this, CIM ensures that those who gain the CIM Certificate, Professional Diploma and Postgraduate Diploma are worthy of the qualification and perceived as such in the view of employers, actual and potential.

Part of what you will need to do within the examination is to be 'examiner friendly' – that means you have to make sure they get what they ask for. This will make life easier for you and for them.

Hints and tips for 'examiner friendly' actions are as follows:

o   Show them that you understand the basis of the question, by answering *precisely* to the question asked, and not including just about everything you can remember about the subject area.
o   Read their needs – how many points is the question asking you to address?
o   Respond to the question appropriately. Is the question asking you to take on a role? If so, take on the role and answer the question in respect of the role.
o   For example, you could be positioned as follows:

'You are working as a Marketing Assistant at Nike UK' or 'You are a Marketing Manager for an Engineering Company' or 'As Marketing Manager write a report to the Managing Partner'.

o   These examples of role-playing requirements are taken from questions in past papers.
o   Deliver the answer in the format requested. If the examiner asks for a memo, then provide a memo; likewise, if the examiner asks for a report, then write a report. If you do not do this, in some instances you will fail to gain the necessary marks required to pass.
o   Take a business-like approach to your answers. This enhances your credibility. Badly ordered work, untidy work, lack of structure, headings and sub-headings can be off-putting. This would be unacceptable in the work situation, likewise it will be unacceptable in the eyes of the Senior Examiners and their marking teams.
o   Ensure the examiner has something to mark: give them substance, relevance, definitions, illustration and demonstration of your knowledge and understanding of the subject area.
o   See the examiner as your potential employer, or ultimate consumer/customer. The whole purpose and culture of marketing is about meeting customers' needs. Try this approach – it works wonders.
o   Provide a strong sense of enthusiasm and professionalism in your answers; support it with relevant up-to-date examples and apply them where appropriate.
o   Try to do something that will make your exam paper a little bit different – make it stand out in the crowd.

All of these points might seem quite logical to you, but often in the panic of the examination they 'go out of the window'. Therefore, it is beneficial to remind ourselves of the importance of the examiner. He/she is the 'ultimate customer' – and we all know customers hate to be disappointed.

As we move on, some of these points will be revisited and developed further.

About the examination

In all examinations, with the exception of Marketing in Practice at Certificate level and Analysis and Decision at Diploma level, the paper is divided into two parts.

- Part A – Mini-case study = 40 per cent of the marks
- Part B – Option choice questions (choice of three questions from seven) = 60 per cent of the marks.

Let's look at the basis of each element.

Part A – The mini-case study

This is based on a mini-case or scenario with one question, possibly subdivided into between two and four points, but totalling 40 per cent of the overall marks.

In essence, you, the candidate, are placed in a problem-solving role through the medium of a short scenario. On occasions, the scenario may consist of an article from a journal in relation to a well-known organization: for example, in the past, Interflora, easyJet and Philips, among others, have been used as the basis of the mini-case.

Alternatively, it will be based upon a fictional company, and the examiner will have prepared it in order that the right balance of knowledge, understanding, application and skills are used.

Approaches to the mini-case study

When undertaking the mini-case study there are a number of key areas you should consider.

Structure/content
The mini-case that you will be presented with will vary slightly from paper to paper, and of course from one examination to the next. Normally, the scenario presented will be 250–400 words long and will centre on a particular organization and its problems or may even relate to a specific industry.

The length of the mini-case study means that usually only a brief outline is provided of the situation, the organization and its marketing problems, and you must therefore learn to cope with analysing information and preparing your answer on the basis of a very limited amount of detail.

Time management
There are many differing views on time management and the approaches you can take to managing your time within the examination. You must find an approach to suit your way of working, but always remember, whatever you do, you must ensure that you allow enough time to complete the examination. Unfinished exams mean lost marks.

A typical example of managing time is as follows:

Your paper is designed to assess you over a three-hour period. With 40 per cent of the marks being allocated to the mini-case, it means that you should dedicate somewhere around 75 minutes of your time to both read and write up the answer on this mini-case. Some students, however, will prefer to allocate nearer to half of their time (90 minutes) on the mini-case, so that they can read and fully absorb the case and answer the questions in the context of it. This is also acceptable as long as you ensure that you work extremely 'SMART' for the remaining time in order to finish the examination.

Do not forget that while there is only one question within the mini-case, it can have a number of components. You must answer all the components in that question, which is where the balance of time comes into play.

Knowledge/skills tested

Throughout all the CIM papers, your knowledge, skills and ability to apply those skills will be tested. However, the mini-cases are used particularly to test application, i.e. your ability to take your knowledge and apply it in a structured way to a given scenario. The examiners will be looking at your decision-making ability, your analytical and communication skills and depending on the level, your ability as a manager to solve particular marketing problems.

When the examiner is marking your paper, he/she will be looking to see how you differentiate yourself, looking at your own individual 'unique selling points'. The examiner will also want to see if you can personally apply the knowledge or whether you are only able to repeat the textbook materials.

Format of answers

On many occasions, and within all examinations, you will most likely be given a particular communication method to use. If this is the case, you must ensure that you adhere to the requirements of the examiner. This is all part of meeting customer needs.

The likely communication tools you will be expected to use are as follows:

- o Memorandum
- o Memorandum/report
- o Report
- o Briefing notes
- o Presentation
- o Press release
- o Advertisement
- o Plan.

Make sure that you familiarize yourself with these particular communication tools and practise using them to ensure that, on the day, you will be able to respond confidently to the communication requests of the examiner.

By the same token, while communication methods are important, so is meeting the specific requirements of the question. This means you must understand what is meant by the precise instruction given. *Note the following terms carefully*:

- o *Identify* – Select key issues, point out key learning points, establish clearly what the examiner expects you to identify.
- o *Illustrate* – The examiner expects you to provide examples, scenarios and key concepts that illustrate your learning.

- o *Compare and contrast* – Look at the range of similarities between the two situations, contexts or even organizations. Then compare them, i.e. ascertain and list how activities, features, etc. agree or disagree. Contrasting means highlighting the differences between the two.
- o *Discuss* – Questions that have 'discuss' in them offer a tremendous opportunity for you to debate, argue, justify your approach or understanding of the subject area – *caution* it is not an opportunity to waffle.
- o *Briefly explain* – This means being succinct, structured and concise in your explanation, within the answer. Make your points clear, transparent and relevant.
- o *State* – Present in a clear, brief format.
- o *Interpret* – Expound the meaning of, make clear and explicit what it is you see and understand within the data provided.
- o *Outline* – Provide the examiner with the main concepts and features being asked for and avoid minor technical details. Structure will be critical here, or else you could find it difficult to contain your answer.
- o *Relate* – Show how different aspects of the syllabus connect together.
- o *Evaluate* – Review and reflect upon an area of the syllabus, a particular practice, an article, etc., and consider its overall worth in respect of its use as a tool or a model and its overall effectiveness in the role it plays.

Source: Worsam, Mike (1989) *How to Pass Marketing*, Croner.

Your approach to mini-cases

There is no one right way to approach and tackle a mini-case study, indeed it will be down to each individual to use their own creativity in tackling the tasks presented. You will have to use your initiative and discretion about how best to approach the mini-case. Having said this, however, there are some basic steps you can take.

- o Ensure that you read through the case study at least twice before making any judgements, starting to analyse the information provided, or indeed writing the answers.
- o On the third occasion, read through the mini-case and, using a highlighter, start marking the essential and relevant information critical to the content and context. Then turn your attention to the question again, this time reading slowly and carefully to assess what it is you are expected to do. Note any instructions that the examiner gives you, and then start to plan how you might answer the question. Whatever the question, ensure the answer has a structure: a beginning, a structured central part of the answer and, finally, always a conclusion.
- o Keep the context of the question continually in mind: that is, the specifics of the case and the role which you might be performing.
- o Because there is limited material available, you will sometimes need to make assumptions. Don't be afraid to do this, it will show initiative on your part. Assumptions are an important part of dealing with case studies and can help you to be quite creative with your answer. However, do explain the basis of your assumptions within your answer so that the examiner understands the nature of them, and why you have arrived at your particular outcome. *Always ensure that your assumptions are realistic.*
- o Only now are you approaching the stage where it is time to start writing your answer to the question, tackling the problems, making decisions and recommendations on the case scenario set before you. As mentioned previously, your points will often be best set out in a report or memo type format, particularly if the examiner does not specify a communication method.
- o Ensure that your writing is succinct, avoids waffle and responds directly to the questions asked.

251

Part B – Option choice questions

Again, with the exception of the Analysis and Decision case study, each Part B is comprised of six or seven more traditional questions, each worth 20 per cent. You will be expected to choose three of those questions, to make up the remaining 60 per cent of available marks.

Realistically, the same principles apply for these questions as in the case study. Communication formats, reading through the questions, structure, role-play, context, etc. – everything is the same.

Part B will cover a number of broader issues from within the syllabus and will be taken from any element of it. The examiner makes the choice, and no prior direction is given to students or tutors on what that might be.

As regards time management in this area, if you used about 75 minutes for the mini-case you should have around 105 minutes left. This provides you with around 30 minutes to plan and write a question and 5 minutes per question to review and revise your answers. Keep practising – use a cooker timer, alarm clock or mobile phone alarm as your timer and work hard at answering questions within the time frame given.

Specimen examination papers and answers

To help you prepare and understand the nature of the paper, go to www.cim.co.uk/learningzone to access Specimen Answers and Senior Examiner's advice for these exam questions. During your study, the author of your Coursebook may have, on occasions, asked you to refer to these papers and answer the questions. You should undertake these exercises and utilize every opportunity to practise meeting examination requirements.

The specimen answers are vital learning tools. They are not always perfect, as they are answers written by students and annotated by the Senior Examiners, but they will give you a good indication of the approaches you could take, and the examiners' annotations suggest how these answers might be improved. Please use them.

The CIM learning zone website provides you with links to many useful case studies which will help you to put your learning into content when you are revising.

Key elements of preparation

One Senior Examiner suggests the three elements involved in preparing for your examination can be summarized thus:

- ○ Learning
- ○ Memory
- ○ Revision.

Let's look at each point in turn.

Learning

Quite often students find it difficult to learn properly. You can passively read books, look at some of the materials, perhaps revise a little, and regurgitate it all in the examination. In the main, however, this is rather an unsatisfactory method of learning. It is meaningless, shallow and ultimately of little use in practice.

For learning to be truly effective, it must be active and applied. You must involve yourself in the learning process by thinking about what you have read, testing it against your experience by reflecting on how you use particular aspects of marketing, and how you could perhaps improve your own performance by implementing particular aspects of your learning into your everyday life. You should adopt the old adage of 'learning by doing'. If you do, you will find that passive learning has no place in your study life.

Below are some suggestions that have been prepared to assist you with the learning pathway throughout your revision.

- o Always make your own notes, in words you understand, and ensure that you combine all the sources of information and activities within them.
- o Always try to relate your learning back to your own organization.
- o Make sure you define key terms concisely, wherever possible.
- o Do not try to memorize your ideas, but work on the basis of understanding and, most important, applying them.
- o Think about the relevant and topical questions that might be set – use the questions and answers in your Coursebooks to identify typical questions that might be asked in the future.
- o Attempt all of the questions within each of your Coursebooks since these are vital tests of your active learning and understanding.

Memory

If you are prepared to undertake an active learning programme then your knowledge will be considerably enhanced, as understanding and application of knowledge does tend to stay in your 'long-term' memory. It is likely that passive learning will only stay in your 'short-term' memory.

Do not try to memorize parrot fashion; it is not helpful and, even more important, examiners are experienced in identifying various memorizing techniques and therefore will spot them as such.

Having said this, it is quite useful to memorize various acronyms such as SWOT, PEST, PESTLE, STEEPLE, or indeed various models such as Ansoff, GE Matrix, Shell Directional, etc., as in some of the questions you may be required to use illustrations of these to assist your answer.

Revision

The third and final stage to consider is 'revision', which is what we will concentrate on in detail below. Here, just a few key tips are offered.

Revision should be an ongoing process rather than a panic measure that you decide to undertake just before the examination. You should be preparing notes *throughout* your course, with the view of using them as part of your revision process. Therefore, ensure that your notes are sufficiently comprehensive that you can reuse them successfully.

For each concept you learn about, you should identify, through your reading and your own personal experience, at least two or three examples that you could use; this then gives you some scope to broaden your perspective during the examination. It will, of course, help you gain some points for initiative with the examiners.

Knowledge is not something you will gain overnight – as we saw earlier, it is not a quick fix; it involves a process of learning that enables you to lay solid foundations upon which to build your long-term understanding and application. This will benefit you significantly in the future, not just in the examination.

In essence, you should ensure that you do the following in the period before the real intensive revision process begins.

- Keep your study file well organized, updated and full of newspaper and journal cuttings that may help you formulate examples in your mind for use during the examination.
- Practise defining key terms and acronyms from memory.
- Prepare topic outlines and essay answer plans.
- When you start your intensive revision, ensure it is planned and structured in the way described below. And then finally, read your concentrated notes the night before the examination.

Revision planning

You are now on a critical path – although hopefully not too critical at this time – with somewhere in the region of between 4 and 6 weeks to go to the examination. The following hints and tips will help you plan out your revision study.

- You will, as already explained, need to be very organized. Therefore, before doing anything else, put your files, examples, reading material, etc. in good order, so that you are able to work with them in the future and, of course, make sense of them.
- Ensure that you have a quiet area to work. It is very easy to get distracted when preparing for an examination.
- Take out your file along with your syllabus and make a list of key topic areas that you have studied and which you now need to revise. You could use the basis of this book to do that, by taking each unit a step at a time.
- Plan the use of your time carefully. Ideally you should start your revision at least 6 weeks prior to the exam, therefore work out how many spare hours you could give to the revision process and then start to allocate time in your diary, and do not double-book with anything else.
- Give up your social life for a short period of time. As the saying goes 'no pain – no gain'.
- Looking at each of the subject areas in turn, identify which are your strengths and which are your weaknesses. Which areas have you grasped and understood, and which are the areas that you have really struggled with? Split your page into two and make a list on each side. For example:

Planning and control	
Strengths	**Weaknesses**
Audit – PEST, SWOT, models Portfolio analysis	Ratio analysis Market sensing Productivity analysis Trend extrapolation Forecasting

o Break down your list again and divide the points of weakness, giving priority in the first instance to your weakest areas and even prioritizing them by giving them a number. This will enable you to master the more difficult areas. Up to 60 per cent of your remaining revision time should be given over to that, as you may find you have to undertake a range of additional reading and also perhaps seeking tutor support, if you are studying at a CIM Accredited Study Centre.

o The rest of the time should be spent reinforcing your knowledge and understanding of the stronger areas, spending time testing yourself on how much you really know.

o Should you be taking two examinations or more at any one time, then the breakdown and managing of your time will be critical.

o Taking a subject at a time, work through your notes and start breaking them down into sub-sections of learning, and ultimately into key learning points, items that you can refer to time and time again, that are meaningful and that your mind will absorb. You yourself will know how you best remember key points. Some people try to develop acronyms, or flowcharts or matrices, mind maps, fishbone diagrams, etc., or various connection diagrams that help them recall certain aspects of models. You could also develop processes that enable you to remember approaches to various options. (But do remember what we said earlier about regurgitating stuff, parrot fashion.)

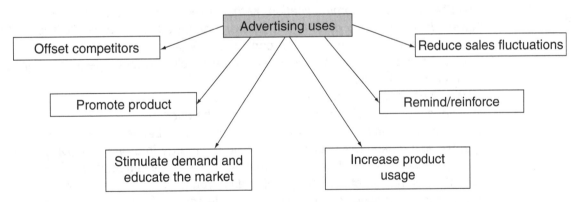

Figure A1.1 Use of a diagram to summarize key components of a concept
Source: Adapted from Dibb, Simkin, Pride and Ferrell (2001) *Marketing Concepts and Strategies*, 4th edition, Houghton Mifflin

Figure A1.1 is just a brief example of how you could use a 'bomb-burst' diagram (which, in this case, highlights the uses of advertising) as a very helpful approach to memorizing key elements of learning.

o Eventually you should reduce your key learning to bullet points. For example: imagine you were looking at the concept of Time Management – you could eventually reduce your key learning to a bullet list containing the following points in relation to 'Effective Prioritization':

- Organize
- Take time
- Delegate
- Review.

Each of these headings would then remind you of the elements you need to discuss associated with the subject area.

o Avoid getting involved in reading too many textbooks at this stage, as you may start to find that you are getting confused overall.

o Look at examination questions on previous papers, and start to observe closely the various roles and tasks they expect you to undertake, and importantly, the context in which they are set.

o *Use the specimen exam papers and specimen answers* to support your learning and see how you could actually improve upon them.

o Without exception, find an associated examination question for the areas that you have studied and revised, and undertake it (more than once if necessary).

o Without referring to notes or books, try to draft an answer plan with the key concepts, knowledge, models and information that are needed to successfully complete the answer. Then, refer to the specimen answer to see how close you are to the actual outline presented. Planning your answer, and ensuring that key components are included, and that the question has a meaningful structure, is one of the most beneficial activities that you can undertake.

o Now write out the answer in full, time-constrained and written by hand, not with the use of IT. (At this stage, you are still expected to be the scribe for the examination and present handwritten work. Many of us find this increasingly difficult as we spend more and more time using our computers to present information. Do your best to be neat. Spidery handwriting is often off-putting to the examiner.)

o When writing answers as part of your revision process, also be sure to practise the following essential examinations techniques:

- *Identify and use the communication method* – requested by the examiner.
- *Always have three key parts to the answer* – an introduction, a middle section that develops your answer in full and a conclusion. Where appropriate, ensure that you have an introduction, main section, summary/conclusion and, if requested or helpful, recommendations.
- *Always answer the question in the context or role set.*
- *Always comply with the nature and terms of the question.*
- *Leave white space* – Do not overcrowd your page. Leave space between paragraphs, and make sure your sentences do not merge into one blur (Don't worry – there is always plenty of paper available to use in the examination).
- *Count* – how many actions the question asks you to undertake and double-check at the end that you have met the full range of demands of the question.
- *Use examples* – to demonstrate your knowledge and understanding of the particular syllabus area. These can be from journals, the Internet, the press, or your own experience.
- *Display your vigour and enthusiasm for marketing* – Remember to think of the Senior Examiner as your Customer, or future employer, and do your best to deliver what is wanted to satisfy their needs. Impress them and show them how you are a 'cut above the rest'.

o Review all your practice answers critically, with the above points in mind.

Practical actions

The critical path is becoming even more critical now as the examination looms. The following are vital points:

- ○ Have you registered with CIM?
- ○ Do you know where you are taking your examination? CIM should let you know approximately one month in advance.
- ○ Do you know where your examination centre is? If not find out, take a drive, time it – whatever you do, don't be late!
- ○ Make sure you have all the tools of the examination ready. A dictionary, calculator, pens, pencils, ruler, etc. Try not to use multiple shades of pens, but at the same time make your work look professional. *Avoid using red and green as these are the colours that will be used for marking.*

Summary

Above all, you must remember that you personally have invested a tremendous amount of time, effort and money in studying for this programme and it is therefore imperative that you consider the suggestions given here as they will help to maximize your return on your investment.

Many of the hints and tips offered here are generic and will work across most of the CIM courses. We have tried to select those that will help you most in taking a sensible, planned approach to your study and revision.

The key to your success is being prepared to put in the time and effort required, planning your revision, and equally important is planning and answering your questions in a way that will ensure that you pass your examination on the day.

The advice offered here aims to guide you from a practical perspective. Guidance on syllabus content and developments associated with your learning will become clear to you as you work through this Coursebook. The authors of each Coursebook have given subject-specific guidance on the approach to the examination and on how to ensure that you meet the content requirements of the kind of question you will face. These considerations are in addition to the structuring issues we have been discussing throughout this Appendix.

Each of the authors and Senior Examiners will guide you on their preferred approach to questions and answers as they go. Therefore, where you are presented with an opportunity to be involved in some activity or undertake an examination question either during or at the end of your study units, do take it. It not only prepares you for the examination but helps you learn in the applied way we discussed above.

Here, then, is a last reminder:

- ○ Ensure you make the most of your learning process throughout.
- ○ Keep structured and orderly notes from which to revise.
- ○ Plan your revision – don't let it just happen.
- ○ Provide examples to enhance your answers.
- ○ Practise your writing skills in order that you present your work well and your writing is readable.

- o Take as many opportunities to test your knowledge and measure your progress as and when possible.
- o Plan and structure your answers.
- o Always do as the question asks you, especially with regard to context and communication method.
- o *Do not leave it until the last minute!*

The writers would like to take this opportunity to wish you every success in your endeavours to study, to revise and to pass your examinations.

Karen Beamish
Academic Development Advisor

appendix 2
assignment-based assessment

Introduction – the basis to the assignments and the integrative project

Within the CIM qualifications at both Certificate and Diploma levels, there are several assessment options available. These are detailed in the outline of modules below. The purpose of an assignment is to provide another format to complete each module for students who want to apply the syllabus concepts from a module to their own or a selected organization. For either qualification there are three modules providing assessment via an assignment and one module assessed via an integrative work-based project. The module assessed via the integrative project is the summative module for each qualification.

	Entry modules	Research & analysis	Planning	Implementation	Management of Marketing
Professional Postgraduate Diploma	Entry module – Professional Postgraduate Diploma	Analysis & Evaluation	Strategic Marketing Decisions	Managing Marketing Performance	Strategic Marketing in Practice
Professional Diploma	Entry module – Professional Diploma	Marketing Research & Information	Marketing Planning	Marketing Communications	Marketing Management in Practice
Professional Certificate		Marketing Environment	Marketing Fundamentals	Customer Communications	Marketing in Practice
Introductory Certificate		Supporting marketing processes (research & analysis, planning & implementation)			

Outline of CIM 'standard' syllabus (© The Chartered Institute of Marketing, September 2003)

The use of assignments does not mean that this route is easier than an examination. Both formats are carefully evaluated to ensure that a grade B in the assessment/integrative project route is the same as a grade B in an examination. However, the use of assignments does allow a student to complete the assessment for a module over a longer period of time than a 3-hour examination. This will inevitably mean work being undertaken over the time-span of a module. For those used to cramming for exams, writing an assignment over several weeks which comprises a total of four separate questions will be a very different approach.

Each module within the qualification contains a different assignment written specifically for the module. These are designed to test understanding and provide the opportunity for you to demonstrate your abilities through the application of theory to practice. The format and structure of each module's assignment is identical, although the questions asked will differ and the exact type of assignment varies. The questions within an assignment will relate directly to the syllabus for that particular module, thereby giving the opportunity to demonstrate understanding and application.

The assignment structure

The assignment for each module is broken down into a range of questions. These consist of a core question, a selection of optional questions plus a reflective statement. The core question will always relate to the main aspects of each module's syllabus. Coupled with this are a range of four optional questions which will each draw from a different part of the syllabus. Students are requested to select two optional questions from the four available. In addition, a reflective statement requires the students to evaluate their learning from the module. When put together, these form the assessment for the entire module. The overall pass mark for the module is the same as through an examination route, which is set at 50 per cent. In addition, the grade band structure is also identical to that of an examination.

Core question

This is the longest and therefore most important section of your assignment. Covering the major components of the syllabus, the core question is designed to provide a challenging assignment which both tests the theoretical element and also permits application to a selected organization or situation. Please ensure that you observe the rubric on the front of the assignment for the word count. This guidance is provided by CIM and should be adhered to as closely as possible. This additional information should be in the form of appendices. However, the appendices should be kept to a minimum. Advice here is that they should be no longer than five pages of additional pertinent information.

Optional questions

There are a total of four questions provided for Certificate level and Diploma level of the syllabus from which a student is asked to select two. Each answer is expected to provide a challenge, although the actual task required varies. The word counts are indicated to you in the rubric in the same way as the core element of the assignment and should be adhered to in the same way. Again, it is appropriate to include appendices where necessary.

These are designed to test areas of the syllabus not covered by the core question. As such, it is possible to base all of your questions on the same organization although there is significant benefit in using more than one organization as a basis for your assignment. Some of the questions specifically require a different organization to be selected from the one used for the core question. This only occurs where the questions are requiring similar areas to be investigated and will be specified clearly on the question itself.

Within the assignment there are several types of questions that may be asked, including:

o *A report* – The question requires a formal report to be completed, detailing an answer to the specific question set. This will often be reporting on a specific issue to an individual.

o *A briefing paper or notes* – Preparing a briefing paper or a series of notes which may be used for a presentation.

o *A presentation* – You may be required to either prepare the presentation only or to deliver the presentation in addition to its preparation. The audience for the presentation should be considered carefully and ICT used where possible.

o *A discussion paper* – The question requires an academic discussion paper to be prepared. You should show a range of sources and concepts within the paper. You may also be required to present the discussion paper as part of a question.

o *A project plan or action plan* – Some questions ask for planning techniques to be demonstrated. As such, the plan must be for the timescale given and costs shown where applicable. The use of ICT is recommended here in order to create the plan diagrammatically.

o *Planning a research project* – Whilst market research may be required, questions have often asked for simply a research plan in a given situation. This would normally include timescales, the type(s) of research to be gathered, sampling, planned data collection and analysis.

o *Conducting research* – Following on from a research plan, a question can require student(s) to undertake a research gathering exercise. A research question can be either an individual or a group activity depending upon the question. This will usually result in a report of the findings of the exercise plus any recommendations arising from your findings.

o *Gathering of information and reporting* – Within many questions, information will need gathering. The request for information can form part or all of a question. This may be a background to the organization, the activities contained in the question or external market and environmental information. It is advisable to detail the types of information utilized, their sources and report on any findings. Such a question will often ask for recommendations for the organization – these should be drawn from the data and not simply personal opinion.

o *An advisory document* – A question here will require students to evaluate a situation and present advice and recommendations drawn from findings and theory. Again, any advice should be backed up with evidence and not a personal perspective only.

o *An exercise, either planning and/or delivering the exercise* – At both Certificate and Diploma levels, exercises are offered as optional questions. These provide students with the opportunity to devise an exercise and may also require the delivery of this exercise. Such an activity should be evidenced where possible.

o *A role-play with associated documentation* – Several questions have asked students to undertake role-plays in exercises such as team-building. These are usually videoed and documentation demonstrating the objectives of the exercise provided.

Each of these questions is related directly towards specific issues to be investigated, evaluated and answered. In addition, some of the questions asked present situations to be considered. These provide opportunities for specific answers relating directly to the question to be asked.

In order to aid students completing the assignment, each question is provided with an outline of marking guidance. This relates to the different categories by which each question is marked. The marker of your assignment will be provided with a detailed marking scheme constructed around the same marking guidance provided to students.

For both the core and the optional questions, it is important to use referencing where sources have been utilized. This has been a weakness in the past and continues to be an issue. There have been cases of plagiarism identified during marking and moderation, together with a distinct lack of references and bibliography. It is highly recommended that a bibliography be included with each question and sources are cited within the text itself. The type of referencing method used is not important, only that sources are referred to.

The reflective statement

This is the final aspect to each module assignment. The purpose of the reflective statement is for each student to consider how the module has influenced him or her as individuals and reflected upon their practice. A shorter piece of work than for other aspects at 500 words (Certificate level) or 750 words (Diploma level), it is also more personal in that your answer will often depend upon how you as an individual have applied the learning from the module to your work and other aspects.

A good reflective statement will comprise a number of aspects, including:

○ Details of the theoretical aspects that you found beneficial within the module, and their reasons. If you have found particular resources beneficial, state this and the reason why.
○ How these concepts have affected you as a practitioner with examples of application of concepts from the module to your work and/or other activities.
○ How you intend to progress your learning further after completing the module assessment.

When looking at the reflective statement, your tutor or an assessor will try to award marks for your demonstration of understanding through the module together with how you have applied the theoretical concepts to practice. They are looking for evidence of learning and application over time, rather than a student simply completing the question because they have a deadline looming. The result of this marking tends to be that students who begin to apply the module concepts early often achieve higher marks overall.

Integrative project structure

The integrative project is designed to provide an in-company approach to assessment rather than having specified assignments. Utilized within the summative module element of each level's syllabus, this offers a student the chance to produce a piece of work which tackles a specific issue. The integrative project can only be completed after undertaking other modules as it will rely on information in each of these as guidance. The integrative project is approximately 5000 words in length and was introduced from September 2002 at the Certificate level. It was introduced from September 2003 at Diploma level with the commencement of the new syllabus. The integrative project is marked by CIM assessors and not your own tutors.

Certificate level assignments – customer communications

Divided into five different elements, the Customer Communications module covers a range of aspects. These present a number of potential questions which can be asked. For each of the five elements, a sample question is given together with an evaluation of the type of answer which would be expected at this level.

Element 1 – Customers and stakeholders

This element of the syllabus covers the role of stakeholders and the importance of internal and external customers. A typical question covering this aspect would be:

For your organization or an organization of your choice, prepare a report for the Marketing Manager which evaluates your organization's stakeholders. From this, select FOUR key stakeholder groups and evaluate the following:

- o Their relationship with the organization
- o The best form of media to communicate with each stakeholder.

In order to answer this question effectively, an answer would consider the following aspects:

- o A clear introduction to the organization selected as a basis for the question.
- o An analysis of the organization using a range of stakeholder mechanisms. This would include a map of stakeholders and a discussion of both internal and external stakeholders. This would include details of their interactions and level of influence on the organization.
- o Plotting of the stakeholders in a diagrammatic representation.
- o An evaluation of each of the stakeholders in order to identify the four key stakeholders. This would be presented best in a table format.
- o The rationale for identifying the key stakeholders.
- o For each of the four key stakeholders, cover in detail the relationship they have with the organization. Are they internal or external. In addition, how do they view the organization's products/services.
- o Drawing in part of element 3 (Implementing elements of the promotional mix), the range of potential media should be considered. From these the most appropriate for each of the four stakeholders identified should be considered. The rationale for each selection also needs to be given.
- o The assignment should be presented as a report, although not in a folder, as per the submission instructions for the module.

Element 2 – Buying behaviour

This element covers the role of the decision-making unit and buyer behaviour, both consumer and organizational. As such, a sample question from this element would be:

For your organization and another one of your choice, make a comparison of consumer and organizational buyer behaviour that will help a graduate trainee, with no marketing experience, understand the differences. Your analysis should address the Decision-Making Process (DMP) and how the communications mix can be used by an organization to influence the DMP.

In order to create an effective answer, two organizations need to be selected to provide a comparison. One needs to provide a perspective of consumer buyer behaviour and the other organizational buyer behaviour. A suggestion for this would be to link up with another student whose organization has the alternative customer base. However, the assignments should be completed separately. An answer to the question would include the following:

- o A background of the organizations selected given, together with a picture of the types of customer(s) each organization has. This needs to provide a basis of comparison for the organizations.

263

o A definition of consumer and organizational buyer behaviour, with the organizations placed into context. This should include the models of consumer and organizational buyer behaviour.

o An explanation of the decision-making process for each organization – one covering the organization with consumers and the other with organizational buyers. This should highlight the differences between each organization's buyers. This could either be displayed diagrammatically or in a table to facilitate understanding and aid comparison.

o The next stage would be to introduce the communications mix, which is drawn from element 3 (Implementing elements of the promotional mix). The differences and similarities between the buyers should be shown. Again, a table would be the best form of representation here.

o Presentation as a report in this instance would be the most obvious choice.

Element 3 – Implementing elements of the promotional mix

There are a wide range of questions which could be asked from this element. The most obvious range around the use of communications mechanisms, as has been included in the previous questions. However, the element covers much more than simply communications, as the sample question below demonstrates:

Your manager has asked you to prepare a presentation to the Sales Team on the value and potential impact of 'below-the-line' methods of promotion to your organization or an organization of your choice. The presentation should take no longer than 40 minutes and include slides plus a handout to aid the sales team.

This question covers a number of aspects, together with drawing a presentation from element 4 (face-to-face communication). The format of the question should not be ignored, nor the additional request. Therefore, an answer should cover the following:

o A background to the organization selected as a basis for the question. This should show the relationship between the sales team and their customers. In addition, a picture of the current use of promotion methods would be helpful.

o The presentation needs to include the different types of promotion, both above-the-line and below-the-line methods. The benefits and drawbacks of each should be highlighted, together with the use of examples.

o From this, the below-the-line methods should be covered in more detail, providing a range of examples to illustrate points made.

o A summary of the presentation is required. In addition, having a question-and-answer session at the end to reinforce learning would be beneficial. Suggestions for this would include a questionnaire or questions relating to each promotional method within the presentation slides themselves.

o Each slide should be legible and understandable. A recommended number of words per slide is 20 +/–5 to aid understanding.

o The format of the presentation covers the use of slides together with the handout. This additional information should include the slides together with documentation relating to above-the-line and below-the-line methods of promotion. It should also include sources of further information.

o A copy of the presentation slides should be included with the answer to the question, together with the handout and a disk containing the presentation.

Element 4 – Face-to-face communication

This element provides some interesting opportunities for questions. They could relate to your own or a given organization. As such, questions drawn from this element may relate to external and internal customer communication, to the handling of meetings, to personal communication or to presentations. An example question would cover:

In recent months, the planning meetings at the local council offices have become heated affairs due to a long-running application to construct an accommodation centre for international refugees. Local and national media have also been covering the arguments that have reigned. In order to improve local relations, you have been asked to advise the council on how their meetings can be better operated.

An answer to this question would require consideration of the contentious nature of the subject. In addition, the question has been placed in a public-sector context and one where feelings are already likely to be running high. There has been global media coverage on the nature of refugees, both genuine and bogus. A significant number of refugees claiming asylum in many countries are genuine, and therefore this should be the context in which the question is placed. An example answer would cover the following aspects:

- o The context of the question should be set, and its nature covered. The situation should be explained in detail in order that there is no confusion.
- o The question needs to cover both communication in meetings together with face-to-face communication.
- o An explanation of communications is required, together with coverage of the different types of communication. This should cover not just voice, but also body language, tone plus listening skills. Barriers to communication would need to be covered in detail within the question.
- o The answer would then move on to explaining the role of meetings. This should include guidance for holding meetings. It is also important here to place the answer in the context of the question.
- o The final element of the answer should cover advice on communication in general with stakeholders, together with recommendations for the next meeting to be held.
- o The most appropriate format for this question would be the use of a report highlighting the communication issues, together with advice on communication and meetings.

Element 5 – Customer service and customer care

Customer service is one of the smaller elements of the Customer Communications module. However, questions are likely to be asked on this element as customer service is a critical aspect of customer communications. A typical question covering this element would be:

More organizations are now using their websites to interact with their customers and to facilitate and fulfil on-line purchasing. You have decided to produce a report for the next marketing meeting to highlight the differences between your own website and those of your THREE main competitors, together with their ease of identification using search mechanisms.

An answer to this question would require the selection of a range of competitors in order to provide a comparison. The organization selected should have a website already although this is not essential. In addition, they would not need to undertake online purchasing.

- o The answer should set the scene by identifying the organization selected together with their industry. The current use of a website within the organization needs discussing.

This should cover the purpose of the website, together with the use of online purchasing if this occurs.

o The three competitor websites should be selected, with a clear rationale for their choice. They may include the key competitors within the market, the largest players are those with the most advanced online purchasing systems.

o The next stage would be to examine potential sources of information regarding the sites. This includes search engines (e.g. Google, Hotbot, Yahoo, etc.), directories (e.g. Yahoo and others), links (trade bodies). Issues within this which need considering are the use of domain names, online promotion and listings. Do competitors use paid-for listings and promote themselves or are they generally listed on a search engine.

o Each of the three competitors' websites should be examined. Areas to be considered are navigation, information searching, customer contact together with their online purchasing system. If possible, follow through an order as a customer. The best way to represent these would be in a table as a comparison. In addition, the organization selected as a basis for the assignment should be included.

o The final stage would be to make recommendations regarding the organization's own website. How does their website reflect in terms of the industry standard. Where can improvements be made to the website.

o This would be best presented as a report, detailing the three competitors' websites. In addition, examples taken from each website would be suitable as appendices.

Assignment regulations

There have been a number of changes to the assignment structure compared with previous years, timed with the introduction of the new syllabi. These have been designed to provide consistency in approach for a student whether they are completing the assessment for a module by examination, assignment or integrative project. The more significant changes include:

o For the current academic year tutors at CIM centres will mark assignments. These are then moderated by CIM assessors. An integrative project is marked by CIM assessors only.

o No resubmission of assignments, as per an examination. In previous years, a range of assignments were being submitted. Where a student does not achieve the 50 per cent pass mark, they are requested to retake the assessment for the module through examination or assignment/integrative project.

o Whichever assessment route selected is fixed rather than having the option to change at the last minute. Past history has shown that students sometimes begin on an assignment route, change to an examination at the last minute due to not meeting a deadline and then score badly in the examination. The paths to an assignment or examination are different and therefore it is unadvisable to switch, which is the reason for the change of rule.

o In the academic year 2002/03, word limits for questions and assignments were introduced. This was introduced due to assignments being submitted which were of a wide variety of lengths. These ranged from under 2000 words to over 25 000 words. Where a student is completing four modules by assignment this would equal over 100 000 words – the equivalent of a medium-sized textbook or novel. As such it became impossible for two assignments to be considered together. Therefore, the word limit guidance was introduced in order to provide equality for all students undertaking assessment by assignment.

o Two sets of assignments per year as with the examination route. With this change students are required to complete the assignment aimed at the nearest examination session. Previously students had between 3 months and 9 months to complete an assignment depending upon whether it was given out in September for a June deadline or March for the June deadline. Therefore, a decision was made to follow the examination route with the intention of giving all students equal time to complete an assignment.

These summarize the key changes which have occurred due to the introduction of new syllabi with the assignment/integrative project route in order that there is parity of assessment at all levels and using all formats. Some of these changes have been significant, others minor. However, all the changes have been considered thoughtfully and with the best intentions for the students in mind.

Use of case studies

For anyone who is not working or has difficulty with access to information on their or another organization, there are a number of case studies available which allow the completion of a module using a case-based approach rather than basing it upon an organization identified by the student. These case studies are provided on a request-only basis through your accredited CIM centre and should only be used as a last resort. Using a case study as the basis for your assignment will not mean an easier approach to the assignment. However, they do provide an opportunity to undertake assignments when no other alternative exists. Each case study comes with a certain amount of information which can be used specifically for the completion of a question. Additional information may need to be assumed or researched in order to create a comprehensive assignment.

Submission of assignments/integrative project

The following information will aid both yourself and your tutor who marks your work and also the CIM assessor who will be moderating your work and the integrative project. In addition, the flow diagram represents the process of an assignment/integrative project from start to final mark.

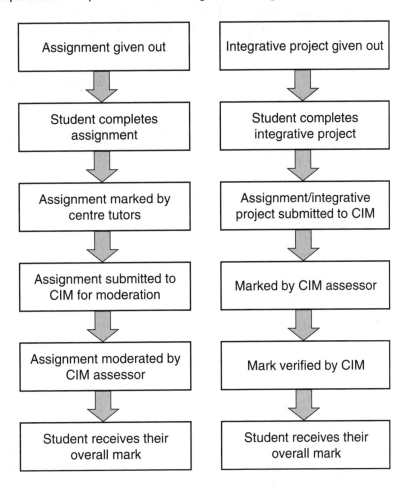

Assignment given out	Integrative project given out
Student completes assignment	Student completes integrative project
Assignment marked by centre tutors	Assignment/integrative project submitted to CIM
Assignment submitted to CIM for moderation	Marked by CIM assessor
Assignment moderated by CIM assessor	Mark verified by CIM
Student receives their overall mark	Student receives their overall mark

When completing and submitting assignments or the integrative project, refer to the following for guidance:

o Read through each question before starting out. Particularly, with the core question there will be a considerable amount of work to undertake. Choose your optional questions wisely.

o Answer the question set and use the mark guidance given regarding the marking scheme.

o Refer to each question within the assignment and use a bibliography.

o Complete all documentation thoroughly. This is designed to aid both the CIM and yourself.

o Ensure that the assignment is bound as per instructions given. Currently assignments are requested not to be submitted in plastic wallets or folders as work can become detached or lost. Following the submission, instructions provided aid both the CIM administrators and the CIM assessor who will be marking (integrative project) or moderating (assignments) your work.

o Complete the candidate declaration sheet showing that you have undertaken this work yourself. *Please note that if you wish the information contained in your assignment to remain confidential you must state this on the front of the assignment.* Whilst CIM assessors will not use any information pertaining to your or another organization, CIM may wish to use the answer to a question as an example.

An assignment will be marked by a tutor at your CIM centre followed by moderation by a CIM assessor. The integrative project will be marked by a CIM assessor as per an examination with moderation by the CIM. To ensure objectivity by CIM assessors there exists a marking meeting prior to any marking in order that standardization can occur. The senior assessor for each subject also undertakes further verification of both examinations and assessments to ensure parity between each type of assessment.

Based on the appendix written by

David C. Lane
Former Senior Moderator (Advanced Certificate)
February 2003

appendix 3
answers and debriefings

Unit 1

Debriefing Activity 1.1

Differentiate – can be used in two ways, first to bring attention to a unique attribute that the product/service can offer such as the Dyson bagless vacuum system, and secondly to try to provide a point of difference between products where very little difference actually exists. For example, Daz washes whiter, Persil cares and Ariel digests stains but they all *get clothes clean.*

Remind – is often used for products in the maturity stage of the Product Life Cycle. Well known and probably used by all at some time, people need to be reminded to use again or to use more frequently, for example Kellogg's cereals, Lemsips, Horlicks, After Eight mints and so on.

Inform – is often used where the potential customers need to make an informed decision about the product service choice they are about to make, because their personal circumstances will mean they need a slightly different product to the next person. Financial products such as pensions, insurance and mortgages fall into this category as well as mobile phones and related airtime packages.

Persuade – often used for luxury items or again products that have very little real difference between them. Think of the strapline attached to the L'Oreal range 'Because you're worth it'. Often used for chocolate and other nice things to eat, for example Mr Kiplings 'exceedingly good' cakes.

Debriefing Activity 1.2

Recently, two large companies have been in the news for allegedly misusing this technique. Cadbury Ltd was accused of encouraging child obesity by linking promotional vouchers to chocolate purchases. Cadbury defended their actions by saying that, as the vouchers were for schools to buy sports equipment, this in fact demonstrated a responsible link by trying to get the 'couch potato' children to become more active.

Walker's crisps were similarly berated for their Books for Schools promotion.

Debriefing Activity 1.3

Stakeholder	Message	Method	Why
Consumers – these would be broken down into various target groups in the consumer and B2B markets	Information about products, persuasive messages to brand the cars and persuade customers to buy	All the promotional mix: advertising, branding, sponsorship, sales literature, direct marketing, public relations and a trained sales force	To raise awareness To increase sales
Shareholders	Performance, dividend payout, future developments	Annual general meeting Annual report PR to financial press	Need shareholder support and need to promote correct image Legal obligation to set out performance information
Employees	Company performance, future plans Training information Improvements in staff facilities Staff news	Internal newsletter, memos, meetings, staff notice board	To maintain good industrial relations and staff motivation
Potential employees	What the company does. What job opportunities are available	Recruitment advertising Corporate image	To recruit from the biggest pool of available staff so will have better selection
Suppliers	Company production plans and requirements	Meetings Tender documents Contracts	To help firms supply best components at the right time and to ensure that the organization and its suppliers work together in partnership
Distributors	Product and technical information	Point of sale material, sales literature and promotional items for branding purposes	To assist dealerships in selling cars
Local community – could be residents who live near factories or local charities	That the firm cares for the local community	PR activities. Sponsorship	Good PR which could help, for example, if the firm applies for planning permission to extend factory premises
The media	Product information and information about company performance	Press releases Events	To raise the company's profile To promote its image

Government – local, national and international	They are an ethical firm and a good employer	Via senior management on a personal level	To establish good relations so can put pressure to bear regarding legislation that might affect the industry
Pressure groups	They are an ethical firm that cares about the environment	PR	To negate effect of conflicting messages from environmental pressure groups
Competitors	To develop strategic alliances	Via senior management on a personal level	To rationalize operations, cut costs and expand into other markets

Unit 2

Debriefing Activity 2.1

With a major purchase we will seek information from a variety of sources: friends, family specialists in that area and so on. The type of information and level of detail will depend upon the product purchased. An expensive item of clothing for that big night out will take a lot of finding but the advice of a friend will probably be the deciding factor. In comparison, changing your car will mean sourcing lots of detailed information such as mpg and fuel emissions. Communications are designed to take us through the purchasing process – a skill which will be developed further within this unit. The Internet has substantially increased the amount of information that we can access in our own homes; organizations have had to consider that carefully when developing their communications plans.

Take care over the period of your study to consider, for a few purchases, the process that you go through and the information you seek. How much of that information is provided to you by the organization and in what format?

Debriefing Activity 2.2

We find that the influences that subconsciously affect us can re-emerge over and over again across a range of different products. Older people are affected by different influences but not so much now as in the past. As a larger section of the population fall into the 54+ age group, advertisers have had to change their views on how this group thinks, dresses and behaves. Today, 60-year-old women will probably have had laser eye surgery and highlighted hair – a long way from the grey-haired, bespectacled, Granny figure we used to associate with that age. Over 50s now have their own lifestyle categories.

- ∘ 'Woofs' – Well-off older folk
- ∘ 'Youthfully spirited' – less well off than Woofs but willing to experiment
- ∘ 'Self preservationists' – Older, more conservative than other groups.

271

Debriefing Activity 2.3

The buying process	AIDA model of communication	Promotional tool
Need recognition	Gain attention	PR
Information search	Stimulate interest	Advertising and point of sale material in car showroom
Evaluation of alternatives	Create desire	Test drives, sales brochure
Purchase decision	Generate action	Sales force
Post-purchase decision	Create satisfaction	Direct marketing material, follow-up calls to check customer satisfaction, warranty material

Debriefing Activity 2.4

The office manager buying air conditioning units is a new buy situation but most likely a one-off purchase. The total buying process will need to be considered. The office manager will refer to stationery suppliers, directories, trade magazines, colleagues and previous discussions with sales people. There are unlikely to be several members of the DMU within the organization, which means that a high level of risk will exist in the mind of the buyer, which communications will need to minimize by giving information and reassurance.

The buyer for the car company will be effecting a straight rebuy. It is unlikely that he will go through the stages of the buying process unless there arises a problem in which case a modified rebuy situation may exist, extending the elements of the buying process that will need to be considered. There will be many members of the DMU, and the personal level of risk felt by the buyer will be low. The orders will be substantial and regular. Communication will be regular and the purpose is to build and continue a mutually beneficial relationship. Internet/extranet use, e-mail and telephone calls are likely to be the most frequently used methods of communication. Corporate hospitality will also be beneficial.

Unit 3

Debriefing Activity 3.1

- o I liked it so much I bought the company – Remington shavers
- o Your flexible friend – Access/mastercard
- o Raise your hand if you are sure – Sure deodorant
- o Scchh … you know who – Schweppes tonic
- o Don't just book it – Thomas Cook it
- o Pleasure you can't measure – Mars Bar – current campaign
- o Work, rest and play – Mars old campaign
- o Vorsprung durch technik – Audi
- o Can hate be good – can hate be great? – Honda diesel engines
- o Have a break have a … – KitKat
- o I'm loving it – McDonald's

How many did you get right? Did those that didn't come to mind quickly remind you, once you saw the answer. What is your view between the two Mars straplines? Have they been successful in establishing a new strapline or do most people think of 'Work, rest and play'? Consider other memorable straplines and collect examples of their use in your communications diary.

Debriefing Activity 3.2

There are quite a few product/service categories where the message content emphasis and encoding changes considerably.

Consider the mobile phone market. The message sent to 16- to 19-year-olds has a significant lifestyle emphasis from being seen to have the latest technology on offer to needing hundreds of text messages to communicate more cheaply. The message sent to a widow over 55 will be based on being prepared for an emergency such as the car breaking down; here the emphasis is based on fear. Consider how these techniques are used in other markets such as insurance, package holidays, alcohol and so on.

Debriefing Activity 3.3

You will probably be surprised by the number of terms you would need to explain that you and your colleagues use on a regular basis. It can also be very much more difficult to write an explanation of a term that you know perfectly well what it means, but have to create a clear explanation for someone who is blissfully unaware. Imagine what a problem this would be if the new recruit did not share the same language as yourself.

Debriefing Activity 3.4

Look at your communications diary and divide the messages into rational and emotional ones. Which do you consider are most memorable and why? Try and consider advertisements that have been used in the past. Why do you remember those particular ones?

Debriefing Activity 3.5

1. You could use a poster campaign along the roads where the tolls will be introduced. As with all poster campaigns, you would need to keep the message simple because people need to be able to take in the message as they go past at speed.
2. You would need to alert the sales force as soon as possible so fax, e-mail or letter could be used depending on what was available. The message may contain scientific proof so written communication will aid understanding and this may be presented graphically so that it can be reproduced for the trade personnel the salesperson is meeting. It may be possible to follow up with more detailed research produced within a document which could be mailed directly to the trade contacts or be shown on the organization's website. The style would be explanatory with the minimum of scientific jargon used.
3. You may write a lengthy, formal report to the director that deals with the problems and suggests solutions. You may adopt an impersonal tone, using a 'third person' style. For example, 'It appears that the road works on the local motorway network have caused significant delays when our vans depart for the mid-morning delivery run.' As you are writing to your line manager, you would not use an authoritative 'tell' style of communication. In your report you would not necessarily avoid longer, more complex sentences or technical terms.

Unit 4

Debriefing Activity 4.1

1. 'I don't actually handle those products but if you hold on ... ' either 'I will transfer you to x in y department who will help you' or 'I will ask x in y department to come down to speak to you if you could just wait for a few minutes.'
2. 'I don't think we have that in stock but I'll just go and check for you. Would you mind waiting for a few minutes?'
3. 'We have sold out at present. Can I take your contact details and ring you when they come in?'
4. 'It is difficult to fit you in at another time as we are so busy today. Would you like to take a seat whilst I go on see the doctor/dentist/hairdresser and find out when they could squeeze you in?'

Debriefing Activity 4.2

Many non-verbal cues are used in communicating 'hidden' messages within the advertising message. Many of these also affect how goods and services are packaged. Here are a few examples.

Family roles – The relative power between the male/female relationship will differ across the world. Many cultures still regard women as the subservient gender. In some countries, the idea of a woman making a financial decision or being out on her own driving a car is totally alien. In China, the 'family' will be depicted with one child only as is the law.

Use of dress/nudity – The amount of nudity and style of dress will differ across the world. Different areas have different levels of acceptability. Scandinavian countries have a much more relaxed attitude to nudity than in the UK. Several Asian countries have costumes relating to many different parts of the body.

Use of graphics and colour – White rather than black is the colour of mourning in some countries. Imagine how this would affect the screening of the Scottish widows' commercial in those countries. The use of flowers also reflects mourning in some European countries.

Debriefing Activity 4.3

There are a number of ways in which you can ensure that you are listening effectively:

1. Be patient and let the person express themselves – do not interrupt or complete sentences for the patient.
2. Use appropriate body language, such as eye contact and nodding, to show interest in what is being said – this will encourage the patient to communicate effectively and to become calm.
3. Ask questions to clarify your understanding of what has been said.
4. At intervals, sum up what the patient has said to show that you have listened and understood.

Debriefing Activity 4.4

To: Fiona Sharp – Admin

From: Martin Brundle, Marketing Manager

Subject: Effective telephone use

Fiona

I have become a bit concerned about your use of the telephone and how you are dealing with the calls that come into the department. It is really important that we deal with calls in a business-like manner as most of the calls are external from customers and suppliers. We want to make sure they have full confidence in us!!!

I have just put a few notes down. Come and see me to have a chat if there is anything you don't understand. And don't worry, you're doing fine in all other areas.

Incoming calls

All calls should be answered by the fifth ring. Too many callers are left waiting for several minutes before their call is picked up.

When calls are answered, it is important that they are dealt with correctly. You should clearly state your name and the department name, followed by the question, 'How can I help you?'

Transfer of calls

It is important that you become familiar with the extension numbers for the department's various staff, so that calls can be transferred quickly and efficiently.

It is apparent that many calls are being cut off whilst they are being transferred. Therefore, it is vital that you ensure that you press the gate (#) button before dialling the extension number they require.

Many suppliers have complained that they are transferred to the wrong person before they have had a chance to say who they want. Before transferring calls, please confirm with the caller who they need to speak to, and ask them to hold whilst you transfer them.

Message taking

If the extension number is engaged or not answered, then it is important that an accurate message is taken. Messages should be noted on the proper message pads only. They should state the date and time of the call, name of the caller (company name, if it is appropriate) and the telephone number of the caller. Messages for staff should state the purpose of the call. All messages should be put in staff pigeonholes immediately.

Thank you for your co-operation and welcome to the Marketing department. I do hope you enjoy working with us.

Debriefing Activity 4.5

The main thing that you need to make clear at the start of the presentation is when questions should be asked – either during the presentation or saved until the end. With a lively lot like the marketing department, I think it's best to let them ask during the presentation so they don't sit there just concentrating on what they want to be answered rather than listening to you.

Whatever you decide, don't let the questioning take over and the flow of the presentation be lost. It's your job to keep focused on the subject. Just a few other tips.

- o Repeat any questions so that the audience can hear and be involved in this part of the session.
- o If the question or comment is relevant, then either answer the question directly or thank the person for their contribution.
- o If the question is rambling or unclear, try to clarify and retrieve one simple question from the narrative.
- o If the question is irrelevant, you could say that it is outside the scope of the presentation.
- o If the question is hostile or you don't agree with the points made, accept as much as you can of the points made but do not get drawn into a long argument.
- o If you cannot answer the question, admit that you cannot but enlist the help of the audience, or you could say that you will get back to the person once you have had a chance to look into the matter.

And finally – enjoy. We are all on your side.

Debriefing Activity 4.6

	Selection interviews	Appraisal interviews	Disciplinary interviews	Customer complaints
Purpose	To find a suitable person for the job and convey information concerning the job, the organization and terms and conditions	To give an employee feedback on their performance and to identify/agree future training needs and issues important for their continued development	Clarify understanding of an incident that has arisen and agree a way of resolving the problem in order that everyone is fairly treated	To determine the necessary details and agree a course of action that leaves the customer feeling satisfied
Audience	Line Manager Job applicant HR representative	Line Manager Appraisee maybe HR representative	Line Manager Appraisee maybe HR representative	Customer Salesperson maybe Sales manager
Structure	Plan of content Briefing of job requirements Q & A Session Tour of offices Next stage explained	Explain procedures and paperwork Agreement on point for discussion Discussion Agreement on actions required	Explain procedures and paperwork Discussion to establish facts and review supporting evidence Agreement on actions required	Introduction of parties attending Q & A to establish basis of complaint Discussion to clarify exact issues to be resolved Agreement on actions required

Style	First interview often informal	If poor performance is an issue then more supportive/ probing style required	Supportive but fair, trying to be non-judgemental to establish relevant facts	Reconciliatory and helpful
	Second interview maybe more formal, more detailed and involve selection panel	Open and restatement questions needed Closed to clarify points	Careful use of body language	Keen to resolve Careful use of questioning – open and restatement mostly
	Consider if table required. Closed questions used to start then all others required to determine ability	Table may be a barrier Constructive and looking to future	All types of questioning used to clarify situation and check understanding Table – dependent on severity of incident	Room layout may be down to client but if possible, can be small meeting table and chairs

Unit 5

Debriefing Activity 5.1

UK Country Cottages

17 Haymill Road

Birmingham BH4 2UT

Dear Miss Murray

As a valued customer of UK Country Cottages in the past, we have your details on our database ready to send out brochures for the 2005 season. The new brochure has approximately 200 new properties and we have managed to increase our coverage of West Wales and West Scotland so that even the most loyal customers will have new pastures to explore. However, one of the problems of our success is that the brochures are becoming rather large to accommodate all the property details we offer you.

It is also possible to access the accommodation details online on our easily navigable website: (www.ukcountrycottage.com). All aspects of the transaction from search through to booking and payment can be facilitated and there are plenty of reminders of our phone number in case you have an unanswered question!

We will of course be offering our usual 10 per cent discount for bookings taken before March 1st. There is also an additional discount of a further 5 per cent for booking online as this allows us to reduce costs on printing and distributing the rather hefty brochures.

Could you please confirm your contact details by returning the tear-off slip below in the prepaid envelope or accessing the home page of the website where you can access the 'Previous Customer' section to confirm your personal details. We would also like to know on both the website and tear-off slip if you wish to continue receiving the annual brochure.

We strive to bring you the best possible value in premium holiday accommodation across the UK and welcome your anticipated co-operation in this activity, which can help us to reduce our operating costs and continue to deliver a premium service to our customers.

Yours sincerely

Agnes Marple

Customer Liason Manager

Debriefing Activity 5.2

Deatties Department Store

Lime Street

Hightown

Herts

14 June 200X

Mrs Beckett

Longley Lane

Northenden

Hightown

Dear Mrs Beckett

Thank you for your letter of 10 June with regard to the quality of service you received during your visit to the Mother and Baby department on 5 June.

I would like to take this opportunity to apologize on behalf of all the staff at Deatties for the unacceptable behaviour by one member of my staff.

Although I am most concerned to hear about how you were treated, I am pleased that you took the trouble to inform me of what happened. I can assure you that the matter was thoroughly investigated and that the member of staff has been disciplined as part of company policy. It is company policy to monitor performance in a case such as this and the member of staff is fully aware of the consequences if there is any repeat of such an incident in future.

I would be very pleased if you would accept a voucher for £20 as a small token for the trouble you have been caused. I look forward to seeing you at the store in the future and would be interested in receiving further feedback so that I can check that the action taken has resulted in the problem not re-occurring.

Again, I would like to express my apologies and hope this incident will not deter you from remaining a loyal and valued customer.

Yours sincerely

Michael Smith

Manager

Debriefing Activity 5.3

e-Mail Communication

To: Sales Managers

From: Meredith Chapman

Date: 19 June 200X

Subject: Internal communication

With the new post-merger sales structure in place, it is vital to establish effective communication between the different regions. Although letters have been traditionally used, we now need to speed up internal communication because there are several disadvantages in relying on the postal system as the sole means of communication.

Problems with sending letters:

- o Letters can be delayed through postal difficulties in certain countries
- o Letters can be quite expensive
- o Letters do not allow for immediate feedback.

It is important for staff to remember that we can opt for a number of different ways to communicate with colleagues in other regions using our existing ICT facilities.

E-mail

Messages go direct to the recipient and can be copied to as many people as required. A hard copy of the message can be printed out if required. It is a quick method of communication and enables our company to protect the security and confidentiality of our internal communication. However, confidential documents should be password protected.

Fax

The fax machine allows immediate communication. Even where there is a time difference and the office you are communicating with is closed, the fax message will be there when staff are next in. It is possible to send hard copies of diagrams and drawings/plans of construction sites quickly and cheaply (for the cost of a telephone call).

Voice mail

This enables the sender's spoken message to be recorded in a digital form by a network computer so the recipient can access the message via a telephone handset at any convenient time. This means that, in spite of the time differences that are experienced in running an international sales operation, colleagues can communicate and express themselves in a way that is not possible with written information.

All electronic communication methods do rely on your updating the out-of-office message for e-mail and voice message for voice mail. We will be undertaking random checks to ensure this is happening. Any one with three offences to their name is required to make a donation of £10 or $15 to charity!!!!!

Unit 6

Debriefing Activity 6.1

Specimen answer

REPORT ON SHOPPING HABITS AND SUPERMARKET ADVERTISING

Report Commissioned By: Managing Director, Robinsons Grocery Chain

Report Written By: Any Candidate

Date: 12 September 200X

1.   TERMS OF REFERENCE

This report is an analysis of the information resulting from a survey on shopping habits and supermarket advertising conducted by 'Food Retailer' magazine.

2.   METHODOLOGY

A total of 1750, mainly female, shoppers selected at random from the electoral register, were interviewed in the north of England. The average age of the respondents was 40, and 78 per cent of those interviewed had children.

3.   FINDINGS

3.1   Shopping habits

The survey showed that most people (60 per cent) do a weekly shop, with 17 per cent shopping twice a week and 11 per cent only shopping once every 2 weeks. The most popular day for shopping was Friday (40 per cent), with 31 per cent doing grocery shopping on Saturday and 24 per cent on Thursday. The least popular day was Tuesday with only 4 per cent of respondents saying they shopped on that day.

Table 1 I have chosen a column/bar chart to represent the data in this table.

How often respondents shop

Figure 1 Shopping for groceries

The main reasons for shoppers choosing a particular day to do their shopping was because it was the most convenient time (45 per cent) while 30 per cent said that it was because it fitted in with when they were paid and 26 per cent because it was a good day for special offers.

Table 2 I have chosen a pie chart to represent this data.

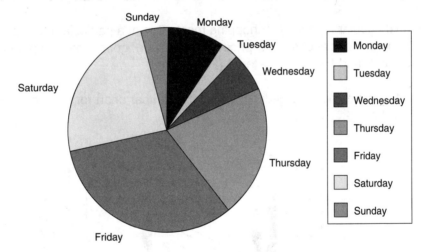

Figure 2 Shopping days

3.2 *Store preferences*

The stores that respondents shopped at most often was Sainsbury (11.2 per cent) and Tesco (10.4 per cent). Robinsons and Fine Fare were sixth in the list with 4.5 per cent of shoppers preferring to shop at these two stores, but 6.9 per cent of respondents shopped most often at the Co-op, 5.7 per cent at Asda and 4.7 per cent at Safeway.

Table 3   I have chosen a standard line graph for the data in this table.

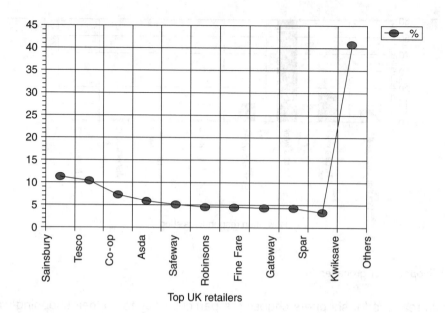

Figure 3 Store shopped at most often for groceries

Gateway, Spar and Kwiksave each attracted about 3–4 per cent of shoppers but just over 40 per cent of respondents cited 'other' smaller stores and shops to do their grocery shopping.

The most popular reasons for shopping most often at a particular store are convenient location (42 per cent), special offers/low prices (38 per cent), good meat (25 per cent), stock all brands (22 per cent) and friendly assistants (20 per cent).

Table 4   I have chosen a 3-dimensional column/bar chart for this data.

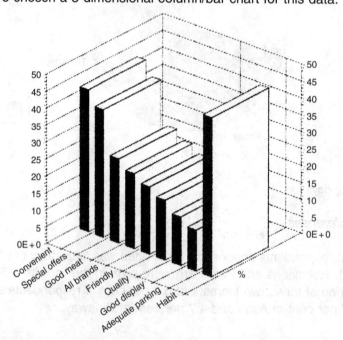

Figure 4 Reasons for shopping at a certain shop

The most popular reasons for not shopping at other stores were high prices (45 per cent), travel distance (27 per cent) and slow checkouts (22 per cent).

3.3 Advertising

Items that are advertised as special offers are frequently purchased by 35 per cent of shoppers although a similar number (38 per cent) never bought them.

Most respondents obtained special offer coupons from newspapers (40 per cent), 25 per cent used store leaflets while only 15 per cent used leaflet drops.

Most respondents preferred Safeway's advertising (20 per cent), with 16 per cent preferring Fine Fare's and 14 per cent preferred Asda's. However, only 2 per cent preferred Robinsons' advertising.

The reasons cited most for liking advertisements were that 'special offers are easy to find' (42 per cent), or that the advertisements were 'eye catching' (38 per cent), 'had large print' (27 per cent) or were 'easy to find specific brands' (17 per cent) or featured 'a variety of items' (15 per cent).

4. CONCLUSION AND RECOMMENDATIONS

The survey presents Robinsons with some interesting findings. From the shoppers surveyed, Robinsons came sixth out of the top ten named stores for grocery shopping. However, 40 per cent of respondents shop most at stores other than the top ten, which indicates that many people are shopping at smaller stores.

This probably links in with the most popular reasons for store choice, which are convenient location and special offers/pricing.

This indicates that Robinsons should further investigate the convenience of its stores to where people live (which may mean looking at 'free' bus rides if stores are not convenient for transport or looking at where stores are located in relation to housing estates).

In addition, Robinsons should compare its prices with those of its main competitors and, if necessary, alter its pricing strategy in order to attract more shoppers.

One reason cited for not using stores was 'slow checkouts', and Robinsons could check the average time checkout staff take to deal with customers and the amount of time shoppers spend queuing to ensure that these factors do not put off potential customers from shopping at Robinsons.

The survey also showed that Friday and Saturday were the most popular shopping days and Robinsons should ensure more staff are on duty on these days.

One important feature of the survey related to advertising. Robinsons' advertising was one of the least preferred from the top ten stores named in the survey. Therefore, advertising needs to be reviewed with a view to making special offers and specific brands more obvious, using large print and making more visual impact on customers.

Media trends showed that newspapers should be the main medium used for special offer coupons' advertising.

Debriefing Activity 6.2

The absolute levels of cost that is £200 000 for Shawcross and £250 000 for Marlbrook are not that important; it is the distribution of those costs across the four given costs that is important. So, it would be best to work on the percentage figure rather than the £'000 figure. This could be illustrated using a multiple column bar chart using the horizontal axis to represent the four categories. However, the relationship of Office costs to Direct labour is also important as, really, in a manufacturing plant Direct labour should show a degree of correlation with the Direct materials. Because the percentage figure that would need to be represented on the horizontal axis would range from 5 to 50 per cent which will result in the relationship between the categories being less easy to quickly assimilate.

There is no timing aspect to this data; therefore a line graph which would be used to show changes over time is not relevant here.

The best way to present this data is using two Pie charts side by side. By using different colours to represent each of the four categories, the piecharts will give a simple pictorial display of the relative sizes of the elements or categories.

By looking at these charts, it is easy to consider that the key issue is the very different relationship between Direct materials and Direct labour in comparison to each other. This relationship needs investigation and explanation.

Unit 7

Debriefing Activity 7.1

Distributors – Petrol stations	You will receive deliveries this weekend. 70% of petrol stations will be covered
	We aim to distribute on a first come first served basis – first fulfilling outstanding orders
Direct customers – Fire/Police/ Hospitals	You will receive deliveries this weekend
	Emergency services will receive priority
Petrol buying customers	Working round the clock to resume normal distribution as soon as possible. Grateful for their understanding
	High price of petrol mainly due to size of tax levy, not us taking advantage
Government	Trying hard to resume normal service in as short a time as possible. Not trying to make additional profit from the situation
Employees – forecourts and Tanker drivers	Need to work hard and be flexible to return to normal
All stakeholders	We have the matter in hand. We are in control and behaving responsibly

Debriefing Activity 7.2

Does your objective start with one of the suggested beginnings in the coursebook? These are commonly associated with communications objectives and so should be used.

Is there a measurable outcome such as raising awareness to 80 per cent? Is that realistic if the product awareness is only 10 per cent currently?

Does the objective have a timed element to it such as 'by the end of May'? Is that achievable?

For example, Cadbury may have an objective to raise awareness of Cadbury's Dream Eggs in the minds of 24 to 34-year-old women from the present level of 30–70 per cent in an 8-week campaign commencing 1st February.

Debriefing Activity 7.3

British Airways is the UK national carrier flying the flag across the world. It stands for quality, reliability, Britishness, high standards and is quietly reassuring as it goes about its day-to-day business. Somewhat arrogant in its dealings in the past it has a core of loyal customers for whom cost is not an issue. It sets out to be, and would maintain it still is, 'the world's favourite airline'. However, being aloof and charging high fares has led to a loss of certain customers as more people move over to the lower cost alternatives.

Virgin entered the industry as a direct competitor and offered different services to customers such as reclining bed seats, limos to the airport and personal DVD choice. Positioned as the new kid on the block with Richard Branson as its figurehead, it very much came to play in the BA playground but set out to win customers over by doing things differently.

easyJet essentially produced another market segment by removing the bureaucracy, paper-work and additional services and cut the cost to a bare minimum. Staff wore T-shirts. The plane became a flying advert with a number on, and it rejected the BA way as being costly and fussy. With Stelios, its founder and Chief Executive, being very visible and trying to break down old established ways of doing things it made Virgin look like the safe option.

Each of these personalities have also manifested themselves in the product/service on offer. Think about the styles of advertising used, the uniforms worn, the very different flying experiences in terms of service offered. All these activities closely support the corporate image.

Debriefing Activity 7.4

Advantages	Disadvantages
Easy way to communicate the values you are portraying	Fashion-led celebrities can have a short shelf life
Clear positioning vehicle in the minds of the consumer	Can put off consumers who do not identify with the face
Consumers' aspirational drives can lead to them becoming brand advocates	Bad publicity for the face will become connected to the organization

Debriefing Activity 7.5

The two main criticisms are that the content is dull and the language is indecipherable.

Somewhere in the text there is possibly a news story but the way it is written makes it difficult to find.

The readers of a local newspaper want to read human-interest stories that relate to the area they live in.

XYZ Farming Ltd is probably a local firm in the area covered by the newspaper, and the writer should make reference to this in the release.

The news story the writer could have developed is that XYZ Farming Ltd has introduced a new product that helps local farmers produce milk that is more popular with consumers, and dairies pay higher prices for it.

To add some human interest to the story, the writer could have found a local farmer who actually had sold more milk to the dairies because of this new product. The writer could then have provided him with a suitable quote in the release, stating his delight with the new product. The firm could then have organized a photograph of the farmer, holding a bag of the miracle new product, standing beside one of his cows.

The press release could also have been improved even further if the writer had avoided jargon and used short, punchy sentences. It would also have been a useful tactic to get the name of the product (Granary) into the first few paragraphs of the release, as presumably the objective was to publicize the Granary feed and the fact that XYZ produced it.

Unit 8

Debriefing Activity 8.1

There are many examples of celebrity use. Gryff Reece Jones has been extensively used as a voice-over. Viewers recognize his voice, it is transferable to radio and it implies values that they want to link into. However, his appearance in a Vauxhall Corsa advertisement as a David Bellamy-type character bombed completely and the TV ad only ran for a short time.

Chris Evans was also used for many voice-overs for similar reasons, however after he left Virgin Radio and disappeared from the public eye for a period, so did the use of his voice.

Carol Vordaman was used by Ariel Washing Powder as the 'Scientific Voice' whilst she was the presenter for the Tomorrow's World programme. The BBC felt this was commercial trading on associations and promptly replaced her as a presenter. The Ariel ad then had little meaning.

Debriefing Activity 8.2

Not all regional areas are served by good local commercial radio stations. Most that are tend to be more urban than rural and are generally better because competition exists due to the large potential audiences. Hence, you will notice that all the major cities in the UK have at least two commercial stations plus the nationals to listen to.

Many rural areas tend to tune into national stations (commercial or BBC) or their local BBC station.

National commercial stations tend to be used by nationally distributed brands, with male targeted ads being placed around drive-time slots (8–9 a.m. and 5–6 p.m.) and more general FMCG stuff being featured during the day. Teenage and younger adults tend to tune in after 8 p.m. and at weekends and so this is where products/services targeted to these groups tend to appear.

Local stations tend to carry a significant amount of advertising for local businesses, for example car dealers and tile shops. Dependent on the size of the business, some with larger budgets will appear in the more expensive drive-time slots, whereas the smaller businesses tend to occupy daytime slots.

Most local advertising can be quite badly produced with annoying jingles or straplines. Unfortunately, these tend to get repeated ad nauseum, hence the listener can choose to 'switch off' some of the smaller commercial stations.

Debriefing Activity 8.3

Specimen answer: The Society for the Prevention of Accidents

To: Ruth Arnold, Marketing Officer

From: Davina Darcy, Chief Executive

Date: 7 May 20XX

Subject: Brief for marketing campaign

Project details

Marketing campaign 8, summer 1999, highlighting health and safety issues in the workplace.

Background information

Government statistics show a rise of 25 per cent in the last 2 years in workplace accidents. A recent Law Gazette article has revealed a dramatic rise in employer negligence cases where damages have had to be awarded and, in some cases, the head of the company has been given a jail sentence.

The SPA has a large database of companies that have requested information on accident prevention, have attended one of our training courses or have been added to our list through our own research into accidents.

Objectives

- o To send out 3000 posters illustrating workplace health and safety hazards.
- o To generate 1000 requests from personnel managers in the industry for leaflets about accident prevention. This information is to be added to our database.
- o To generate 1000 requests from managers in the construction industry for leaflets about accident prevention. This information is to be added to our database.

Target audience

- o Companies on SPA's database
- o Personnel managers in the industry
- o Managers in the construction industry.

Message to be conveyed

- o Government statistics show a 25 per cent rise in workplace accidents over the last 2 years.
- o Accidents can result in employers paying substantial damages and they can be held criminally negligent.
- o More accidents than ever before are happening in the construction industry.

Media

- o Posters illustrating health and safety issues in the workplace to be sent to all the companies held on SPA's database. Each poster to be sent with a covering letter addressed to health and safety officers highlighting the penalties and pointing out methods of prevention. A copy of the letter should be provided so that the health and safety officer can give it to the company's Managing Director.
- o Advertising and PR campaign in *People Management* with a direct response mechanism for personnel managers to request more information about accident prevention.
- o Advertising and PR campaign in *Construction News* with a direct response mechanism for senior managers to request more information about accident prevention.

Timescale

Campaign should run from the beginning of September to the end of October 20XX.

Budget

A total budget of £8000 is available.

Unit 9

Debriefing Activity 9.2

ICT developments have changed the way people communicate as follows:

- o E-mail has become a major means of internal and external communication and large documents can be sent as attachments quickly, which reduces time and cost on paper distribution.
- o In offices that do not have access to scanners or e-mail, or sending visual information, fax machines are still used.
- o Mobile telephone use means staff on the move can keep in touch with colleagues and customers.
- o Laptop technology means sales staff have remote access to information when out in the field with clients.

- o Laptop computers ensure sales staff can give quality presentations to clients.
- o Videoconferencing means excess travel to meetings is reduced but that staff working at different sites can communicate almost face to face without too much advance notice.
- o Databases are used to track customer purchases and to mail merge documents when sending out mail shots to different groups of customers.
- o An EDI system means that when outlets in the network use up materials, re-stocking requests are automatically received which reduces paper and telephone calls.
- o An intranet can be set up for managers to access information on previous projects and client requirements easily and quickly.
- o Internet research means that information can be found more quickly and easily.

Unit 10

Debriefing Activity 10.1

Consider your own organization. What processes do customers go through to decide upon and purchase the product/service in question? How long have these systems been in place? How could they change and how would this enhance the customer experience? How would you communicate this change to the customer so that they could understand what to do and how this helped them?

This activity is essentially very personal to your own situation. However, it might help to know the problems McDonald's had when they tried to change a process. In-store research recorded that queues were most often delayed because of non-standard orders, which had to be cooked fresh (e.g. burger with no relish). McDonald's instituted an express queue, which was designed to fastrack people who only wanted standard menu items. They communicated this by putting an Express Banner above the till on the far right-hand side of the serving area. Unfortunately, customers did not know the criteria that represented an Express purchase, so some who could have used it, didn't, as they were unsure. Some who only wanted one meal, but different to standard, thought it was for them, and held0 up the queue. In the end McDonald's realized that so many customers were asking for non-standard items that the Express checkout delivered no benefit.

Debriefing Activity 10.2

It may be helpful to graphically represent the process of dealing with the complaint, for example

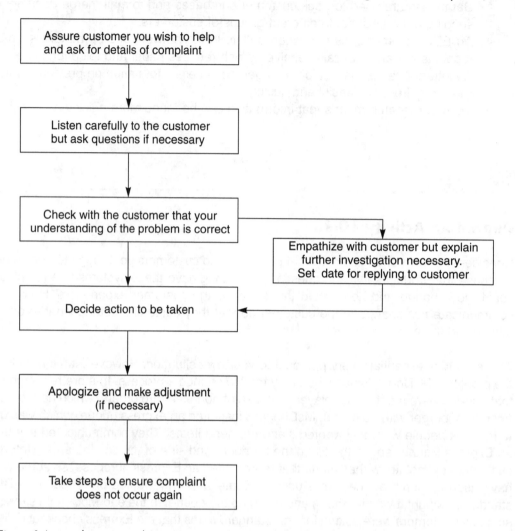

Figure 1 A complaints procedure

There are a number of general approaches that can be adapted to help deal with difficult situations where customers are dissatisfied and a complaint needs to be handled in a sensitive way. Here is a list of helpful approaches:

- o Listen and say nothing until the customer has stated his grievance.
- o Give the customer your name so they are assured that you are committed to resolving the problem.
- o Use appropriate body language to show empathy with the customer.
- o Use an empathic tone of voice.
- o Use diplomatic phrases to calm angry customers, for example 'This is obviously an unsatisfactory situation' or 'I'm sorry you're upset about this situation'.
- o Apologize for the fact that there has been a problem – this does not mean you are accepting full blame.
- o Do not interrupt the customer and use effective listening skills to get an overview of the problem and show that you are taking the customer seriously.
- o Clarify the problem by checking details and making notes so that you can fully investigate the complaint.
- o Be positive, not defensive. So, for instance, you could thank the customer for telling you about the situation because you need to know about the problem if it is to be rectified.

- Tell the customer what steps you are going to take so that they know they have not just sounded off and wasted their time.
- In cases of serious allegations you may need to explain that you cannot take the matter at face value and that you must investigate to verify the allegations.
- Call for management help with customers who remain angry or dissatisfied.

Debriefing Activity 10.3

Tesco Baby Club Card

Pregnant women are encouraged to apply for a club card and the reward is money-off coupons for baby products. The mother-to-be completes an application form, providing information such as name, address, information about the family and the baby's expected birth date.

The money-off coupons encourage repeat purchase at Tesco's stores. The card means the company can record each customer transaction and establish a customer profile. The company can then target the customer with information about relevant products and services. The organization can also sell this information to other organizations wishing to communicate with customers of a certain age, living in a certain area, who have a particular purchase history.

The baby club card scheme also features a frequent customer contact programme. Mothers are sent magazines with hints and advice to coincide with the various developmental stages that babies go through. So, for example, when the baby is aged 4 months old, the mother is sent a magazine which gives advice on how to wean babies onto solid food and contains advertising and money-off coupons relating to first-stage baby food products.

In this way, both the organization and the customer receive benefits from the relationship that is about timing and delivery!

appendix 4

past examination papers and examiner's reports

The Chartered
Institute of Marketing

Professional Certificate in Marketing

Customer Communications

20:	**Customer Communications**
Time:	**14.00 – 17.00**
Date:	**6th December, 2004**

3 Hours Duration

This examination is in two sections.

PART A – Is compulsory and worth 40% of total marks.

PART B – Has **SIX** questions; select **THREE**. Each answer will be worth 20% of the total marks.

DO NOT repeat the question in your answer, but show clearly the number of the questions attempted on the appropriate pages of the answer book.

Rough workings should be included in the answer book and ruled through after use.

© The Chartered Institute of Marketing

Professional Certificate in Marketing

PART A

Mintel

The following extract was reproduced and adapted with kind permission from Mintel.

Despite a dwindling birth rate (and hence customer numbers) and advertising restrictions, the baby food and drink market's value has grown almost 20% in recent years. This growth is a reflection of modern times - working patterns, shopping and eating habits, consumer views on food, higher disposable income and aspirations for their children. More mothers are working, thus spending more on convenience and timesaving products. They are now buying more jars of baby food than previous generations, who generally made more meals themselves because they were not working.

More mothers are also trading up to premium organic baby produce amid food safety scares, in an attempt to ensure that what they are feeding their baby is safe, wholesome and tasty. Consequently, the sector is becoming increasingly mainstream with a rash of new suppliers entering the market and big baby brands going organic. Organic baby food has taken off in recent years to reach a value of £27.4 million in 2003, more than five times higher than in 1999. Baby food is a particularly buoyant sub-sector of the organic food market, indicating that consumers are not deterred by higher prices when it comes to purchasing for their infants. Figure 1 details value trends for organic baby food.

UK retail sales of organic baby food, 1999-2004

	£ million	% of total baby food and drink market
1999	5.0	1.6
2000	7.2	2.3
2001	9.0	2.7
2002	12.0	3.4
2003	27.4	7.5
2004 (est)	39.6	10.6

Figure 1 - Source: Adapted from Mintel, "Baby Food and Drink"

The total market for baby food and drinks can be segmented into four main sectors; milk, meals, drinks and finger foods. In terms of volume consumed, baby meals comprise by far the largest sector, accounting for three quarters of total units sold. Baby milks assume far more importance than volume because the unit cost is much higher, with more servings per pack. Consequently, there is little difference in value terms between the two sectors. Drinks and finger food (mainly rusks) account for 9% of sales by value and 11% by volume. Figure 2 gives trends by sector.

UK volume retail sales of baby food and drink, by product type, 2001-2004.

	2001 Million Units	2002 Million Units	2003 Million Units	2004 Million Units(est)	% change 2001-2004
Baby meals	208.7	220.0	216.8	224.9	+7.8
Baby milks	36.8	38.4	40.6	42.0	+14.1
Baby drinks	22.6	23.5	26.1	20.9	-7.5
Baby finger foods	7.1	7.8	7.9	12.0	+69.0
Total	275.2	289.7	291.4	299.9	+9.0

Source: Adapted from Mintel, "Baby Food and Drink"

Hipp Nutrition has made the most of the burgeoning demand for organic baby foods in the UK, building a healthy 58% share of the market in 2003 with sales of £16 million. This share is expected to grow to around 62% by the end of 2004. For example, Hipp's infant milk and follow-on milk (for babies over 6 months of age) are the only organic baby milk formulae on the UK market at the current time.

Between them, Hipp Nutrition and Baby Organix have pioneered the organic baby food market; in 2003 the companies were dominant, although Heinz and Cow & Gate are now making good headway in the market. Baby Organix, however, has been rather less successful in building on that strength.

Hipp Nutrition has made gains with its propositions of choice and value for money, while Baby Organix presents a premium offering.

Figure 3 looks at manufacturer's shares in organic baby foods.

Manufacturer/brand shares in the UK organic baby foods market, 2003-2004.

	2003		2004 (est)		% change 2003-2004
	£ million	%	£ million	%	
Hipp Nutrition	16.0	58	24.5	62	+53
Baby Organix	10.2	37	11.2	28	+10
Boots	0.4	1	0.5	1	+25
Others	0.8	3	3.4	9	+325
Total	27.4	100	39.6	100	+45

Source: Adapted from Mintel, "Baby Food and Drink"

PART A - Compulsory

Question One

a) You are a marketing assistant in a major supermarket chain. The supermarket is considering developing its own range of organic baby food and/or drink. By extracting relevant information from the data given, write a formal **REPORT** to your marketing manager, which evaluates the case for your supermarket chain developing this new product range.

(25 marks)

b) Include the following three appendices in your report:

   i) A line graph showing the trend of UK retail sales of organic baby food 1999-2004

(5 marks)

   ii) A bar chart showing percentage change for UK volume retail sales of baby food and drink, by product type, 2001-2004

(5 marks)

   iii) A pie chart showing the estimated manufacturer/brand shares in the UK organic baby foods market, 2004.

(5 marks)

(Total 40 marks)

PART B - Answer **THREE** questions only

Question Two

You work for a company who is about to launch a new type of lubricating oil for cars. The new oil will be launched at a forthcoming exhibition in Frankfurt.

a) Draft a press release for the business press announcing this new product launch.

(10 marks)

b) Write an email to staff that will be attending the exhibition, reminding them of the importance of tone of voice, body language and listening skills.

(10 marks)

(Total 20 marks)

Question Three

You work as a promotions assistant for a hair shampoo manufacturer.

a) Identify **FOUR** members of the decision making unit (DMU) for a female, aged 15-18 years of age, and the role that each member of the DMU may play as she decides whether or not to buy your brand of shampoo.

(10 marks)

b) Identify **FOUR** methods of promotion that you would use in an integrated communications campaign for a brand of hair shampoo aimed at females aged 15-18 years of age.

(10 marks)

(Total 20 marks)

Question Four

As a communications assistant for a large local veterinary practice, your job is to keep your customers/animal/owners up-to-date with the services your veterinary practice provides.

a) Draft an advertisement for your local newspaper, announcing that your veterinary practice now offers a full dog-training service.

(10 marks)

b) Your veterinary practice anticipates a high volume of demand will be generated as a result of your advert for the dog training service. You are to attend a meeting to be held with the employees of the veterinary practice, to enable you to put forward proposals for ways to use information and communication technologies (ICT) to promote further the services practice offers.

Draft an agenda for the meeting. Include at least **TWO** motions with proposers and seconders.

(10 marks)

(Total 20 marks)

Question Five

You work in a large cinema as a customer care assistant and recently you have been receiving more complaints than usual from unsatisfied customers. The main focus of the complaints appears to be the lack of customer care and attention.

a) Write a standard letter of apology to these unsatisfied and very unhappy customers and offer them an appropriate recompense.

(8 marks)

b) Write a memo to staff, advising them of the importance of customer care and relationship management within the cinema.

(12 marks)

(Total 20 marks)

Question Six

You work for a UK based company that produces exclusive bed linen. A new market opportunity has been identified by one of your agents over in a foreign country that has very different cultural values from the UK. You need to prepare a presentation to your sales representatives who will be trying to sell your bed linen to prospective buyers in this foreign country.

a) Draft notes for yourself on how to write and deliver a good presentation.

(10 marks)

b) Draw up **TWO** slides with presenter's notes for your presentation. One slide should highlight the communications process and the other slide should show the key problems that may occur in this process, with particular reference to your company in the foreign country.

(10 marks)

(Total 20 marks)

Question Seven

You work as a marketing assistant in a large bookstore who would like a new corporate catalogue designed to promote the range of books sold. You now have to write a design brief for your new corporate catalogue, so that a design agency may provide you with their proposal for the "look" of the catalogue and an approximate price for them to undertake the work.

Your brief should indicate your design requirements, such as your target audience, the ways in which your bookstore aims to keep their customers satisfied and the corporate image you wish to portray.

Furthermore, your brief should include a description of print requirements, such as the number of catalogues needed, the quality of paper required and any other information you think is relevant.

(Total 20 marks)

The Chartered
Institute of Marketing

Professional Certificate in Marketing

Customer Communications

20:          Customer Communications

SENIOR EXAMINER'S REPORT FOR DECEMBER 2004 EXAMINATION PAPER

**SENIOR EXAMINER'S REPORT FOR
DECEMBER 2004 EXAMINATION PAPER**

MODULE NAME: CUSTOMER COMMUNICATIONS

AWARD NAME: PROFESSIONAL CERTIFICATE IN MARKETING

DATE: DECEMBER 2004

1.   General Strengths and Weaknesses of Candidates

This session has gone fairly well, mainly because students seemed to (more or less) have made better attempts at the formal reports and graphs, which is cheering. Most UK centre candidates attempted four questions however, many overseas candidates attempted fewer, and this is clearly a contributory factor in the lower pass rate for these candidates. There is a definite sign of improvement with regards to the understanding of the topic by a large number of candidates. Many of them seem better able to apply the theory and work in context.

Having said that, there are still many students who fail to provide definitions and only provide lengthy discussions (particularly evident on question three). General weaknesses are not understanding/knowing the basics like letter layout, and how to "sell" an advertisement. These should be regarded as basics for good communication.

Too many candidates are leaving the case study until the end and therefore not having enough time to complete the very important section of the paper. A lot of valuable marks were lost in this part thus lowering the candidates chances of passing or achieving a better grade.

There are still too many students who fail to fill in the front cover of the exam script and finally, the instructions to commence each answer on a fresh page were often ignored.

Finally, I would continue to impress upon study centre tutors to remind candidates of the importance of past exam papers, marking schemes and specimen answers.

2.   Strengths and Weaknesses by Question

Question 1- Case Study

Same problems reoccur from year to year – students re-writing the case study material with litter analysis and context – the question asks for evaluation and very few students were able to do this. The graphs were reasonably well done – although many candidates did not identify the source and there still appears to be a lot of confusion between a histogram and a bar-chart.

Question 2 – Press Release and Email re. Tone of Voice, Body Language and Listening Skills

The question was answered by many candidates and answered well. Formats remain a problem, especially quotes and double spacing. Some candidates failed to make the relationship between the exhibition in Frankfurt and the needs of the email, i.e. tone of voice and any cultural differences.

Question 3 – Decision Making Unit and Integrated Marketing Communications

Lack of definition of Decision Making Unit (DMU) and Integrated Marketing Communications (IMC). A few still confused DMU with Decision Making Process (DMP). Candidates need to discuss their answers more fully. When the examiner asks for IMC, I expect to see the candidate exhibiting an understanding of what integration would mean in practice.

Question 4 – Advert and Agenda (ICT)

This was not a popular question and when it was attempted it was generally poor. This should have been an opportunity for creativity and originality, but the majority of adverts were disappointing and some did not even include contact details. The agenda was generally handled well, which reflects the rote learning of usual agenda headings – weaker candidates didn't include relevant motions with proposers/seconders.

Question 5 – Letter and Memo (Customer Care and Relationship Marketing)

A popular question but surprisingly, not many candidates earned the full two marks for format or marks for tone in the letter. With regards to the memo, definitions of customer care and relationship marketing were either non-existent or weak. Discussion of relationship marketing was weak, although the importance of customer care was well answered.

Question 6 – Presentation Notes and Slides re. Effective presentations and communication problems.

The better answers did use the PASS format for the presentation notes, however few answered in context and the majority ignored the context.
The slides were very poorly done in the majority of cases – most were drawn crudely and candidates failed to adopt an appropriate layout. There was a good understanding of the communications process but, again, a lack of context with just theory reproduced.

Question 7 – Design Brief

This was the least popular question on the exam paper. Candidates generally managed to include a reasonable proportion of the content needed in order to give the relevant instructions. Careful reading would have ensured higher marks – all the clues were there!

3.   Future Themes

I do feel it is important that candidates have a better understanding of the links between all of the areas of the Customer Communications syllabus, rather than merely each separate part on its own. Candidates should therefore expect to see a greater requirement for this kind of understanding and its subsequent application (in the given context), in future exam papers. I will also expect candidates to provide clear, concise definitions in their answers – this is an area of great weakness for many.

The Chartered
Institute of Marketing

Professional Certificate in Marketing

Customer Communications

20:        Customer Communications
Time: 14.00 - 17.00
Date: 6 June, 2005

3 Hours Duration

This examination is in **TWO** sections.

PART A - Is compulsory and worth **40%** of total marks

PART B - Has **SIX** questions; select **THREE**. Each answer will be worth **20%** of the total marks

DO NOT repeat the question in your answer, but show clearly the number of the questions attempted on the appropriate pages of the answer book.

Rough workings should be included in the answer book and ruled through after use.

© The Chartered Institute of Marketing, 2005

Professional Certificate in Marketing

Customer Communications

PART A

The following extract is reproduced and adapted with kind permission of Mintel.

Most of us are taught the importance of a good breakfast when we are children, yet much of this advice is neglected as we get older. Furthermore, changing lifestyles dictate changing morning routines. The Home-Grown Cereal Authority (HGCA) which represents cereal farmers and processors in Britain, claims that approximately 14 million people (equating to around 23% of the UK population in 2004) go without breakfast at home on a regular basis. It also claims that over half of all workers (around 14 million, of total population in employment of 28.5 million in 2004) never eat breakfast at all. Of particular reference to this report is the HGCA's claim that: "Recent independent studies show that cereal skippers (people who do not eat cereal at breakfast) generally feel more stressed, less energetic and tend to be fatter than people who start the day with the traditional bowl of cereal, slice of toast or bacon sandwich".

The UK market for breakfast cereals can be segmented into two categories (see Figure 1). Firstly, there are ready-to-eat (RTE) cereals; these are commonly poured from a packet straight into a bowl and milk added. Secondly come hot cereals, which comprise oat and instant hot-cereal products. In this instance these do not include RTE cereals served with hot milk. As Figure 1 shows, the market remains overwhelmingly dominated by RTE products. Hot cereals have shown marginal value growth over the review period, outperforming the slowing rate of growth seen in RTE (figure not shown). The generally poor market performance since 2002 is a result of breakfast's decline as a key meal and consumer take-up of alternative products (eg cereal bars).

Figure 1: UK retails sales of breakfast cereals, by category and volume, 2002 - 2006

	2002		2004		2006(est.)		% change 2002-2006
	000 tonnes	%	000 tonnes	%	000 tonnes	%	
RTE	350	91	343	91	345	91	-1.4
Hot	36	9	35	9	35	9	-2.8
Total volume	386	100	378	100	380	100	-1.6

Data may not equal totals due to rounding.
Source: Fictional

During the latter part of the 1990's the UK breakfast cereal market was characterised by high levels of advertising spend. However, tighter margins has resulted in a fall in advertising spend of around 25% in recent years and is symptomatic of a sector struggling to continue expensive campaigns. Below-the-line campaigns are increasingly being used in this sector; below-the-line

305

campaigns can increase volumes, although not necessarily penetration, and can help to stimulate growth in overall market size. Promotional support for some of the larger cereal brands during November 2004 included "33% extra free", "Free cinema tickets" and merchandise for new film releases at cinemas.

The influx of convenience-oriented breakfast bakery items (eg toaster and microwaveable pastries, muffins, breakfast cereal bars) has also had a major impact on the cold RTE breakfast cereal market in recent years. The main response has been developing products that cater better for convenience snacking. Other trends have centred on healthier positioning and fruitier flavours.

Compared to cold RTE breakfast cereals, the hot cereals market is very small in global terms. Indeed, it is nearly non-existent outside of the UK, North America and parts of Asia. Furthermore, only a small number of new products are introduced into this market every year, on a very seasonal basis. The most active region for hot cereals is North America.

Figure 2 shows a forecast for the UK breakfast cereal market, showing growth of 5% over the coming years to attain a market value of £1.1 billion by 2009. The introduction and expansion of organic, indulgence (intended for pleasure) and convenience products will drive demand and growth within the market. Products perceived as being healthy or exclusive will command higher prices.

Figure 2   Forecast of the UK breakfast cereals market, 2004-2009

	RTE £ million	Hot £ million	Total £ million
2004	990	50.0	1, 040
2005	1, 024	52.0	1, 076
2006	1, 032	53.0	1, 085
2007	1, 040	54.2	1, 094
2008	1, 043	55.6	1, 099
2009	1, 040	56.9	1, 097

Source: Fictional

The above data has been based on a fictitious situation drawing on a variety of events and do not reflect management practices of any particular organisation.

PART A - Compulsory

Question 1

As a marketing assistant for a cereal manufacturer, you believe you have identified a market opportunity promoting your cereal ranges directly to elderly people.

a.
  i. Write a formal report to your board of directors, evaluating the case for the company to promote to this sector. Your report should include relevant data extracted from the case

  ii. Identify and justify within your report **TWO** key above-the-line and **TWO** key below-the-line methods of promotion, suitable for targeting the elderly market

(25 marks)

b. Include the following **TWO** appendices in your report:

  i. A line graph showing the forecast of the UK breakfast cereals market, 2004-2009

(5 marks)

  ii. A Gantt chart showing your proposed above and below-the-line promotion campaign aimed at the elderly

(10 marks)

(Total 40 marks)

PART B - Answer **THREE** questions only

Question 2

You work as a marketing assistant for one of the largest confectionery manufacturers in the world, who is about to launch a new confectionery product aimed at women aged 25-40 years of age.

a. Write a short report to your marketing manager, highlighting the role and importance of logos, packaging, point of sale display and merchandising for this new product

(10 marks)

b. Write a press release for the consumer press, informing them of the forthcoming launch of this new confectionery product

(10 marks)

(Total 20 marks)

Question 3

a. Discuss the stages of the decision making process a consumer may go through when considering the purchase of a new computer

(10 marks)

b. Discuss the role of **FOUR** possible members of the decision making unit for a large engineering company, who are considering purchasing computers for their 300 employees

(10 marks)

(Total 20 marks)

Question 4

A new product assistant has joined your company. Your company manufactures cable for a variety of electronic products, including computers, printers and scanners. She has never been involved in leading and conducting internal meetings before. Send your new product assistant an email with an attachment that contains draft explanatory notes that help her to understand:

a. The role of meetings

(5 marks)

b. The different types of meeting that occur within your company

(5 marks)

c. Leading meetings, and the role that non-verbal communication plays in this process

(5 marks)

d. The documentation used in meetings

(5 marks)

(Total 20 marks)

Question 5

You work as a promotions assistant for a kitchen appliance manufacturer. The company are now going to add cookers/stoves to their range of products.

a. Identify **FOUR** methods of promotion that you would use to promote this new product range, within an integrated marketing communications campaign. Justify your choice of promotion relevant to the likely target market

(10 marks)

b. As this is a new product, you realise that you may have queries and complaints from customers. Describe how to plan and establish a customer care programme for customers who buy this new product

(10 marks)

(Total 20 marks)

Question 6

The communication process can sometimes be difficult.

a. Explain the elements of the communications process, using examples from products/services of your choice to illustrate the terms – noise, distortion, encoding and decoding

(10 marks)

b. Explain how **FOUR** methods of information and communication technologies (ICT) can assist in internal communication

(10 marks)

(Total 20 marks)

Question 7

Customers are often accused of being more demanding today and because of this, marketers must clearly understand who their customer is and what they really want in order to satisfy them. As a marketing assistant in a service organisation:

a. Draft notes for a presentation to the marketing director, where you define the terms "customer", "stakeholder" and "user" and discuss the importance of "customers" to your organisation, using a service sector organisation to illustrate your points

(10 marks)

b. Write an email to the sales team, where you discuss the importance of tone of voice, listening and verbal skills in developing and maintaining good customer relations

(10 marks)

(Total 20 marks)

The Chartered
Institute of Marketing

Professional Certificate in Marketing

Customer Communications

20:     CUSTOMER COMMUNICATIONS

SENIOR EXAMINER'S REPORT FOR JUNE 2005 EXAMINATION PAPER

© The Chartered Institute of Marketing, 2005

SENIOR EXAMINERS REPORT FOR

JUNE 2005 EXAMINATION PAPER

MODULE NAME:	CUSTOMER COMMUNICATIONS
AWARD NAME:	PROFESSIONAL CERTIFICATE IN MARKETING
DATE:	JULY 2005

1. General Strengths and Weaknesses of Candidates

General Strengths

- Generally seems to be a good understanding of some relevant concepts, i.e. the communications process, the decision making process (DMP) and the decision making unit (DMU).
- Generally seems to be a good understanding of the layouts that are required, namely reports, press releases, presentations and so on.

General Weaknesses

- Many candidates' examination technique was poor – apparently running out of time for the last question and not having a clear focus on the question.
- Marks lost because context was ignored.
- Marks lost because definitions were not included.
- Many candidates did not seem to acknowledge the mark breakdown given for the various parts of a question.
- Three specific areas provided problems for many candidates – namely, the Gantt chart, merchandising and Integrated Marketing Communications.

2. Strengths and Weaknesses by Question

Part A

Question 1 – The Case Study

1a (i)
Candidates spent valuable time reproducing much of the case study and in doing so ran out of time to answer the question properly. Although most students were able to organise information under the correct headings, they are still confused by the difference in meaning between "conclusions" and "recommendations." Also, they failed to focus on the word "promote" in 1a (i), and failed to gain marks for discussion of market opportunities.

1a (ii)
Most candidates were able to identify above and below-the-line methods of promotion but failed to justify their answers.

1b (i)
Encouraging ability to draw the correct chart (line graph), however, key marks were lost by not providing a key, title or a source.

1b (ii)
Many candidates failed to produce a Gantt chart at all and many of those who did really did not fully understand what a Gantt chart was. Again, many candidates failed to include the basics, like a source or a title. Better candidates produced a realistic Gantt chart, which reflected the recommendations they'd made within their reports for above and below-the-line promotions. Unfortunately, many candidates appear to have a poor understanding of how the different marketing tools can be used to support each other in an integrated campaign. This final point was also very evident in Question 5.

Part B

Question 2

This was not really a popular question.

a. Report format was generally okay. This question was a classic example of a problem which ran through many candidates' papers; namely lack of definitions. The areas of logos, packaging, point of sale display and merchandising should all have been clearly defined before discussing and contextualising their relative role and importance. Many candidates seemed confused with merchandising, with some completely missing it out.

b. The quality of answers for how a press release should be set out, plus tone, relevancy etc, was again of a disappointing standard. Major areas where marks were lost were:

- relevant quotes missed
- double spacing ignored
- no heading, no date and no key information in the first paragraph
- little real understanding of the purpose of a press release.

Question 3

By far this was one of the most popular question and many candidates made a reasonable attempt. It would appear that my comments in previous Senior Examiner reports have been taken on board, as there seems to be a vast improvement in candidates' knowledge, understanding and subsequent contextualising of both the Decision Making Process and the Decision Making Unit. However, many lost marks for not providing definitions and contextualising was lacking in some. Some candidates did confuse the DMP with AIDA; however, many of the stronger candidates discussed the two together, producing some very fine answers.

Question 4

In terms of format, many candidates did not indicate that there was an attachment with the email. Nevertheless, many candidates tackled this question and demonstrated a good knowledge of meetings and associated theory. Contextualising was an issue here, with many candidates making little reference to electronic products.

Question 5

This was a popular question with some valiant efforts.

a.   Most candidates could identify four types of promotion, but often failed to define each method of promotion and they could not justify their choice in the context of a kitchen appliance manufacturer. My **overriding issue** with this question was the dearth of definitions of "Integrated Marketing Communications" and its subsequent discussion AT ALL, never mind in context! Tutors and candidates MUST develop a comprehensive understanding of this area of the syllabus, as it **will** come up time and time again.

b.   The majority of candidates failed to define customer care.

Question 6

By far the most popular question, with many candidates achieving high marks for their efforts.

a.   The content of the communications process was usually accurately drawn, with evidence that candidates understood what noise, distortion, encoding and decoding was. Explanations of barriers to communication were usually adequate but often poorly expressed and incomplete. Lack of contextualising was an issue here.

b.   As in question 5 above, many candidates failed to define Information and Communication Technology. Nevertheless, many candidates did produce some very good answers.

Question 7

Another popular question but again many candidates lost marks for lack of context.

a.   Considering the title of this subject, a surprising number could not define "customer" and "user" and understand the difference. Some also found difficulty in commenting on their importance. Presentation format was, in most cases, appropriate.

b.   This email was generally handled well but few gained marks for discussing good customer relationships. Tone of voice, verbal and listening skills were discussed but the application to good customer relations in context was lost.

appendix 5
curriculum information and reading list

Aim

The Customer Communications unit provides the entry level skills and application in the development and use of communications for the Professional Certificate. It aims to provide students with a working knowledge of customers' buying behaviour and the promotional mix as well as communications techniques.

Students will be expected to be conversant with the content of the Marketing Fundamentals unit before undertaking this unit.

Related Statements of Practice

Cb.1   Develop direct or indirect communications
Cb.2   Deliver direct or indirect communications
Gb.1   Support the management of customer relationships
Gb.2   Deliver effective customer service

Learning outcomes

Students will be able to:

5.24.1   Recognize organizations as open systems and explain the importance of relationships between the organization and its suppliers, intermediaries, customers and other key stakeholders in a changing environment.

5.24.2   Explain why it is important for marketers to understand consumer and industrial buying behaviour for marketing decisions.

5.24.3   Explain the elements of the promotional mix and its fit with the marketing planning process.

5.24.4   Explain the advantages and disadvantages of the range of communications tools available to an organization.

5.24.5 Develop internal and external communications using appropriate tools to suit a variety of target audiences and using an understanding of customer behaviour and customer information.

5.24.6 Select appropriate verbal and non-verbal communications with people inside and outside the organization.

5.24.7 Demonstrate the importance of customers and customer service and apply customer care principles to create positive relationships with customers in a variety of contexts.

Knowledge and skill requirements

Element 1: Customers and stakeholders (20 per cent)

1.1 Explain what is meant by the terms 'customer', 'stakeholder' and 'user'.

1.2 Demonstrate the fundamental importance of 'customers' to all forms of organizations, including services and the need to clearly identify them.

1.3 Describe the link between the marketing concept, a customer focus and relationship marketing.

1.4 Appreciate the need for effective internal and external customer communications and their link to and role in maintaining customer focus, developing and sustaining good customer relations and relationship marketing in creating loyalty and customer retention.

1.5 List the factors that cause change in customers and the subsequent impact on marketing programmes.

Element 2: Buying behaviour (10 per cent)

2.1 Explain the difference between consumer buyer behaviour and organizational buyer behaviour.

2.2 Explain the importance of understanding buyer behaviour.

2.3 Describe the decision-making unit (*DMU*) and the roles of its constituents.

2.4 The decision-making process (*DMP*) for consumers and organizations.

2.5 The impact and effect of the *DMU* and the *DMP* on the communications mix.

Element 3: Implementing elements of the promotional mix (50 per cent)

3.1 Explain the concept of, and need for, an integrated marketing communications approach and the links between communications and marketing planning.

3.2 Explain the role and importance of promotion in marketing.

3.3 Explain the structure and function of the communication process.

3.4 Describe the tools of promotion (the promotion mix).

3.5 Explain the planning process for developing and implementing promotional strategies and individual elements of the promotional mix.

3.6 Explain how above-the-line and below-the-line activities are used.

3.7 Explain the key stages and considerations when developing and designing advertisements.

3.8 Describe the role and scope of PR and its contribution to the promotional mix.

3.9 Explain the role of corporate identity, brand image and logos in corporate communication with customers.

3.10 Distinguish between the different forms of integrated mail media, such as direct mail leaflets and mail-order advertising.

3.11 Explain the role of point of sale (*POS*) material and how it is developing in response to changing customer needs.

3.12 Explain the role of packaging in the promotions mix.

3.13 Describe the role of exhibitions as a communications tool and their role in promotions.

3.14 Explain the role of information and communications technology (*ICT*) in communications, including digital TV and interactive marketing.

3.15 Describe current trends and developments in promotions and their impact on organizations.

Element 4: Face-to-face communication (10 per cent)

4.1 Describe the communication process and explain the importance and the advantages and disadvantages of different types of communication in a variety of face-to-face situations.

4.2 Identify barriers to communication and explain how they can be avoided and overcome.

4.3 Explain the communications planning process to produce effective strategies for improving alternative communications formats.

4.4 Explain the importance of effective body language, tone, verbal and listening skills in communication and strategies for developing and improving verbal, non-verbal and listening skills.

4.5 Interpret, summarize and present oral, written and graphical information.

4.6 Explain key communication factors to consider in meetings, including arranging and convening a meeting, documentation involved and strategies for conducting a meeting.

4.7 Plan, prepare and deliver a presentation using appropriate and effective visual aids and media.

4.8 Use a variety of formats to communicate with internal and external customers including telephone, letters, memoranda, notices, reports and e-mails.

Element 5: Customer service and customer care (10 per cent)

5.1 Explain the concept of customer care and its importance in consumer, business-to-business, not-for-profit and public sector organizations.

5.2 Explain the importance of quality and customer care and methods of achieving quality.

5.3 Explain the relationship between customer care, customer focus and relationship marketing.

5.4 Explain the importance of obtaining customer feedback and devising contingencies for dealing with customer complaints.

5.5 Describe how to plan and establish a customer care programme.

5.6 Demonstrate an understanding of how ICT is used in customer service, for example through the use of databases.

Related key skills

Key skill	Relevance to unit knowledge and skills
Communication	Select appropriate communications for different audiences
	Develop internal and external communications (written or oral)
Application of number	Forecast likely response rates
	Carry out calculations for budgets and measures
Information technology	Exchange information with others
Working with others	Develop relationships in the marketing function
Improving own learning and performance	Apply planning techniques to agree targets and plan how these will be met (methods, timescales, resources)
	Select and use a variety of methods for learning
	Manage time effectively
	Seek feedback to monitor performance and modify approach
	Review progress and provide evidence of meeting targets
Problem-solving	

Assessment

CIM will offer two forms of assessment for this unit from which study centres or students may choose: written examination and an assignment. CIM may also recognize, or make joint awards for, units at an equivalent level undertaken with other professional marketing bodies and educational institutions.

Recommended support materials

Core texts

Blundel, R. (2004) *Effective Organizational Communication: Perspectives, Principles and Practice*, 2nd edition, Harlow: Prentice Hall.

Syllabus guides

Jones, M. (2006) *Customer Communications*, Oxford: BH/Elsevier.

BPP (2006) *Customer Communications: Study Text 2006*, London: BPP Publishing.

Supplementary readings

Daffy, C. (2000) *Once a Customer, Always a Customer*, 3rd edition, Dublin: Oak Tree Press.

Fiske, J. (1990) *Introduction to Communication Studies*, London: Routledge.

Foster, J. (2005) *Effective Writing Skills for Public Relations*, 5th edition, London: Kogan Page.

Godin, S. (2002) *Permission Marketing: Turning Strangers into Friends and Friends into Customers*, London: Simon and Schuster.

McQuail, D. and Windahl, S. (1993) *Communication Models for The Study of Mass Communications*, 2nd edition, Harlow: Longman.

McQuail, D. (2005) *McQuail's Mass Communication Theory*, 5th edition, London: Sage.

BPP (2006) *Customer Communications: Practice and Revision Kit*, London: BPP Publishing.

BH (2006) *CIM Revision Cards: Customer Communications*, Oxford: BH/Elsevier.

Overview and rationale

Approach

The ultimate significance of the Customer Communications unit is based on the importance of both customers and communications to the success of organizations. Without identifying who customers are and their buying habits, we cannot begin to understand them. Without this fundamental understanding, we cannot develop appropriate and effective communications.

Therefore, the rationale for the unit is that it provides marketers with a comprehensive range of communication tools aimed at establishing and maintaining relationships with our customers, both internal and external. In addition, it emphasizes the role that we have to play in nurturing and developing our relationships.

The syllabus has now been greatly refined, ensuring both horizontal and vertical separation and integration.

- o *Horizontally* – the unit includes customer behaviour and customer care moved from the Marketing Fundamentals unit of the previous Certificate syllabus. The use of marketing research, previously included in this unit, has been moved to Marketing Environment to avoid overlap. The practical application of communications skills is reinforced in Marketing in Practice.
- o *Vertically* – this unit provides a foundation for Marketing Communications at the Professional Diploma, which builds on this unit by developing higher level of knowledge and understanding for communicating.

Syllabus content

This unit, like the other units across all levels of the CIM syllabus, has been modified and improved. These modifications have tried to take into account the changes to the Marketing Customer Interface, to be renamed Marketing Communications, the Professional Diploma unit which is a logical follow-on and progression from Customer Communications.

With this in mind, the percentages for indicative weightings are:

- o Customers and stakeholders (20 per cent)
- o Buying behaviour (10 per cent)
- o Implementing elements of the promotional mix (50 per cent)
- o Face-to-face communication (10 per cent)
- o Customer service and customer care (10 per cent)

Those tutors already familiar with the previous Customer Communications syllabus will be able to identify key changes to the content, particularly the inclusion of and greater emphasis on buying behaviour and customer care, previously covered in Marketing Fundamentals although both areas were covered in the previous syllabus to an extent, and building relationships with stakeholders.

Element 1 – Customers and stakeholders

The key message that needs to be communicated to students is the importance of customer-centred organizations. Tutors need to differentiate between the different types of 'customers' that marketers communicate with. The difference between internal and external customers should be reinforced and the differences between customers and consumers should be emphasized. The link and the importance between good communications and maintaining and nurturing good relationships with customers should be discussed along with the many factors which cause changes in customers and the subsequent impact on marketing programmes. Tutors should introduce the concept of relationship marketing and its importance, although this will be covered in greater depth in Element 5. The key message here is the role of communication in managing this relationship, to guiding and supporting customers through changing circumstances and situations, including for example, the need to develop new products in response to changing consumer attitudes.

Element 2 – Buying behaviour

The concepts of the decision-making units and the role of stakeholders should be introduced in relation to the communication process. At a basic level, students should be able to understand and identify the needs of different target audiences in both not-for-profit organizations and a variety of business sectors. Students need to have a good understanding of buying behaviour within decision-making units and the impact of the DMU on both the decision-making process and ultimately on the communications mix.

Element 3 – Implementing elements of the promotional mix

The key point here is that students should be aware of basic theories about the communication process and customer behaviour so that students can design effective customer communications at a basic level.

Consequently it would be appropriate to introduce the encoding/decoding process of communication. In addition, it would be appropriate to introduce students to a simplified black box model of consumer behaviour and combine it with the various influences on consumer behaviour.

Students should develop a comprehensive understanding of the range of promotion tools available to them and be able to develop and implement promotional activities and individual elements of the promotional mix. Therefore, practical exercises around developing advertisements, planning exhibitions, developing effective sales promotion and devising PR campaigns would all be useful practical measures to deepen understanding and assist in application.

The role of ICT should be discussed, including digital TV and interactive marketing. Students are not expected to have technological expertise in this area. Tutors should impress upon candidates to be aware of developments in this area and of their dynamic nature and impact by reading appropriate marketing magazines and the quality press. Key points for discussion will include how digital technology will impact upon media decisions and how developments in digital technology (for example interactive catalogues, newsletters and video conferencing) will influence media decisions and improve communication.

A basic knowledge of consumer behaviour can be applied so that students are capable of drafting a variety of communications, bearing in mind their target audience, and the use of appropriate tone and language.

The concept of and need for an integrated marketing communications approach should be introduced as a way of pulling together this element. It will introduce students to the strategic role of communications however, more importantly, it will encourage students to view and consider each element of the promotional mix as part of a cohesive whole, whose individual elements go towards creating an overall picture.

Finally, students should look beyond current practice and give consideration to trends and developments in promotions and their impact on organizations.

Element 4 – Face-to-face communication

Tutors will again describe the communications process and explain the importance and the advantages and disadvantages of different types of communication in a variety of face-to-face situations. Tutors will explain the importance of effective body language, tone, verbal and listening skills in communication and strategies for developing and improving verbal, non-verbal and listening skills. Students must also develop the skill of interpreting, summarizing and presenting oral, written and graphical information. Good practice for students would be to write reports that interpret customer data, market trends and issues relating to electronic methods of communication.

Students should be able to identify barriers to communication and be able to explain how they can be avoided and overcome.

Key communication factors to be considered in planning key communications events must be given due consideration, for example, the key communication factors involved in planning and conducting meetings or planning and preparing a presentation. This could involve approaches to pitching for work from clients or dealing with presentations from suppliers. Tutors should also encourage students to look at the importance of effective listening.

Tutors should also highlight the variety of formats used to communicate with internal and external customers, including telephone, letters, memoranda, notices, reports and e-mails.

Element 5 – Customer service and customer care

Customer relationship marketing is important in marketing today. As such, it is critical that students understand the concept of customer service and customer care and its importance in consumer, business-to-business, not-for-profit and public-sector organizations.

Tutors should explain the importance of quality and customer care and methods of achieving quality of service. Tutors should also explain the relationship between customer care, customer focus and relationship marketing.

Students should be able to devise contingency plans for dealing with customer complaints in the context of a well-planned customer care programme. As a result of this, students will be better informed at to how to develop and establish a customer care programme.

Finally, students should demonstrate an understanding of how ICT is used as part of the delivery of customer service, for example building customer databases and using Customer Relationship Management (CRM) software programmes as part of automated customer handling processes.

Delivery approach

Marketing Communications should ideally be taught either in conjunction with or following Marketing Fundamentals, as Fundamentals will provide the basic knowledge required regarding the marketplace and customers and their role. Furthermore, the teaching of the Marketing Environment will emphasize the role of different stakeholders within marketing and also the key external factors, which impact upon these very groups of people. This understanding will aid in appreciating the need for establishing appropriate forms of communication for different target audiences and for different communications circumstances.

As stated earlier, this unit provides a good grounding for the Marketing Communications unit at Professional Diploma, which logically follows on from this one. Therefore, it is fundamental that students assume a good grasp of the knowledge and skills components covered within this unit. Furthermore, it is recommended that tutors devise or utilize a variety of practical exercises to allow students the opportunity to practise their new-found knowledge.

The form of assessment for this unit will be by examination or assignment. This should be taken into consideration when developing the teaching strategy for the unit.

Additional resources (Syllabus – Professional Certificate In Marketing)

Introduction

Texts to support the individual units are listed in the syllabus for each unit. This Appendix shows a list of marketing journals, press and websites that tutors and students may find useful in supporting their studies at Professional Certificate.

Press

Students will be expected to have access to current examples of marketing campaigns and so should be sure to keep up to date with the appropriate marketing and quality daily press, including:

- *Campaign* – Haymarket
- *Internet Business* – Haymarket
- *Marketing* – Haymarket
- *The Marketer* – Chartered Institute of Marketing
- *Marketing Week* – Centaur
- *Revolution* – Haymarket.

Websites

The Chartered Institute of Marketing

www.cim.co.uk	CIM website containing case studies, reports and news
www.cim.co.uk/learning zone	Website for CIM students and tutors containing study information, past exam papers and case study examples; Also access to the marketer circles on-line

Publications on-line

www.revolution.haynet.com	Revolution magazine
www.brandrepublic.com	Marketing magazine
www.FT.com	A wealth of information for cases (now charging)
www.IPA.co.uk	Need to register – communication resources
www.booksites.net	Financial Times/Prentice Hall Text websites

Sources of useful information

www.acnielsen.co.uk	AC Nielsen – excellent for research
http://advertising.utexas.edu/world/	Resources for advertising and marketing professionals, students, and tutors
www.bized.com	Case studies
www.corporateinformation.com	Worldwide sources listed by country
www.esomar.nl	European Body representing Research Organisations – use-ful for guidelines on research ethics and approaches
www.dma.org.uk	The Direct Marketing Association
www.eiu.com	The Economist Intelligence Unit
www.euromonitor.com	Euromonitor consumer markets
www.europa.eu.int	The European Commission's extensive range of statistics and reports relating to EU and member countries
www.managementhelp.org/research/research.htm	Part of the 'Free Management Library' – explaining research methods
www.marketresearch.org.uk	The MRS site with information and access to learning support for students – useful links on ethics and code of conduct
www.mmc.gov.uk	Summaries of Competition Commission reports
www.oecd.org	OECD statistics and other information relating to member nations including main economic indicators
www.quirks.com	An American source of information on marketing research issues and projects
www.statistics.gov.uk	UK Government statistics
www.un.org	United Nations publish statistics on member nations
www.worldbank.org	World bank economic, social and natural resource indicators for over 200 countries. Includes over 600 indicators covering GNP per capita, growth, economic statistics, etc.

Case sites

www.bluelagoon.co.uk	Case – SME website address
www.ebay.com	On-line auction – buyer behaviour
www.glenfiddich.com	Interesting site for case and branding
www.interflora.co.uk	e-commerce direct ordering
www.moorcroft.co.uk	Good for relationship marketing
www.ribena.co.uk	Excellent targeting and history of comms

© CIM 2005

Index